Hacker States

The Information Society Series

Laura DeNardis and Michael Zimmer, Series Editors

Hacker States

Luca Follis and Adam Fish

The MIT Press
Cambridge, Massachusetts
London, England

This book was set in Stone Serif and Stone Sans by Jen Jackowitz. Printed and bound in the United States of America

Library of Congress Cataloging-in-Publication Data

Names: Follis, Luca, author. | Fish, Adam, author.
Title: Hacker states / Luca Follis and Adam Fish.
Description: Cambridge, MA : MIT Press, [2020] | Series: Information society
    series | Includes bibliographical references and index.
Identifiers: LCCN 2019019587 | ISBN 9780262043601 (hardcover : alk. paper)
Subjects: LCSH: Hacktivism. | Cyberspace--Political aspects.
Classification: LCC HV6773 .F65 2020 | DDC 364.16/8--dc23 LC record available at
    https://lccn.loc.gov/2019019587

10 9 8 7 6 5 4 3 2 1

Contents

Contents

Acknowledgments

A book begins with a collection of multiple lines of inquiry, dispersed ideas, and research trajectories that predate the research itself and seek to extend beyond it. When it is the product of collaborative work, the synthesis and clarification of ideas is perhaps more challenging but also significantly more stimulating, and I would like to thank my coauthor Adam Fish for being a thoughtful, imaginative interlocutor during the years we spent researching and writing this book. Throughout this process, I have drawn significant inspiration from the interdisciplinary spirit that animated my PhD years at the New School for Social Research in New York and the critical focus on the themes of democracy, crisis, and resistance that characterized my time there. The guidance, mentorship, and support of a theoretically agile and politically engaged group of scholars—Andrew Arato (to whom I owe a tremendous intellectual debt), Oz Frankel, Eiko Ikegami, Jeffrey Goldfarb, Elżbieta Matynia, and José Casanova—is reflected in many of the pages of this book.

In Lancaster and beyond, many colleagues generously gave their time and effort to comment on, discuss, and otherwise significantly improve various drafts of this book. In particular, I would like to thank Monika Buscher, Mark Lacy, Daniel Prince, Majid Yar, and Maxigas. Others helped provide the vibrant and collegial research environment that allowed this project to develop. Sue Penna, Corinne May-Chahal, Alisdair Gillespie, Sigrun Skogly, Catherine Easton, Sarah Kingston, Gary Potter, and Steven Wheatley deserve special thanks. Security Lancaster and the Faculty of Arts and Social Sciences at Lancaster University provided funding at various stages of this research and the law school facilitated a timely research sabbatical during which the final draft of this manuscript was completed. I would also like to extend our gratitude to our informants, in particular Lauri Love and Naomi Colvin, who gave us access to their time—under incredibly stressful conditions—so that we could write this book. Our editor at the MIT Press, Gita Devi Manaktala, and four anonymous readers also contributed to making our manuscript better.

Finally, I would especially like to thank my parents Eugenia and Fabrizio Follis, who regularly provide a respite from the storm of academic commitments and are an unwavering source of support and encouragement, as well as Marco Follis, Anna Maria Notaro, Jolanta Zagrodzka, and Jerzy Szmagalski, whose enthusiasm, engagement, and warmth throughout the writing of this book kept me grounded. Above all this project would not have been possible without my travel partner in life, academia, and all else. I would like to thank Karolina Follis, whose encouragement, love, and boundless imagination powers our little family, as well as the restless and incandescent spirit of our two children, Benjamin and Matilda. When they smile, the worries of the world fade away.

—Luca Follis

I would like to sincerely acknowledge the creative work of my coauthor Luca Follis. His dedication to grounded realism, steady discipline, and playful theorizing made this project possible. A community of fellow anthropology hackers—Christopher Kelty, Gabriella Coleman, Maxigas, and Paula Bialski—inspired this research. I appreciated the opportunity to present drafts of this research at the Digital Social Research Unit, Umeå University, Sweden; Disconnections Symposium, Uppsala University, Sweden; ZeMKI Centre for Media, Communication and Information Research, University of Bremen, Germany; and Hackademia: Empirical Studies in Computing Cultures, Lüneburg Summer School for Digital Cultures, Leuphana University, Germany. I thank the ZeMKI Centre for Media, Communication, and Information Research for a 2018 fellowship that supported this research. My family, Robin, Io (Isis Viola Lune Moxie), and Jennifer Fish, made this and all work meaningful. I dedicate this work to Richard Lee Fish (1947–2018), a hacker in spirit.

—Adam Fish

1   Hacker States

The smell of pinecones roasting on black basalt rock. Icy creeks replenishing free-flowing rivers, where salmon swim to peak-side spawning grounds. On a sandy beach, prints of bighorn sheep scatter away from an ambush by a mountain lion. Situated in central Idaho, between Montana and Oregon, this is the largest roadless area in the lower forty-eight United States. It is one of the only remaining intact ecosystems large enough to support ambulatory and predatory megafauna like wolverines, gray wolves, lynx, mountain lion, and likely grizzly bears. This wilderness is protected on the grounds that it sustains biological richness, allows scientists to observe ecological principles, inspires a freedom-seeking zeitgeist, reminds people of commonly shared responsibilities, and serves as a sacred space (Nash 1976). Authors from Henry David Thoreau to Edward Abbey have noted the dialectic between internal wildness and external wilderness that exists in the American psyche, a co-determining relationship between a people's values and what a nation cherishes. An immense wilderness in Idaho might seem an unlikely place to begin a book about computer hacking. Yet the internet—and the sprawling network of servers, computers, and other devices that constitute it—forms its own kind of wilderness. Fin de siècle computer viruses, self-replicating worms, and other malware swim in the fiber-optic streams of this "wild." As an untamed region far removed from the sandbox of computer laboratories and research facilities, the hacker wilderness is the space where security researchers, cybercriminals, and hacktivists meet and mesh. Thinking about the relationship between the nation-state and the wild offers important insights into today's fight for the cyber commons.

The Frank Church River of No Return Wilderness Area described above was named after Idaho Democratic senator Frank Church, who served from

1957 to 1981. Church grew up fishing and hunting around the capital of Boise and sponsored numerous conservation bills, including the 1964 Wilderness Act, which set aside and protected 9.1 million acres of federal land. He was not only an environmentalist but also a progressive. Church was a vocal opponent of the Vietnam War and advocated governmental transparency and military restraint in the aftermath of the Gulf of Tonkin Resolution. He famously told his mentor, US president Lyndon B. Johnson, "In a democracy you cannot expect the people, whose sons are being killed and who will be killed, to exercise their judgment if the truth is concealed from them" (Bumiller 2010). His enduring legacy is bound up in the work of the US Senate Select Committee to Study Governmental Operations with Respect to Intelligence Activities (1975–76). The Church Committee, as the body came to be known, presided over a multiyear investigation into the covert surveillance practices engaged in by American intelligence agencies, including the Federal Bureau of Investigation (FBI) and the National Security Agency (NSA).

Senator Church helped to establish a wilderness area that challenged ecological homogeneity, while the Church Committee's work challenged state attempts to force political conformity through the disruption and stifling of political dissent. Church's heritage is vigilance against forced conformity in nature and society. A 1974 *New York Times* investigation by journalist Seymour Hersh into the Central Intelligence Agency (CIA) classified "family jewels"—an eight-hundred-page compilation of agent reports concerning illegal activities committed by the agency—informed the Church Committee's work, as did whistleblower Christopher Pyle's earlier revelations of plainclothes US Army troops conducting domestic political surveillance operations on antiwar protesters (Zwoof 2013). Hersh documented how between the 1950s and 1970s, the CIA routinely conducted covert activities outside its legislative charter, including domestic spying, illegal wiretapping, assassination plots, domestic surveillance, unjust detainment, warrantless entry, human experiments involving LSD, and the aggressive targeting of numerous political groups (Hersh 1974). Church targeted these covert and clandestine incursions on the rights of citizens.

The Church Committee uncovered egregious and shocking details of state-supported analog hacking and surveillance, many of them reminiscent of documented practices. For example, under the NSA's SHAMROCK program (1952–75), the agency enjoyed direct access to daily microfilm copies of all telegrams initiated via Western Union, the Radio Corporation of America (RCA), and International Telephone and Telegraph (ITT), which it then sifted for the communications of US citizens on its "watch list." At the program's height in 1973, this watch list contained some six hundred names, including celebrities, activists, and ordinary US citizens who had attended political demonstrations (Snider 1999–2000). According to the committee's report, SHAMROCK, which involved the collection of approximately 150,000 messages per month, was "probably the largest government interception program affecting Americans ever undertaken" (US Senate 1976, 765)—that is, until the dawn of internet communication enabled the collection of billions of records.[1]

The most infamous revelation was the disclosure of the FBI's Counterintelligence Program (COINTELPRO), a widespread and largely illegal attempt to disrupt, discredit, and destroy dissent and social justice movements. COINTELPRO began under FBI director J. Edgar Hoover in 1956 as a project designed to erode support for the US Communist Party, but it quickly broadened its scope to "disrupt groups" and "neutralize" individuals (US Senate 1976, 10) deemed threats by the FBI director. These included civil rights leaders, critics of the FBI, student activists, the Black Panthers, the Old and the New Left, the Socialist Workers Party, and the American Indian Movement. Besides engaging in warrantless surveillance, harassment, and intimidation of these groups, the agency sought to break up marriages, get targets fired from jobs, and incite animosity and mistrust among them by labeling group members as government informers. Most famously, the FBI "employed nearly every intelligence-gathering technique at its disposal" to "destroy Dr. King as the leader of the civil rights movement" (US Senate 1976, 11), including attempting to blackmail him into committing suicide.

COINTELPRO was exposed by the Citizens' Commission to Investigate the FBI after they broke into an FBI field office in Media, Pennsylvania (Pilkington 2014). The bureau would later admit that it had committed some 238 burglaries under COINTELPRO, and the Citizens' Commission to Investigate the FBI clearly drew on the FBI's own tactics and methods to expose them (Donner 1980, 130). The group copied all the documents in the files, including memos and directives from Hoover ordering surveillance dossiers and outlining specific targets in the African American community and among antiwar demonstrators. The trove, which the group then sent to

newspaper outlets and two congressmen, also included a routing slip with
the codename COINTELPRO. This single acronym and a query about it in
the form of a Freedom of Information (FOI) request revealed the entirety of
this dubious program.

The activities of American intelligence agencies throughout this period
illustrate the continuities between contemporary surveillance practices and
those that dominated much of last century. They also testify to federal law
enforcement's early and enthusiastic adoption of emergent technologies
as means of social control and tools of disruption, whether through the
bulk collection of incoming, transiting, and exiting telegraphic data or
breaking into residences and hotel rooms to plant bugs and tap phones.
The state that appears in the Church Committee report hacks communications and breaches physical spaces, compiles dossiers and assembles
"watch lists," stigmatizes dissent, and detains without warrant. In short,
it concentrates, monopolizes, and deploys various species of capital (force,
coercion, technological, informational, and symbolic) in the construction
and maintenance of its field of power (Bourdieu 1994, 4–5). At the same
time, as much as this state represents itself as the preeminent crystallization
of power and knowledge (Poulantzas [1978] 2013, 59), it remains caught
within and shaped by the dialectics of resistance and social change its own
actions target. COINTELPRO was discovered thanks to the Citizens' Commission to Investigate the FBI—which adopted illegal state tactics to disrupt
the FBI's illegal operations—and several other transparency activists and
journalists who filed FOI requests and civil cases against the government.
In the wake of the Church Committee, Congress passed the 1978 Foreign
Intelligence Surveillance Act (which set up a secret court to vet and autho-
rize NSA surveillance), imposed term limits on the FBI directorship of ten
years, and brought the agency under permanent congressional oversight
(Snider 2008).

Yet alongside these important changes, state actors continued to deploy
technological resources to further national security and social control. As
we document in the chapter that follows, within the United States, these
efforts developed under different governmental agencies connected with
the military (most notably the US Air Force) and national security (the
NSA). Throughout the 1980s federal law enforcement increasingly played
a role in the criminalization of hacking and hackers, but in the wake of
the 9/11 attacks, official hacking operations mushroomed and shifted from

being primarily focused on foreign threats to targeting the domestic sphere as well.

September 11 provided the impetus for an organizational and theoretical rethinking of the relationship between military, law enforcement, and intelligence. For example, the 9/11 Commission commented in its report on the numerous missed opportunities to foil the 9/11 plot, when law enforcement or intelligence actors were in possession of critical information (Kean 2004, 353–360) but failed to capitalize on it or to share it more broadly than the immediate agency in possession of it. The commission recommended the abandonment of the "old mainframe or hub-and-spoke" approach and argued that "information be shared horizontally, across new networks that transcend individual agencies" (Kean 2004, 418). Besides the emergence of NSA bulk data collection and surveillance programs, as disclosed by former NSA subcontractor Edward Snowden, this period also saw a dramatic growth in the sheer size of the national security apparatus. Billions of dollars ($40 billion in 2001, $36.5 billion in 2002, and $44 billion in 2003) were committed to global action against al-Qaeda and domestic defense, alongside significant institutional expansion. For example, at least 263 organizations were created or reorganized in response to 9/11, bringing the vast footprint of the secret state to 1,271 government organizations and 1,931 private organizations working on counterterrorism, homeland security, and intelligence programs (Priest and Arkin 2010). The Global War on Terrorism and the characterization of al-Qaeda as a "networked, dynamic enemy" (Yoo 2007, 572) by President George W. Bush's administration set the stage for including cyberattacks within the wider category of asymmetric threats posed by terrorists.

In 2008 President Barack Obama's campaign was the first to be hacked by a foreign power, and the incoming administration took over a sprawling and deeply embedded surveillance state from Bush, as well as inheriting a covert cyber operation called Stuxnet, targeting Iran's nuclear weapons program (Kaplan 2016, 198, 201). Indeed, the cyber threat as national security and economic concern figured prominently early on and drove a systematic rethinking of the legal, technological, and organizational issues surrounding cybersecurity (Mueller 2010, 179). For example, alongside a more hawkish cyber posture (against Iran and China), the administration also presided over an unprecedented crackdown on official whistleblowing and leaking. Before Obama, it was unusual for leakers to be charged for publicly disclosing classified information without authorization: under all previous presidents combined, there had been only three prosecutions of this kind, but the new administration brought criminal charges against nine leakers (Savage 2016, 358). Among these were two whistleblowers—US Army intelligence officer Chelsea Manning and Edward Snowden—whose disclosures introduced a technological sea-change in the distribution, scale, and scope of official leaks.

In conjunction with an aggressive legal pursuit of whistleblowers (which shares important corollaries with hacktivist prosecutions under the Computer Fraud and Abuse Act), the administration also targeted a key outlet and source of legitimation for leaks: the press. The nine Obama leakers were charged under the 1917 Espionage Act—an arcane legislation that carries lengthy prison sentences and bars the use of a public interest (or whistleblowing) defense at trial (Savage 2015, 365). The administration also successfully argued on appeal before the Fourth Circuit Court in Richmond, Virginia, that there is no First Amendment shield for reporters and news organizations that would protect them from being compelled to testify about their sources in criminal proceedings concerning illegally leaked information (Savage 2015, 404–405).[2]

While the Obama campaign was the first to be hacked by a foreign power, US president Donald Trump's election campaign was the first to directly benefit from a hack by a foreign power. As we detail in chapter 3, during the election Russian hackers exfiltrated thousands of emails from the Democratic National Committee (DNC) and passed the material to transparency activists WikiLeaks. Throughout this period, longtime Trump advisor Roger Stone was in communication on Twitter with Guccifer 2.0, the hacker that claimed responsibility for the breach (Sanger, Rutenberg, and Lipton 2018). According to the February 27, 2019, congressional testimony of Trump lawyer and fixer Michael Cohen, Trump received a phone call from Stone, who informed both Cohen and Trump that he had spoken with WikiLeaks editor Julian Assange, and that Assange planned to release hacked emails that "would damage the Hillary Clinton campaign." According to Cohen, Trump responded, "Wouldn't that be great" (Bump 2018). Days later on the campaign trail, Trump implored, "Russia, if you're listening, I hope you're able to find the 30,000 emails that are missing." Trump said, "I think you will probably be rewarded mightily by our press" (D. A. Graham 2018).

Despite Trump's request for help, FBI special counsel Robert Mueller worked to identify any potential links between the president's campaign and Russian hackers. In July 2018, he and his team indicted twelve Russian military intelligence agents associated with the DNC hack (Polantz and Collinson 2018). And most of the revelations disclosed in Cohen's public testimony were likely already known by Mueller's investigators. The role of Russian state hackers in breaching democratic institutions during the 2016 US presidential election, alongside the active incitement of then candidate Trump and his allies, caps this brief history of state hacking and provides the impetus for unpacking what appears to be a jumble of code, hackers, politics, and the state.

What Is Hacking?

Recent years have seen a remarkable proliferation of hackers and hacking. Life hackers, place hackers, education hackers, business hackers—hackers of all sorts—now join the archetypal computer hacker. Indeed, the cultural meaning of hacking has so broadened that it now encompasses virtually any activity that subverts the conventional way of doing things with digital technologies. In this sense, hacking has become a cognate of *disruption*, a term that references the challenges networked technology poses to incumbent forms of political, social, and economic organization. Our framing of hackers and hacking draws on the wider cultural significance that hacking has assumed: a set of material and technical practices set in open conflict or opposition with established modes of doing.

According to sociologist Tim Jordan, hacking is a material practice that "creates difference" in computer communications and network technology (Jordan 2009), and although we reject reducing the hacker to a single "type" among many, in this book we focus on hackers as people who break into software systems. The hacktivists and hackers we describe in the chapters that follow are exfiltrators. That is, individuals involved in the unauthorized access and transfer of data from computers through networks, software, and/or hardware (we also include those that write or design software and code for these same purposes). Exfiltration forces alterations in computers and networks by subverting their routine functioning to provide opportunities for unintended access and illicit use.

We define hacktivism as a digital form of activism that involves the exfil-tration of data and code toward explicitly political ends—no matter how loosely framed the latter may be. We understand the mobilization of these alterations in computers and networks as encompassing a wide variety of digitally mediated objectives, including political disruption, dissident sup-port, symbolic protest, active subversion, and radical transparency. Not all hacktivists are exfiltrators, but most of the instances of hacktivism we discuss involve the extraction of data, either by activists or by state agents. At the same time, we do not advance a definitive interpretation of hacking, as the diversity exhibited within this culture has already been amply cataloged (e.g., Coleman 2014; Jordan 2008; Kelty 2008). Instead, we focus on the culture that exists where exfiltration, political activism, and state practice intersect.

The politics that animate exfiltration span the political spectrum and can take a right-wing, left-wing, democratic, authoritarian, libertarian, or revolutionary character. Moreover, these affiliations visibly shift over time: progressive hackers may have libertarian moments; they may hack author-itarians and later become proponents of fragile democracies. And not just the ideology is mobile, but the software, code, and exploits they use are on the move as well, often flowing from democracies to dark market cap-italists and on to dictators. Over the course of our research and fieldwork, we witnessed these ideological transformations, strange bedfellows, and contradictory practices, as well as the use of similar tactics and software by oppositional parties. In other words, the hacker field is fluid by defini-tion, and its politics can appear itinerant or even fickle. This is not unlike other forms of "cultural activism" (Ginsburg 1997) and "strategic indigene-ity" (Lewallen 2003), where communities intentionally place culture into greater relief to advance particular claims or to pursue strategic goals. As anthropologists Luis Felipe R. Murillo and Christopher Kelty note:

> There are multiple and intersecting moral and technical orders inhabited by peo-ple who self-identify or are identified by peers as hackers—from the underground hacker collectives to "grey hat" security researchers to spam-slinging criminal actors to the hard-core free speech and privacy cryptography defenders; from the diehard Free Software activist to the business-oriented Open Source evangelist; from the uber-cool Northern European design artists to the goofy-but-terrifying Anonymous hackers, and so on. (2018, 105–106)

Elsewhere (Fish and Follis 2016) we term this flexible hacker practice *subjectivation* and contrast this effort with law enforcement attempts to frame hacker subjectivity through processes of *subjection*. We characterize the playful deployment of subjectivity in hacker communities as *versioning* and analyze those instances when hackers "come out"—shed their pseudonymous masks and reveal their actual identities—to add credence and sincerity to a political project. Finally, we note that *doxing*—that is, the release of personal documents or the forceful exposure of an individual's identity—is also a tool of radical transparency activism, political disruption, and state repression (Follis and Fish 2017). The above modes of tactical engagement illustrate hackers' strategic performance of identity and their entanglement with state practices of categorization and containment. In this book we explore how the practice of hacking (as well as the ideological performances that are connected to it) intersects with and comes to be bound up in the state's own tactical adoption of hacking as a resource in the deployment of state power.

Media depictions often portray hackers as technological wizards, high-tech pranksters, or virtual criminals (Thomas 2002), a view that is often reinforced by the numerous firsthand accounts that appear in the literature (e.g., Assange 2014; Mitnick 2012). Where scholars have approached hacking from a more theoretical position, they have focused on how hackers interface with the open source community (Kelty 2008) or self-organize impressive political campaigns (Coleman 2015). Few have explicitly situated hacker practice in the context of state power, although multiple scholars have analyzed and theorized the growing political impact of hacking. Media studies scholar McKenzie Wark (2004), for example, has argued that hackers constituted a novel political, even revolutionary, class, who implicitly challenged state-based representational politics and the commodification of information. Jordan's work on hackers, which spans nearly two decades, situates their actions in terms of social movement theory and political protest (Jordan and Taylor 2004; Jordan 2015). Jordan and Paul A. Taylor (2004) argue that the antiglobalization movement of the late 1990s and early 2000s played a decisive role in the emergence of hacktivism and electronic civil disobedience. Similarly, political scientist Jessica Beyer (2014) has described the hacker collective Anonymous as an example of new digitally mediated—and anonymized—forms of protest. Finally, media studies scholar Molly Sauter (2014) analyzed the practice of distributed denial of service attacks, a form of electronic civil disobedience favored by Anonymous, and physical forms of protest in light of the state's criminalization of dissent.

In each of the above studies, hackers are no longer independent and nonaligned actors, but figures close, far, or opposed to state power. For example, communications professor Douglas Thomas (2002, 170) has argued that hackers' position within a broader cultural shift from material culture to information subcultures affords them novel semiotic strategies to forge subcultural identity and new modalities of resistance to dominant cultural forms. In this view digital space is increasingly virtual, and the online culture it produces is fluid and resistant by default. For Thomas the contrast between this and law enforcement's aggressive prosecution and investigation of hackers underscores the latter's "obsession with the corporeal" (177). Hacker prosecutions and investigations are efforts to materially and corporeally reinscribe hackers and their offline identities within disciplinary and regulatory spaces that sustain state power (182). Hackers are viewed as threatening and dangerous because through their mastery of technology, they are uniquely positioned to disrupt a core pillar of social order: the connection between those who control technology and those who deal out punishment (180).

Anthropologist E. Gabriella Coleman's (2015) ethnography of Anonymous presents a complementary reading of the relationship between hackers and law enforcement. In her account, state agents are a looming presence, both as increasingly frequent targets of the collective's actions and as a coercive force that seizes property, arrests Anonymous members, and develops informants from within their ranks. Coleman's work focuses on the genesis of Anonymous and its overall trajectory from a collection of pranksters to reluctant activists but devotes little space to fleshing out "the state." In contrast, criminologist Kevin Steinmetz's (2016) account views hackers through the lens of cultural criminology and political economy. He argues that hackers are subjects for crime control because some of the behaviors attributed to them (e.g., violating intellectual property, breaching tech infrastructure, or advocating political resistance) directly or potentially disrupt the operation of capital (2016, 173). Steinmetz's account is valuable in that it charts one way in which the state legitimates and maintains its extension of public authority over digital space—even if in this reading, the state is reduced to a hegemonic tool in the service of capital. In the section that follows, we examine how the state, instead of opposing hackers as a criminal underground, has harnessed hacking as a tool of governance.

What Is State Hacking?

State hacking is premised on the generation, identification, and mainte-nance of vulnerabilities it can exploit; whether these vulnerabilities are located in hardware or software, state hacking thrives under and promotes states of digital insecurity. At the same time, the material and offline lives of its citizens are more and more interwoven with the digital; whether one speaks of social media, the internet of things, driverless cars, the automa-tion of work, or critical infrastructure, connected and networked technol-ogies cross into the lives of citizens in intimate and highly specific ways bound up in the (re)production of material, economic, and political life. In this sense, it would be a mistake to characterize the current era of cyber warfare and state hacking as another cold war. True, there are proxy skir-mishes, instances of corporate espionage and intelligence spying, as well as robust systems of signals intelligence collection, but such a depiction fails to capture the full impact and potential of state hacking on international and diplomatic relations, digital capitalism, and democratic governance.

Several recent scholarly accounts seek to describe this new geopolitical reality. For example, according to international relations scholar Lucas Kello (2017), hacking technologies are nothing short of revolutionary in terms of their influence on the rational and moral world order. For Kello, the current situation is defined by a stubborn predicament: technologically superior nations that effectively harness hacking technologies to further economic, military, and social objectives remain the most vulnerable entities to these same threats. As a result, geopolitical relations are characterized by a self-perpetuating state of "unpeace": an ongoing dynamic of mutual aggression and competition among states that remains below the threshold of destruc-tion and violence (i.e., war) but that nonetheless generates harmful dis-ruptions beyond what is tolerable in a state of peaceful competition (Kello 2017, 78). Not only does this scramble conventional strategies of defense, but it also undermines and neutralizes the modes of deterrence states tra-ditionally adopted to deal with the aggressions of adversaries. For example, in an analog context, deterrence frameworks combine a mixture of denial and punishment. The former essentially increases the cost to an adversary of using weapons (e.g., arms control treaties or the erection of defensive perimeters like antiballistic missile defense systems), while the latter works by threatening equivalent, severe penalties in the case of attack. Yet for a host of reasons, including the difficulties with attributing attacks, the problems with identifying an attack in real time and anticipating its impact, as well as issues with quantifying its effects (in terms of determining a proportionate response), traditional deterrence approaches do not work when applied to the cyber realm (Kello 2017, 197–200).

A similar point is made by *New York Times* reporters David Sanger and Robertson Dean (2018), who describe how cyber conflict revolutionizes the conduct of war and transforms geopolitical relations. For Sanger and Dean, much like Kello, conventional threat and escalation scenarios developed during an era when nuclear weapons were states' primary concerns do not fit the contemporary situation. Moreover, the fact that much of this state-sponsored hacking takes place under the rubric of national security (and is thus shrouded in secrecy) also greatly hampers the ability of states to develop new, realistic codes of conduct and effective response scenarios. Despite this, it is particularly important to address and debate these questions now while they remain visible, because in the near future, much of this state hacking activity will likely become automated (Sanger and Dean 2018; Cox 2018). Artificial intelligence will significantly quicken the potential for escalation and response; humans will struggle to intervene effectively in scenarios when the situation becomes irrevocably escalated. Sanger and Dean's solution, much like Kello's, is nonstate directed. They argue that the computer and software industry should take the lead by drafting and enlisting state support for a Digital Geneva Convention along the lines of what has been adopted for conventional weapons (Sanger and Dean 2018).

Ben Buchanan's (2017) diagnosis of the contemporary period echoes some of the positions already discussed. Buchanan notes that cyber threats scramble the traditional options states have used to address the "security dilemma" problem in international relations: when states undertake to strengthen their defensive posture (e.g., build up troops on a border or deploy naval ships in a region for exercises), their adversaries will potentially read such an act as hostile or aggressive and respond in kind. To mitigate against the potential for runaway escalation such a scenario presents, states developed standards and norms that aid in differentiating aggressive from nonaggressive conduct, and they became very good at signaling their intentions to one another so that their actions would not be misinterpreted.

In one sense the cyber realm is not very different. According to Buchanan, technologically advanced states do have a defensive interest (they must defend themselves against the aggression of other states) in conducting network intrusions against rivals, but almost all such intrusions are invariably interpreted as aggressive. Yet because within the field of state hacking, a shift in aggressive or defensive posture similarly involves the breach of an adversary's networks, this effectively renders the distinction between these two activities moot. Such intrusions are regarded as a threat by default and mitigated against as such, which increases the risk for runaway escalation. According to Buchanan this has led to a situation very much characteristic of the United States' cautious (and some might argue paralyzed) approach to Russian and Chinese intrusions. Yet this is a fundamentally unstable situation, since paralysis and inaction breeds boldness in one's adversary, and Buchanan argues that states need to address this dilemma by building trust in formal terms (e.g., through bilateral and multilateral agreements) as well as informally, by being more transparent about their objectives so as to minimize the potential for misinterpretation.

All three of the above accounts of cyber conflict effectively diagnose how the advent of networked technology disrupts traditional forms of statecraft and ushers in a new, seemingly unresolvable geopolitical stand-off. Yet despite their insightful assessment of this new reality, as well as the dearth of normative and legal frameworks for successfully navigating it, their analysis remains focused on intrastate activity and does not stray far from the traditional terrain of international relations and geopolitics. States remain the main actors in this arena. One notable exception is international relations expert Tim Maurer's (2018) analysis of the increasing role that cyber mercenaries play in the field of state hacking.

Maurer defines cyber power in terms of the capacity to leverage unauthorized access into computer networks and argues that it is increasingly deployed through cyber proxies: "intermediaries that conduct or directly contribute to an offensive cyber action that is enabled knowingly, whether actively or passively by a beneficiary" (2018, 31). He analyzes the different forms that state/nonstate proxy relations take (i.e., delegation, orchestration, and sanctioning) and links them to the degree of official control wielded by a beneficiary. For example, *delegation* involves the largest degree of direct control (as in the case of the United States and its contractors), while *orchestration* may include logistical and financial support to a proxy that shares the state's aims and ideology (e.g., Iran's Revolutionary Guard and its hackers). Finally, *sanctioning* is the least directed activity in the sense that it is characterized by state inaction or toleration of a proxy's activities (e.g., Russia's FSB and cyber criminals). Maurer's analysis also sheds light on how different models of cybersecurity affect state decisions about the character of proxy relationships and thus dictate the sort of operating latitude these groups may have. Thus while the United States and Europe view cybersecurity as essentially guarding from destructive harm and intelligence gathering, he argues that actors like Russia and China are primarily interested in control over information, which shapes their hacking activity. Ultimately for Maurer, as for the authors discussed above, proxy relationships feed the problems of threat escalation and the legal ambiguity that surrounds state hacking activity in international law: such activity continues to fall below the threshold of physical, weaponized contact.

The strength of Maurer's analysis is that it seeks to unpack the "state" and account for the heterogeneous medley of actors working in the field of state hacking: technological heavyweights like China, Russia, and the United States employ a host of proxies, as well as fielding their own hacking and intrusion teams from multiple governmental domains. At the same time, some contractor relationships are exclusive (e.g., the United States and its revolving-door relationship with contractors like Booz Allen Hamilton or Raytheon), but others, like Hacking Team, are broadly accessible to anyone with financing. There are also diverse contingents of hacktivists, like the Shadow Brokers and Phineas Fisher, whose motivations and origins are opaque. And finally, within the context of this shadow work is also an emergent industry of ethical hackers (based in the UK and the United States), who seek contracts with states, banks, and corporations in a bid to turn the weapons of black-hat hackers into state cybersecurity and surveillance tools. Maurer's account sheds light on this diverse field but remains largely concerned with state/nonstate dynamics; it seeks to problematize the distinctions between the public and private sphere but fails to transcend the categories of international relations.

Hacker States

This book builds on the theoretical and empirical ground developed in the hacker and cyber-conflict literature described earlier. As we already noted, there have been many sociological and ethnographic accounts of hackers that focus on hacking's growing political impact. Yet to the extent that they consider the state's relationship to hacking, they view this relationship in largely oppositional terms (i.e., criminalization) and fail to develop an account of the state's own increasing use of hacking. In contrast, the approach within the cyber-conflict literature centers on how hacking technologies disrupt the strategic posture of states, and although hackers are sometimes presented as nonaligned agents, it largely folds their efforts into the overall machinations of the state and geopolitics. We advance a theoretical framework that seeks to bridge the above approaches and anchor the book's four substantive chapters.

The *boundary* is a governing concept in this book. The state and the hacker are best understood relationally. Between any two monads that are not indistinguishable and unified exists a boundary. This membrane, however thin and permeable or thick and impenetrable, differentiates the institutions of the state and the hacker lifeworld. Our contention is that traffic exists in unique and troubling ways across the envelope that partitions states and hackers. At different times and locations, the trade across this boundary is co-productive, resulting in mutual benefit, and at other times it is a tangle—a knot of people, law, and technology. In the period of our investigation, the movement across this boundary followed an arc that began with state actors responding to subversive and oppositional forces in the digital realm and ended with state attempts to co-opt hackers. But instead of this being a finalized relationship, relations across the state-hacker boundary are more versatile, because technological elaboration and practical invention routinely outpace legal mechanism and law enforcement. Perhaps it will always be that way.

The relationship across boundaries has been theorized in sociology. One contribution of *Hacker States* is the development of a novel theory of the boundary through a concrete convergence of sociology and science and technology studies (STS). This scholarship began with the work of sociologist of science Thomas Gieryn and his research on the "boundary work" of scientists differentiating themselves from religion in nineteenth-century England. Gieryn identifies this in terms of delineating science from other intellectual activity—a problem approached by everyone from Auguste Comte to Karl Popper. It is an ideological process that attributes select qualities to the "institution of science (e.g., to its practitioners, methods, stock of knowledge, values and work organization) for purposes of constructing a social boundary that distinguishes some intellectual activity as 'non-science'" (Gieryn 1983, 782).

For Gieryn, boundary work is largely a rhetorical strategy for publicly performing the values of science in the press. One example is particularly salient for this book's concern with the relationship between computer science and national security. Gieryn focuses on the boundary work performed by scientists who need to differentiate their work from the state and its regulation, oversight, and control. Specifically, the scientific community defended its craft against those in the administration of US president Ronald Reagan, who claimed that one cause of Soviet military strength was the exploitation of openly available American technology and science. Affirming the necessity of open communication in the scientific community, the importance of basic research, and independence—while blaming others for the leaks of scientific military secrets—the scientific community defended itself by patrolling the boundary separating the "scientific field" (Bourdieu 1975) from the state. Our case is a mirror of Gieryn's in which the state is doing the policing against perceived threats from the hackers at the gates. Gieryn describes several ways in which boundary work can function as a resource:

> (a) When the goal is expansion of authority or expertise into domains claimed by other professions or occupations, boundary-work heightens the contrast between rivals in ways flattering to the ideologists' side; (b) when the goal is monopolization of professional authority and resources, boundary-work excludes rivals from within by defining them as outsiders with labels such as "pseudo," "deviant," or "amateur"; (c) when the goal is protection of autonomy over professional activities, boundary-work exempts members from responsibility for consequences of their work by putting the blame on scapegoats from outside. (1983, 791–792)

As subsequent chapters detail, the state's boundary work with respect to hacking is expansive, monopolizing, and driven by the imperative of protection. Much of this work involves expanding or manipulating borders and boundaries to enfold or expel hackers and their practices. The clearest way this occurs is by the state recruiting and hiring hackers, as we report in chapters 2 and 5. The state monopolizes professional authority by marginalizing nonstate forms of hacking. The prosecution of hackers, as witnessed in chapter 4, is another clear example. Finally, the state protects the hacker territory it has accrued by exempting itself from critique while drawing international attention and activity to the rogue hacking activities of others. As we see in chapter 3, the US state's hacking operations are seemingly legitimate, but Russian (and one might add Chinese) hacking is not.

We develop a conception of state hacking as *boundary work*, understood as a selective and logistical redrawing of borders within the state and between state and society to bring certain material practices and processes into closer proximity (and hence alignment) with state objectives, while selectively keeping those same practices at a distance in other domains of practice. In this sense we view the criminalization of hackers and hacktivists, as well as their enlistment in state cyber conflicts and network penetration efforts, as two sides of the same coin. Both represent twin manifestations of the state's logistical and tactical realignment in the face of networked technology, but they also shed significant light on the different governance strategies regarding hacking technologies pursued within different state domains (e.g., national security, military, and law enforcement).

This book offers a multimethodological account of the entanglements between hackers and the state. It seeks to contribute to both the literature on hacker culture and international relations theory by bringing the two into theoretical and methodological engagement. We draw on ethnographic and digital archival methods from fields as diverse as anthropology, criminology, sociolegal studies, and STS. We adopt a legal ethnographic approach in and around courtrooms in London to interrogate how extraterritorial legal instruments (e.g., extradition treaties) and mutual assistance policing frameworks are deployed to criminalize, stigmatize, and quell the digital dissent and activism of hackers. We use a similar ethnographic approach to document the trajectories of cybersecurity professionalization under way in "ethical hacking" workshops and hacker conferences, where much of the groundwork for transforming dissident hackers into pro–social security researchers unfolds.

We supplement the above ethnographic and participatory accounts with digital archival methods. The internet is a vast archive, and we draw on the staggering array of data that hacking produces, including a voluminous compendium of primary legal documents (e.g., court transcripts, skeleton arguments, witness statements, digital evidence, criminal affidavits, grand jury indictments, etc.), primary accounts (i.e., social media posts and narratives, opinion pieces) and secondary sources (i.e., investigatory journalistic accounts, documentaries), but also state documents (e.g., internal investigations and reports, press releases, congressional and parliamentary hearings and testimony). Finally, we combine archival methods and legal ethnography with STS and platform studies to closely examine the hacker's toolkit and the epistemological practices hackers draw on to do their work. For example, we conduct close software studies and readings of exploit platforms and audit tools, such as Metasploit and Kali Linux, as well as other penetration-testing software. These complementary methodological approaches generate a thick account of hacker-state relations as they play out on the body of the hacker in the courtroom, in the wider field of online and print culture, and in the tools and technologies dissident and state hackers use.

Networks have transformed how we interact with one another, conduct business, and are exposed to information in both important and trivial ways. But how networks provide distinct challenges and opportunities to states is little understood. Chapter 2 introduces the many ways in which nation states have historically supported and presently attempt to control the powers of the internet through harnessing hacking and hackers as resources for the expression of state power. On the one hand are nonstate hackers who use networks to challenge the state, its monopolies on technological force, and its attempts to dominate information flows. On the other, states channel power through proxies, develop intrusion technologies, and deploy criminalization campaigns to govern this new reality.

In chapter 2 we present a genealogy of the practices states have adopted in their bid to colonize, co-opt, and neutralize hacker power. We examine the rich assemblage of processes developed by the hacker state as both a tool and a resource for governance. To do this we begin with the prehistory of US state-supported hacking and how it was made possible by US Department of Defense funding to the Advanced Research Projects Agency (ARPA). While the networks developed by ARPA were largely legal and formal, less formalized practices—email, for example, as well as creative forms of network exploration—also provided momentum for the development of an underground hacking culture. As the network expanded outside ARPANET and into the wild, hacking began to take on contemporary forms, and the illegal and problematic activity that came with it became the subject of prosecution. In the 1980s and 1990s hacking emerged as a problem of governance (incubated within the domain of national security), and state authorities began to crack down on unauthorized or illegal hacking. Media hysteria and Hollywood valorization contributed to public concern, and hackers were aggressively pursued—both as criminals and as potential employees. State authorities recognized that while control through funding and punishment through the courts where both partially effective, hackers could also be important allies in military operations. We conclude chapter 2 by applying the boundary framework to a series of examples from states throughout the world: Chinese, Russian, Latin American, and corporate hackers all engage in variants of boundary work while existing in the liminal zone between crime and patriotism.

We now live in high breach societies. Hackers work outside, inside, alongside, and against state forms; they hack for gain, profit, and the fun of it. Leaks of information, breaches of cybersecurity, dumps of massive troves of data—these actions have populated headlines and generated anxiety among citizens, politicians, and businesspeople for decades. The ubiquity of these occurrences, their frequency and sheer scale, confirms that all facets of digital life are susceptible. In chapter 3 we investigate the political consequences of leaks and hacks. We begin by situating the well-known cases of Chelsea Manning, Edward Snowden, Anonymous, and LulzSec within a discussion of how their leaks were packaged to the public. The quantity of the information, the timing with which it was revealed, and the identity of the messengers—the clandestine WikiLeaks or the legitimate *Guardian* newspaper—are important and misunderstood qualities that affect how hacked and leaked information influences the press and ultimately citizens worldwide.

Hacks and leaks are the raw fuel for debate because they make public information whose political meaning would be silenced in private. This is an example of radical transparency—the ideological belief in transparency for the powerful and secrecy for the citizen with little power. Personal information revealed through the practice of *doxing* is an example of radical transparency and is a way that information is weaponized through acts of visibility (Trottier 2017). Thus chapter 3 investigates how radical transparency interacts with agents in the public sphere, namely citizens, the press, and the state. These include the 2013 Offshore Leaks, 2014 LuxLeaks, 2015 Panama Papers, and 2017 Paradise Papers, which are massive archives of information about offshore accounts and the dark world of tax evasion. Along with the vastness of the terabytes released with these scandals comes the rise of data journalism and multinational newspaper partnerships that try to make sense of this big data.

But while networks, hackers, and leakers fueled a renaissance of journalism, transparency, and accountability, a similar set of technological forces were creating the conditions for fake news, bot armies, and algorithmic opacity. Enter Russia into the 2016 US presidential elections. That nation's information warfare campaign makes clear that not only are the tax shelters of the rich and famous susceptible to leaking for political gain but so are the institutions of democracy. Finally, in chapter 3 we look closely at the Russian hacking of the DNC's email servers, continuing to reveal how the timing and volume of leaks affect politics. We conclude this chapter by examining a more traditional form of boundary work, the attempts by US Congress to manage the role played by Facebook in the Russian hack— and the proliferation of false and misleading information leading up to and beyond the 2016 US presidential election—through governmental regulation and public hearings. Facebook CEO Mark Zuckerberg's testimony before the US Senate and House of Representatives in 2018, suggesting that artificial intelligence might help differentiate fact from fiction, makes clear that the volume and temporality of leaks and hacks is something that technology companies, like the US state, cannot fully control.

The state's attempts to monopolize hacking as an exclusive resource extend from exfiltrating and leaking damaging private information to other institutions of society, such as the courts. In chapter 4 we focus on how the British court system becomes a theater for the execution of state power over hackers. The story that grounds this interpretation begins in an unlikely location, when a UPS courier arrives at a priest's home in Suffolk in late 2013. He knocks, needing a signature. As the unsuspecting inhabitant comes to the door, gives his name, and exits the home to stand on the front porch and sign for the unsolicited goods, he is handcuffed. Fourteen officers exit their unmarked vehicles and march around the suspect and into the house. For the next five hours, they collect every computational device they can find—twenty-nine in total: tablets, laptops, discs, hard drives, and so forth. And so began the multiyear ordeal of hacktivist Lauri Love, a series of events that illustrate the mechanics of state boundary practices as they move beyond networks and data to a more traditional cast of characters, such as the police, lawyers, courts, and other executors of justice.

For the UK's National Crime Agency (NCA), this was a success. The suspect was in custody, and computers were seized before they were encrypted. Yet boundary work is never quite so simple. Although the NCA was pursuing its own investigation, it was also acting as a proxy for a bevy of US law enforcement authorities that wanted to extradite Love. When the NCA case stalled, the agency and the Crown Prosecution Service (now repositioned as US proxies) embarked on a five-year effort to extradite Love to the United States. He was accused by the United States of hacking into ninety-seven government computers, including fifty-three US Army computers, twenty-six US Navy computers, and sixteen NASA computers. The activist project Love was likely involved in was the Anonymous-led #OperationLastResort, an act of retaliation against state authorities for the suicide of American Aaron Swartz, an internet activist who hanged himself while being prosecuted for downloading an archive's worth of scientific articles from an academic database (JSTOR) using his credentials at MIT's library. In Swartz's case, Malcolm Feeley (1992) is correct, the "process is the punishment." Among internet freedom, open information, and antisurveillance culture, Swartz's death was considered the result of an overzealous state enforcing out-of-date laws with ridiculous punishments. Love similarly faced a staggeringly long criminal sentence if prosecuted in the United States.

As social scientists, we followed this case, sitting through long, opaque, and sometimes passionate hearings in court 1 at Westminster Magistrates' Court in London. Along the way we got to know Love and his supporters—LulzSec hackers Mustafa al-Bassam and Jake Davis, hacker lawyer extraordinaire Tor Ekland from the United States, and Naomi Colvin from the Courage Foundation, who also represents Chelsea Manning, Julian Assange, and Edward Snowden. As observers, we collected data about how US and UK authorities use threats of lifelong and difficult incarceration, labored and prolonged adversarial proceedings, and other court processes to govern and contain hacking forms that have been labeled "dangerous." And we witnessed how hackers like Love mobilize their skills as a potential benefit to the state (as ethical hackers or boundary workers) in their public self-presentation. Courtrooms can become locations for spectacles where state power is performed and executed, and hackers and other political figures become important components of future boundary practices.

An important part of Love's defense involved his autism, a disorder that made the possibility of incarceration in the United States particularly troubling and potentially inhumane—at least from the perspective of human rights (which the Human Rights Act 1998 incorporates into UK law). In mobilizing autism as a defense, Love had a precedent in the British hacker Gary McKinnon—charged as Love was with breaking into the US National Aeronautic and Space Administration (NASA). McKinnon's motivations were not as political as Love's; he wanted to discover whether the United States had evidence for the existence of UFOs. The result was "the biggest military hack of all time" (Broadbridge 2009, 12). But concern for McKinnon's autism caused a public outcry, which resulted in a "forum" bar and gave courts the power to refuse extradition if the UK was a more appropriate place for a trial. It worked in McKinnon's case, as he was not extradited to the United States, and Love hoped it would work for him. Nonetheless, the UK prosecutor, appearing on behalf of US authorities, argued that Love was exaggerating his condition and using it "as a shield to extradition."[3] Extradition seemed inevitable and the threat of a lengthy US custodial sentence loomed large over a hearing process characterized by untested evidence and prosecutorial accusation. In early 2018, however, Love succeeded in fighting extradition to the United States, and in the process, the more radical political applications of his hacking talents were redirected toward prosocial and state-supporting activities. As chapter 5 makes clear, the market, like the court, can be used to rehabilitate hackers into pro-state actors.

The state's pursuit, prosecution, and punishment of hackers is but one form of boundary work geared toward containing and controlling the power of hacking. In addition to recruiting hackers to work directly on its payroll, it uses the private sector to find, cultivate, and deploy skilled hackers indirectly. The industry of hacker privateers working for the state and for corporations falls under the rubric of ethical hacking. By *ethical* these hackers define themselves as morally aligned with dominant institutions and against hacker criminals and hacktivists. Ethical hacking as a service offered for a fee might include testing the network security of a bank, an armed force, or a university. In undertaking this practice, ethical hackers adopt tactical perspectives, practices, and software similar to those deployed in criminal or politically motivated hacking. The privatization of hacking is in line with other historical processes widely considered under the banner of neoliberalism, by which state responsibilities—in this example, network security and offensive cyber intrusions—shift to private firms and individuals. The rise of ethical hacking is itself a modality of state boundary work in that it exposes how state agencies encourage the recruitment of hackers through market incentives, and with it, the development of less-accountable private cyber armies.

This privatization of hacking and attacking is paired with another neoliberal process in the global digital economy, understood variously under the terms *free labor* (Terranova 2004), the *gig economy*, and other types of unre-munerated work within communicative or surveillance capitalism (J. Dean 2009). As much of ethical hacking is unpaid, it can be seen as volunteer or precarious networked work that is made possible by the personal interests in tinkering and problem solving associated with hackers (Coleman 2013b) and further incentivized through opportunities for creating social capital around reputation, status, and prestige. In addition to these efforts at find-ing inexpensive cyber-security work, the state attempts to recruit and pay hackers. These dual neoliberal approaches to hacker privatization and paid or underpaid hacking dovetail with the broader transformation of work practices within capitalism more generally. They also exhibit the adaptive ways in which the state solicits and rewards action on its behalf.

The contradictions of ethical hacking, and by extension the paradoxes of the state's support for hacker privateers, can be encountered via sev-eral different methods and at various locations. In chapter 5, we map sev-eral instances of ethical hacking by investigating the creation of an ethical hacking industry, the people involved in ethical hacking, the efforts to teach ethical hacking, the recruitment of hackers at a major hacking con-ference, and other efforts to fold hackers into state boundary work. Our multisited approach provides insights into the diverse ways in which this industry manifests itself through marketing, recruitment, pedagogy, and networking.

Our research took place between 2015 and 2019, an eventful period in the privatization of state hacking and an era characterized by events that call to mind Paul Virilio's notion of the global "accident" (Crosthwaite 2013). The 2017 WannaCry bug outbreak infected more than two hun-dred thousand computers in nearly one hundred countries. The FBI and other federal authorities struggled to recruit enough hackers to stem what seemed like a relentless barrage of networked intrusions. The state, the dig-iterati, and the private sector each mounted efforts to counter the trend of increasing cyber insecurity and decreasing cyber defenders. In this chapter we again follow the work of Lauri Love, described above as facing extradi-tion for illegal hacking, as well as that of Marcus Hutchins, a British cyber-security expert. Both hackers volunteered their time and skill to attempt to stifle the WannaCry bug. In the end, both succeeded: Love in avoiding extradition, and Hutchins in defusing WannaCry. While Love avoided jail in the United States, Hutchins is currently awaiting sentencing in the US after pleading guilty to two counts under the Computer Fraud and Abuse Act and the Wiretap Act in connection with developing and selling the powerful "Kronos" banking malware. The notoriety he received from his "free labor" drew the FBI's attention to previous crimes and his apparent multiyear career as a teenage black hat hacker. Thus, his "ethical" free labor directly affected his own incrimination. In this case, the state needs hackers but also actively works to keep them at a distance. These examples illustrate one of the paradoxes of ethical hacking—displaying one's hacking skills to do "ethical" work can lead to exposure and the possibility of prosecution for past misdeeds.

As a new practice, ethical hacking marks out an area of competence and a domain of activity in pedagogical workshops and recruitment initiatives. For example, the National Cyber Security Centre (NCSC) and Government Communications Headquarters (GCHQ) run Cyber School Hubs in several Gloucestershire, UK, high schools, where would-be hackers are found early in their career and directed toward prosocial applications of their talents. Bug bounty markets, computer bug hunting or capture the flag games, and hacking marathons are efforts to gamify and moralize the work of ethical hacking for the "good guys." To further document how ethical hacking is devised as a "moral technical imaginary" (Kelty 2008, 170)—that is, how its embodied techniques and ideological dimensions are interlinked—we participated in two environments. At Hacker House's "Hands-on Hacking" workshop in Manchester in 2017, we worked with Matthew Hickey, a.k.a. HackerFantastic, and his teaching assistant Dragos, where we learned how to use Kali Linux, a free and advanced penetration-testing platform used by legitimate and illegitimate practitioners. The use of such a software kit exposes again the methodological overlaps and technological dependencies that link state actors and criminal offenders. Here the very tools used to hack the state and corporations are repurposed to train ethical security professionals.

Later that year we participated in DEF CON 25, the largest hacker conference in the world, hosted every year in Las Vegas. DEF CON has been a space for the meeting of black- and white-hat hackers, where hackers are aggressively recruited or even apprehended by the law. The presence of the "feds"—state agents from the security services, such as the NSA—fluctuates from year to year. In 2012, General Keith Alexander, then head of the NSA and US Cyber Command, gave the keynote address. In 2013, immediately after Edward Snowden and Glenn Greenwald revealed the PRISM project, wherein major technology companies provided the NSA backdoor access to the personal data of their subscribers, the feds were barred from entry. In 2017, the year of our participation, the feds were back, along with members of the US Congress. In sessions titled "Meet the Feds" and "Hack the Pentagon," we participated in talks by government officials and their sympathizers speaking in glowing and collaborative terms to the amassed security workers. We documented US congressmen James Langevin (D-RI) and Will Hurd (R-TX) in rare bipartisanship, addressing, thanking, and making peace with hackers. As in the examples discussed, the privatization of hackers and the proximate relationship between the state, could-be criminals, and potentially criminal software underscore the inherent contradictions in ethical hacking and ethical capitalism more generally.

Through our efforts to examine the times, people, practices, and geographies of ethical hacking, we position this practice within the overarching contradictions of neoliberal capitalism—a form of value creation that exploits free labor, co-opts political activism, and reinforces the status quo of security first and foremost for the state and its contracted corporate forces. If some contradictions exist—reliance on unscrupulous hackers and their weapons, conflation of market and civic duties, hanging with the enemy—then so be it. State officials reserve the right to recode legal protocols as well as the normative and moral frameworks around which what is and what is not "ethical" is rendered intelligible.

In the conclusion a final story reinforces the insights of this book and illustrates how state hacking affects the present. We identify some of the enduring problems associated with state hacking before reflecting on how the exponential growth of the network technologies that make it possible will likely magnify the complex of ontological and systemic insecurities that characterize high breach societies. We begin by mapping the movement of hacker code exfiltrated out of the NSA, allegedly by either an NSA employee or a Russian hacker group, and how that code was ostensibly morphed by North Korean hackers into a ransomware called WannaCry, which took over hundreds of thousands of computers around the world before being defused by an ethical hacker. A narration like this advances our argument about what French sociologist Pierre Bourdieu might call the "fuzzy coherence" (1990, 87) of the hacker state. In this flexible arrangement, state hacking emerges as an aggressive practice situated in liminal spaces between states and criminals, justice and lawlessness, and certainty and ambiguity. While the movement and application of code is sometimes unruly and may appear universally malicious, it remains a central and largely unchecked resource for state forms.

Hacker states seek to dominate the direction and application of exfiltration but their actions may have unintended and ultimately deleterious effects on how democratic political systems function. We focus on how state hacking affects core institutions of social, political, and economic organization. For example, the opaque dark state within both democratic and authoritarian states may be reinforced by the rise of in-house hacking. The judicial system, already under executive strain, may become a venue for political performances of power in addition to dealing justice. Vulnerabilities in software that runs much of the world's business, digital culture, and government functions might be harbored by state hackers who have found these vulnerabilities and will not disclose them. The *ethicality* of ethical hacking might be compromised by the growth in the market for these vulnerabilities. Finally, state-on-state hacking can threaten the legitimacy of elections when states seek advantages over opponents through chaos or by helping oppositional candidates.

Taken together, these new manifestations of the dark state, performative judicial systems, software vulnerabilities, ethical hackers, and election tampering may contribute to the erosion of democracy. Responses by civil society have ranged from protest to a rather defeatist "surveillance realism," which accepts the state's new hacking raison d'état (Dencik 2015). We go a step beyond this concern and return to the technologies that make the hacker state possible. We conclude by focusing on how three laws of digitalization—the laws of ever-increasing computational power, information, and information infrastructure—will mark a future of more, not less, insecurity, not only because they powerfully augment state tactics but simply because of the momentum inherent in digital networks. Hacker states will not abandon the opportunity to defend and expand in this new world.

2 Hacking the State Boundary

Hacking is in a persistent state of flux. It is pervaded by normative and legal ambiguities surrounding the status of the practices, software, artifacts, and actors that operate in this field. Not only do actors in the digital sphere have different rights and responsibilities under the law, but the relationships, processes, technologies, and practices that produce the cybersecurity foundations of our collective digital reality are also poorly understood, undercodified, decentralized, and piecemeal. Indeed, it is striking that while security expert Bruce Schneier (2013) once popularized the notion that the "golden triangle" of "people, process, and technology" was central to stable cybersecurity, today he concedes security expert David Lacey's (2013) point that in an era of "big data," people and procedures are increasingly unreliable and incapable of meeting contemporary challenges. According to Lacey and increasingly much of Silicon Valley, the above equation should be rebalanced in favor of automation.

Part of the problem is that the layers of code, software, and hardware tying together our world have been assembled too quickly, stitched with an eye for speed and optimization rather than securing the "very infrastructure of our lives" (Tufekci 2018). But it also flows from the persisting enigmas surrounding what sort of "space" cyberspace really is (Mosco 2004). Whether we call it "networked space" or the "space of flows" (Castells 2000), cyberspace increasingly disrupts or transforms the way geographies of power have traditionally functioned (Cohen 2007). The internet not only enables borderless communication by default but also actively ruptures parameters of speed and scale (Mueller 2010). While the former transforms the political, logistical, and economic costs associated with censorship and surveillance, the latter alters the efficacy, shape, and potential effects of political and state action. In this sense states that seek to deploy power through information networks are shifting the spatial premises and territorially bounded imaginaries on which the exercise of that power rests.

One prominent aspect of this reconfiguration has involved the criminalization of hackers and their position as boundary objects against which a new topography of state practice has been drawn and expanded. Yet in this chapter we argue that criminalization represents but one in a series of governance strategies and adaptations simultaneously pursued within different state domains. For example, outside the law enforcement sphere, state agencies frequently draw on the hacker skill set and, when logistically expedient, assimilate these "rogue" groups as a state resource.

Philosopher Michel de Certeau's (1984) distinction between strategies and tactics illustrates the transformative impact of cyberspace on how state hacking is conceptualized. According to de Certeau, strategies are the purview of institutions; they presuppose resources and power, but above all they impose a Cartesian understanding of place, a "break" between one's space or base of operations and everything else (1984, 36). This axial division forms the basis of control over other organizational vectors like time (a secure base allows independence from contingency), vision (observation, measurement, and therefore control of objects from a fixed place as a form of panoptic practice), and knowledge (the accumulation of strategic knowledge practices through which space becomes legible and manageable). If strategies flow from mastery of place, tactics are determined by the absence of a "proper" place. Without a space to collect its forces, plan a campaign, and surveil the landscape, tactics are limited by contingency and the moment. They are weapons of the weak, and they exploit one of the most obvious constraints of power: its own visibility. As de Certeau notes:

> The space of the tactic is the space of the other. . . . [I]t must play on a terrain imposed on it and organized by a foreign power. . . . It takes advantage of "opportunities" and depends on them, being without any base where it could stockpile its winnings. . . . [T]his nowhere gives a tactic mobility . . . but a mobility that must accept the chance offerings of the moment. (1984, 37)

In our view de Certeau's discussion of tactics and strategies is particularly apt in illustrating the difficulty in conceptualizing (and pursuing) cyberspace as a strategic space. The sort of traditional maneuvers and strategies that become accessible to power once space has been territorially conquered are not available. Indeed, as international relations expert Lucas Kello has noted: "Because machines and networks of them pervade modern society, security threats permanently reside at its core. . . . [I]n the past, the enemy's presence in essential domestic terrains signaled the failure of security policy; today it is a starting axiom" (2017, 5–6).

Thus if cyberspace is a predominantly tactical space, then this "absence of place" has a leveling effect on the exercise of power. This fact allows solitary individuals or groups of hacktivists to act with impact on the international stage once reserved for nation-states. This dynamic also magnifies the capacity for force projection and the influence of smaller states who may lack scale in the traditional fields of war (i.e., air, sea, and land) but gain new scalar capacities through networked technology. Finally, this situation also potentially transforms the entire breadth of our collective digital reality (including consumer social media platforms) into a series of confrontational zones or potential fronts where disruptive and destabilizing attacks are copious, multipronged, and seemingly omnidirectional.

Under the above predicament, the more open, uncensored, and unqualified a country's embrace of networked technology, the more targets it makes available for attack. In this sense, authoritarian and nondemocratic states like Russia, China, and North Korea (to the extent that they support heavily firewalled, censored, and monitored intranets) emerge as the more flexible and nimble actors, capable of applying pressure abroad while leaving fewer targets domestically. Such states seek to transform their cyberspace into a sort of strategic stronghold or base of operations.

In the tactical field of state hacking, however, monopolies of code, software, and digital violence are difficult to concentrate and even more difficult to sustain. As we illustrate below, states behave as if they can obtain such monopolies: they stockpile vulnerabilities, exploits, and cyber weapons as if they were an arsenal of nuclear weapons or the latest military tech. Yet this is an ecology determined by an assortment of heterogeneous actors that depend on a compromised sharing of code, personnel, and hardware practices. As much as the field of state hacking resituates power asymmetries, states (while eminently vulnerable and breachable) remain the best positioned to take advantage of them. After all, far more hackers are in private security firms and the government working on defensive and offensive security than laboring for free or under principle as hacker activists. Yet, as we argue below, it would also be empirically incorrect to view the hacker state as a well-defined and coherent entity with a unified rationale and strategy. The state we describe in the discussion that follows remains in a process of adaptation and assemblage, steered by the quantum pace of technological change and by the concrete imperatives, practices, and resources of its different domains of governance.

The Crisis of the State in the Networked Age

The state is deep in the throes of an adaptive challenge, where many of the traditional functions of statecraft, as well as the core founts of state legitimacy, find themselves significantly upended by new connective technologies and networked forms of action and resistance. Several scholarly accounts focus on the historical and geopolitical shifts generated by the emergence of networked technology and globalization but offer divergent characterizations of the state's response to these challenges. Communications scholars Manuel Castells and Matthew Carnoy (2001) argue that late twentieth-century nation-states reconfigured how they exercised power in the wake of globalization, protracted shifts in the representation of politics, as well as the labor market and the economy. States built international, regional, and supranational institutions to collectively manage globalization and initiated a series of decentralization and devolution initiatives to shift power and resources to substate, regional, and local governments or NGOs in a bid to better represent the social diversity of their constituents (Castells and Carnoy 2001, 13). These changes began the process of replacing the vertical and hierarchical modes of structuring state power prominent in the twentieth century with something akin to a network, where all the constituent nodes (at supranational and subnational levels) interact and remain important for the performance of functions.

Building on a similar set of concerns but locating state crisis in the obsolescence of traditional modes of warfare and the new vulnerabilities generated by the information age, military strategists David Ronfeldt and John Arquilla (2001) advance a theory of "netwar." In their view, there is a fundamental tension between the hierarchical, compartmentalized, and jurisdictional organization of national security and crime-control efforts on one side and the networked and horizontal form increasingly favored by nonstate adversaries, activists, and dissidents. The latter use digital technology as both a weapon and a coordination tool, "swarming" in coordinated strikes from all directions or adopting "electronic pulse systems" (i.e., DDoS software) to overwhelm government and corporate websites (Ronfeldt and Arquilla 2001, 12–13).

Similarly, media scholar Taylor Owen (2015) describes how "disruptive innovation" challenges core functions of the international system, which have been largely controlled by nation-states and international organizations since their inception. Technological disruption (e.g., the actions of hacktivists Anonymous or the emergence of cryptocurrencies) transforms the attributes and strengths of the hegemonic functions of the Western democratic state (e.g., the rule of law, the existence of political ethics and norms of behavior, the structuring of power through hierarchies and bureaucracies) into constraints and therefore weaknesses (2015, 6). In Owen's view, digital technologies level geopolitical power relations: they empower nonstate actors in decentralized networks access to capacities once monopolized by nation-states and large organizations. Simultaneously, though, the same disruptive technology presents new opportunities for state control through, for example, innovations in cyber warfare or the sort of bulk surveillance programs disclosed by NSA subcontractor Edward Snowden.

Finally, communication scholars Shawn Powers and Michael Jablonski (2015) argue that states have responded to the challenges posed by digital technology by expanding their sovereign claims to the informational realm. Democratic and nondemocratic governments alike have increasingly adopted national intranets (i.e., firewalls that restrict access to their local networks and restrict domestic access to global networks) to control the information flows within their territories (2015, 165). To be sure, there is a high variability in how states balance the drive for control alongside questions of privacy and free speech. For example, although China tolerates a significant level of public debate and digital activism, its internet still sits behind a firewall. In contrast, while the United States espouses the internet as a "public space," it has also engaged in a broad array of hacking tactics, including the NSA's efforts to hack encryption technologies and NSA/ GCHQ efforts to hack the anonymity protections in The Onion Router, or Tor (Powers and Jablonski 2015, 187–191). According to the authors, these efforts—by no means unique to Americans but similarly adopted by their European and British counterparts—point to a dramatically reinvigorated state. Governments operating under the mantle of national security routinely persuade or compel private-sector cooperation in surveillance, security, and control activities, even though most of the internet remains controlled and operated by private companies (2015, 194).

In Castells and Carnoy (2001) we encounter a reconfigured state characterized by diffuse and decentralized chains of decision making. Ronfeldt and Arquilla (2001) describe a networked and nimble enemy that wields the digital means of asymmetric warfare against what is essentially an ossified military bureaucracy. Owen's (2015) democratic nation-state is characterized less by its capabilities than by its prerogative and presence on the geopolitical scene. Finally, Powers and Jablonski's (2015) state is stitched together from fiber-optic cables, bulk surveillance programs, and foreign policy pronouncements. Yet these portraits, as much as they present the state as a unified rational actor bending social and economic processes to its will, also present very different visions of the state (an American Western state at that). How is this possible? And what do these accounts tell us about how hacking (a central technology in these narratives) moved from an area of state concern and a problem of governance to an increasingly prominent state resource? We argue that the problem is not that these characterizations are incorrect but rather that they (and many others) are indeed accurate. There are many hacker states, often asserted simultaneously from within the state's own competing spheres of power. Our aim in this chapter is to unpack this disparate assemblage of processes, practices, and imperatives that have shaped our image of the hacker state. In its place we seek to develop an account of the emergence of hacking as a resource and tool of state governance.

Assembling the State

The very notion of the state—as a unitary, bounded entity distinct and set apart from a society on which it acts—has been under scrutiny for some time. Some have labeled it a "mystification" or "reification" (Abrams [1977] 1988, 63, 77) whose ideological representation works to justify political action. Others have noted that the state is best characterized as a "powerful, metaphysical effect" (Mitchell 1991, 94), the result of concrete material practices whose coordination seemingly points to an idealized central structure or framework. For these authors the state is an ideological construct, and its analytical value lies in how this representation is mobilized to achieve different modalities of governance (Midgal 2001; Migdal and Schlichte 2005; Carroll 2009; Mayrl and Quinn 2016).

One important way in which states achieve this act of cultural projection is through drawing borders and boundaries, beginning with the axial distinction between state and society. Yet as Timothy Mitchell (1991) has argued, although it is common among state scholars and in state discourse to posit a clear division between state and society, it is often difficult in empirical terms to locate the line where one ends and the other begins. In Mitchell's view, the state has no concrete exterior edge but is rather a bundle of complex internal processes of governance oriented toward the minutia of spatial and temporal regulation as well as the practices of supervision and surveillance through which social life is steered. The cumulative effect is the impression of an independent status: a machine greater than the sum of its parts (Mitchell 1991, 93). Importantly, if state boundaries and borders are relatively fluid (in the sense that they have no fixed exterior edge), then this also means that they are mobile and that the staging of the state's exteriority is a cultural project that functions as another resource within a state's governance practices. We adopt the term *boundary work* to describe this strategic redrawing of boundaries and borders within state domains and between the state and society. Boundary work brings certain practices and processes closer to state forms while selectively keeping others at arm's length.

The above view is echoed by international relations scholars Joel Migdal and Klaus Schlichte (2005), who emphasize the dichotomy between the image of the state and the practices of state workers. In this definition, the state remains a field of power characterized by its use and threat of violence (2005, 15), but the shape of the state is contingent on the interaction and tension that unfolds between its image and its material practices. Yet these are not necessarily aligned in a coherent or unidirectional fashion. For example, the day-to-day practices of officials, bureaucrats, agents, and officers of the state might work to bolster and strengthen its image, but they also provide opportunities for resistance and friction given that competing strategies and tactics might work against that very image (19–20). The image of the state shifts depending on the concrete practices against which it is projected and the set of problematics of governance those practices have emerged to address.

Sociologist and science studies scholar Patrick Carroll's (2006, 2009, 2012) reworking of the state also addresses the gap between image and practice by describing the inanimate and nonhuman objects state practices emerge from, act through, and operate on. For example, Carroll (2012) focuses on the process through which water became an object of concern and governance for the state of California. He argues that over time, water served as a "boundary object," positioned between government and science. Water became a problem with multiple material and conceptual facets that helped articulate and differentiate new areas of governance around which networks of scientific experts, water infrastructures, and hydro technologies coalesced to form a technoscientific state. The state that emerges is a "heterogeneous assemblage of human and non-humans: of land, dams, levees, aqueducts, maps, meters, organizations, discourses, individuals and so on" (2012, 490). Paradoxically, the more complex this assemblage becomes, the more it is represented in clear-cut, simplified, and unitary terms that are sharply delineated from society.

In this chapter and throughout this book we argue, following Carroll, that the hacker state is a dynamic complex stitched from a heterogeneous assemblage of humans (e.g., security researchers, hackers, programmers, military cyber operatives, private security contractors) and nonhumans (e.g., various forms of software, code, zero days, malware, exploits, and viruses) but also material infrastructures composed of thousands of miles of terrestrial fiber optics and submarine cables, computer servers, and internet exchange points, as well as a collection of more formal bureaucratic structures like cyber response command centers and computer emergency response teams. Hacking is both a target of governance through this complex and ultimately a core resource for the expression of state power.

Hacking, beginning perhaps most importantly with hackers themselves, is a boundary object that increasingly sits at the edge of many shifting state-society domains. It is linked to technological innovation and economic development but also generates exposure in the area of economic espionage. It is a strategic resource in the area of national security and domestic law enforcement, but it remains a challenge to public safety whether the target is critical infrastructure or voting in a democracy. Finally, hacking is both a target of ongoing criminalization and a bundle of highly sought-after skills, which are very much in demand in the public and corporate sectors.

Our focus on hacking as a problematic and a resource of state governance echoes sociologists Patrick Joyce and Chandra Mukerji's (2017) point that a core facet of the state's power involves its control over nonhuman "things."

Much like Carroll, Joyce and Mukerji describe the state as a human, non-human assemblage that relies on material formations acting as "distributed tools of governance" (2017, 2). What is distinctive about the state in this view is as much its material infrastructures (e.g., territory, law, bureaucracy) as its superior use and deployment of logistical power. State power is both material (felt by citizens and visible in symbols and emblems), impersonal (furthered through systems, routines, and principles of calculation), and indirectly deployed through "things" (Joyce and Mukerji 2017, 4). Finally, the state is also distributed: it is defined as much by the multiplicity of sites, domains, and locales different government bodies address as by the different modalities of logistical power they exercise in these domains to consolidate authority and wield influence.

Throughout this book we explore the different processes of coordination through which the borders between hacker states and the shifting domains of technoscientific governance are produced and reproduced. In the section that follows, we describe the array of US state strategies that have emerged in relation to hacking as a set of material technological practices. We argue that, although varied, these were part of a broader set of state initiatives aimed at the governance of hacking. We detail an ensemble of strategies that sought to govern hacking as a new technological object with innovative economic and scientific potential, a new crime problem for law enforcement, and a new resource for state national security and military strategy as well as domestic social-control initiatives. Our aim is not to be exhaustive but rather to underscore the multiple and often competing state objectives and governance practices that come bundled under the heading of *hacking*.[1] Nor is our aim to use the example of the United States as a stand-in for how these practices have developed and manifested themselves throughout the rest of the world. On the contrary, as we illustrate in our discussion of Chinese and Russian hacker states later in this chapter, there is significant value in pursuing genealogies of how other hacking states pursue their own versions of boundary work.

Hacking as an Object of Governance

The early history of hacking and networked technology is entwined with the history of the national security state. The decision by telephone companies in the mid-1960s to replace live human operators with computer switching exchanges created the preconditions for phone phreaking and the early crackdown on hackers in the mid-1980s, but it was an earlier connection between the Massachusetts Institute of Technology (MIT) and the Department of Defense (DOD) in the 1960s that hewed the first building blocks of hacker ethics and praxis from the programming activities of MIT's Tech Model Railroad Club (Levy 2010). In 1958, the DOD founded ARPA, a small bureau whose purpose was to maintain America's technological dominance and prevent technological surprises like the Sputnik crisis (Abbate 2000). ARPA was the core research arm for the DOD and commanded a $3.2 billion annual budget (Powers and Jablonski 2015, 55). In pursuing its mandate, the agency primarily relied on outsourcing research to universities and defense contractors, as well as coordinating and strengthening the links between the public and private domains of its research partnerships.

In 1962, ARPA established the Information Processing Techniques Office (IPTO) with an initial budget of $7 million, which by 1969 would balloon to $28 million a year (Fong 2001, 225). Although the IPTO represented a miniscule fraction of ARPA's overall budget, it financed the first graduate computer science programs in the country and supported most of the computer-related research at universities like MIT, Stanford, Utah, Berkley, and Carnegie Mellon. For example, in 1963 it funded MIT's Project MAC (multiple access computing), with a budget of $3 million per year, but also provided the group of programmers and hackers that coalesced around this and other computing research with prototypes, salaries, and eventually (with the creation of MIT's Artificial Intelligence Lab) a bespoke lab known as Technology Square (Levy 2010). This state agency's heavy investment in computer-related research at MIT was mirrored elsewhere: Stanford opened the Stanford Artificial Intelligence Lab in 1965 and several other universities set up computer research institutes or labs during this period (Abbate 2000). In other words, state funding and logistical support formed the basis for the early development of computer science and the associated technical tinkering and hacking, which gave the nascent discipline its motive force.

The relationship between these early hackers and Defense Department investment remained strong despite significant student unrest and activism connected with the Vietnam War. As Steven Levy describes the links between the two groups, "It was only the rarest hacker who called the ARPA funding 'dirty money'" (2010, 131). Almost everyone else, even people who opposed the war, recognized that ARPA money was the lifeblood of the hacking way of life. Or as the then-director of the MIT AI Lab, Marvin Minsky, put it:

> There's nothing illegal about a Defense Department funding research. It's certainly better than a Commerce Department or an Education Department funding research . . . because that would lead to thought control. I would rather have the military in charge of that. . . . [T]he military people make no bones about what they want, so we're not under any subtle pressures. . . . The case of ARPA was unique, because they felt that what this country needed was people good in defense technology. In case we ever needed it, we'd have it. (quoted in Levy 2010, 131)

The apolitical alignment between these early hackers and the Defense Department also provides a marked contrast with the later representation of hackers as political activists, criminals, or even antistate disruptors. From the beginning ARPA situated itself as an obligatory passage point (Callon 1984) for computer-based innovation, and this position was strengthened post-1969 with the development of ARPANET and the gradual linking of hundreds of universities, research laboratories, and defense contractors into a transnational computer network.

Yet the point here is neither to rehash the early days of hacking nor to follow ARPANET'S role in the development of the internet; those histories have been well documented elsewhere (Hafner and Lyon 1998). Rather our aim is to illustrate that in its organizational structure and broad scope of activity, ARPA provides one example of the logistical deployment of state power and the coordination of researchers, programmers, hackers, and planners—but also technological infrastructures like research sites, laboratories, and telephone networks—into an expansive technoscientific assemblage. The agency was small, flexible, and horizontally organized. Its managers had significant autonomy to select research projects and relative freedom from bureaucratic control. Besides its central role in developing the technological infrastructure that would eventually produce the internet, the agency also played an important role in coordinating the development of the Alto (IBM's first office computer and the precursor to both Microsoft Windows and the Mac). For example, Robert Taylor (the director of IPTO between 1964 and 1969) left the agency in 1969 to head IBM's Palo Alto Research Center, where the Alto was developed and around which ARPA-sponsored researchers coalesced (Fong 2001). In other words, the agency stitched together decentralized packet-switching networks to connect its numerous university-based research labs and its defense contractors; it coordinated the research trajectories of more than one generation of computer scientists and dramatically shaped the material preconditions and communication infrastructures that today's hackers use and deploy.

In the above examples, hacking is a boundary object for the state: it is connected to significant innovations in programming across different iterations of mainframe and microcomputers; it weaves together a program of activity and ethos linked to developing computer languages and refining material technological practices, but it also accounts for significant unstructured, untethered, and technically unauthorized activity (e.g., exploring the ARPANET telecommunications network or using electronic mail for socializing or recreation). In this sense, hacking is at the cusp of new technological possibilities, an object of diffuse coordination and an assortment of material practices that have yet to be problematized. This is not to say that the diffuse coordination of hacking and hackers is not itself a form of governance. We understand governance, in the spirit of Michel Foucault (1991) and Mitchell Dean (1999), as a range of state steering and coordination activities that operate at a distance and take a horizontal form, cutting across a range of institutions (among them economic, social, and scientific) and focused on shaping incentives, developing strategic partnerships, and providing the bases for cooperative action in response to a range of problematic or, indeed, beneficial activities.

Hacking as a Problem of Governance

Hacking and hackers appeared in the optics of governance as a law enforcement problem in the 1980s. This was linked to a shift in the cultural visibility of hackers and the wider availability of computer technology in the home (and not just at work or in universities). The DIY hobbyist and computer self-assembly kits that grew out of the experiences of the Homebrew Computer Club and the manufacture of fully assembled personal computers like the Commodore 64 or the Apple Macintosh made computers accessible and increasingly affordable. The invention of smart modems (which allowed users to connect with other computers more quickly and more easily) broadened the reach of this new computer community and helped to generate a thriving information-swapping exchange centered on bulletin board systems (BBS; Steinmetz 2016, 16).

BBS served as meeting and information sites where users could upload and download files (e.g., free software), have discussions, post information about exploits, send messages and announcements, as well as play games (Coleman 2013b, 30–31). BBS were numerous (e.g., one source estimated 3,400–4,500 BBS were active in 1985) and importantly, their membership could be open or closed (Soma, Smith, and Sprague 1985, 572). Finally, smart modems also provided users with the means to explore telephone networks and seek out connections with other computers for fun, exploration, or exploitation. From time to time, these network surveyors would come across largely unguarded government and corporate servers to explore. The phone numbers and modes of access for these computers were then frequently circulated among hackers on BBS or through word of mouth (Steinmetz 2016, 17).

The "hacker crackdown" (Sterling [1992] 2013) by law enforcement during this period rode on the coattails of previous federal scrutiny of electronic toll fraud committed with blue boxes against telecommunications giant AT&T in the mid-1960s. These efforts initially targeted gambling bookmakers using blue box technology (essentially routing boxes that allowed a user to make free calls through the telephone system) to evade the long-distance toll records that federal authorities used as evidence in their prosecutions. Yet federal scrutiny quickly broadened to include the vibrant *phone phreaking* movement, an assortment of telecommunications hobbyists and enthusiasts who manipulated (i.e., hacked) the phone company's 2,600 hertz signaling tone to set up clandestine conference calls, explore the telephone system, and place free long-distance calls (Lapsley 2013). Smart modems gave computer hackers the capacity to explore the telephone networks and seek out server connections much like the phone phreakers had done in an earlier era. Yet while phone phreakers remained a subcultural phenomenon, hackers quickly ascended to the status of a new criminal class.

On June 3, 1983, United Artists released *War Games*, starring Matthew Broderick as teenage hacker David Lightman. Lightman is a computer geek who likes exploring the phone network and is not above breaking into his high school's computer system to change his grades. One day, while searching the phone network looking for computer games, he inadvertently accesses a US military supercomputer originally set up as a simulation to predict the outcomes of a nuclear war. Lightman thinks the simulation is a game and decides to play. Yet the computer is linked to the nuclear weapons control system, and in playing out the scenario, the pair come a hair's breadth from starting World War III.

Alongside the box office popularity of the film, its debut coincided with significant news coverage of recent FBI raids on teenage hacking groups engaged in activities not entirely different from the movie's premise. The 414s (so named because of the Wisconsin area code where the group was based) were the most prominent of these hacking outfits, and its de facto spokesperson, Neil Patrick, was featured on the cover of *Newsweek* and appeared on *The Phil Donahue Show*, *The Today Show*, and *The CBS Morning News*. Indeed, it was the media attention surrounding the group's activities that spurred Democratic congressman Dan Glickman to organize congressional security hearings to discuss an "entirely new underground of people known as computer hackers who continuously try to defeat the security measures programmed into modern computers" (US House 1983, 2).

The hearings began with a four-minute clip of *War Games* and were followed by the testimony of Patrick, then a seventeen-year-old high school student. He described the various computers and networks the 414s had accessed, including an unclassified computer at Los Alamos National Laboratory (where the atomic bomb was developed), a computer monitoring the radiation treatment for 250 patients at Sloan Kettering Cancer Center (a hack that happened on the same day *War Games* opened), and a computer at the Security Pacific Bank in Los Angeles. Patrick confirmed that the group had simply been exploring the networks and that it had no criminal or malicious intent, but he also described the ease with which simple hacking techniques could be deployed to leverage access to highly sensitive computers. He noted that BBS were a particularly useful informational resource: "Not all people on bulletin boards are in hacking, as they call it, but that's probably the best place to get information about accessing computers, because of the fact that everybody . . . who uses bulletin boards is interested in computers in one way or another." When asked what sort of information was available on BBS, Patrick replied: "Various ways of accessing computers, such as passwords that could be tried. Default passwords are probably the easiest way of accessing computers because of the fact that every—or large numbers of computers around the country would have the same passwords because the system operators may not take out that time to change the passwords" (US House 1983, 15).

Not long after the hearings another dramatic government raid of hackers made national news. On October 12, 1983, the FBI carried out a series of coordinated raids on more than a dozen homes in nine states. Their target was the Inner Circle, a group of mainly teenage hackers from Southern California, New York, Detroit, Tucson, Oklahoma City, and Virginia that had been accessing and exploring General Telephone and Electronic's Telemail system (which hosted email services for companies like Raytheon, Coca-Cola, Citibank, BMW, and NASA) and the ARPA network (ARPANET), which was still mainly used by university researchers and government defense contractors. The group was caught in 1983 after an FBI informant befriended some members on a BBS and then organized an elaborate sting to identify the key players. When the FBI raided their homes, it seized their computers, modems, and notebooks, which contained copious notes on host lists and techniques for accessing the networks (Novak 2016).

The next year, the US Congress passed the first computer crime law as an amendment to the Comprehensive Crime Control Act of 1984. The Counterfeit Access Device and Computer Fraud and Abuse Act (CFAA) would be amended in 1989, 1994, and 1996, as well as expanded under the Patriot Act and the 2008 Identity Theft Enforcement and Restitution Act. At the time, the act criminalized accessing sensitive government information connected with foreign relations or national security, accessing certain types of financial information from financial institutions, and improper access of information on government computers (US Pub. L. 98-473 [1984]). The act gave jurisdiction over computer crimes to three state policing entities: the Secret Service, the FBI, and the Internal Revenue Service (IRS). In practice this meant that the IRS took jurisdiction over crimes involving computer-assisted tax avoidance; the FBI focused on bank fraud, organized crime, national security, and terrorism; and the Secret Service took over everything else. This federal assault on hacking was mirrored at the state level: although only six states had computer crime legislation in 1979, by 1989 forty-eight states had adopted it (McEwen 1989, 7).

BBS in particular came under heavy government scrutiny and were the subject of elaborate sting operations. In 1985, the Technical Crimes Investigation Unit of the Maricopa County (AZ) Sheriff's Office set up a bulletin board for twelve months and yielded fifty arrests for telecommunications fraud (McEwen 1989, 20). That same year, the Freemont Police Department (CA) established a bulletin board to gather intelligence on hackers and phreakers in the area with aid and funding from the telephone, banking, and credit card sectors (VISA, MCI, ITT, Sprint, Western Union, and Wells Fargo Bank). Over the course of three months, agents established and advertised their new "phreak board," amassing more than 130 regular users. They convinced elements of the user base of their hacking credentials by boasting of hacked long-distance codes and stolen credit card numbers and readily gained access to pirate and clandestine BBS in the area (where they found a treasure trove of stolen credit card numbers, long-distance access codes, and passwords for many government, education, and corporate computers). In total, authorities charged fifteen teenagers in California and other states with possession of stolen property, trafficking in stolen long-distance access codes, and theft from credit card accounts (McEwen 1989, 102–103). Dramatic government raids on hacking groups intensified in the following decade, beginning with Operation Sundevil on May 8 and 9, 1990, when the Secret Service executed twenty-seven search warrants in fourteen different states, confiscating computers and charging several hackers with using and selling stolen credit card numbers, phone access codes, and other information from BellSouth. Some hackers received fourteen-month sentences and steep fines totaling about $233,000 (Halbert 1997).

The above cases describe the early boundary work of state law enforcement in its attempts to draw on the symbolic and cultural weight of criminal law to reify state-society boundaries and to provide the practical means for sanctioning increasingly common (if relatively nonserious) breaches of government and corporate infrastructures. It signaled a growing awareness among lawmakers (and agents in the field) of the growing disruptive potential of hacking technology and the increasingly networked (and insecure) character of governmental and economic processes. Yet these efforts were only marginally directed at making the public or the consumer safer, since the laws were clearly meant to shore up state and corporate power (really only criminalizing breaches of government and financial institution computers). Finally, as is often the case when state-society boundaries are redrawn by criminal law, these activities designated a new category of dangerous and threatening subjects capable of serving as examples of state vigilance as well as justification for future state overreach.

Hackers and Hacking within the State

The law enforcement crackdown on hackers during the 1980s and 1990s provides a window into the early variegated state response to the problems posed by hacking. Rather than a centralized unitary approach to hacking and hackers, state actors and agencies during this period were responding to different organizational imperatives, proceeding along multiple fronts of engagement and generating diverse tactics of intercoordination. Indeed, outside the sphere of federal and state law enforcement, different forms of boundary drawing were already under way within the state's own domains. For example, in 1981, the DOD set up the DOD Computer Security Center, a unique entity within the NSA to coordinate cybersecurity within the department. Although it started with a small staff of thirty-one security researchers, this number had swelled to more than ninety full-time staff two years later, and the center planned to double this number by 1985 (Klein testimony, US House 1983, 405).

The DOD Computer Security Center illustrates both the scale of state resources deployed within the field of hacking and the divergent trajectories that these projects inevitably took: DOD state actors were not overly worried about teenage hackers getting into their systems. As Robert Morris (a twenty-year veteran at DOD R&D contractor Bell Laboratories, who did consultancy work for the Air Force and the NSA) pointed out in his 1983 congressional testimony:

> The notion that we are raising a generation of children so technically sophisticated they can outwit the best efforts of the security specialists of America's largest corporations and of the military is utter nonsense. . . . [T]he technological content of the highly publicized events of the last few months and indeed of the last 2 or 3 years, is really the moral equivalent of stealing a car for joy riding . . . purposes when the keys are left in the ignition. (Morris testimony, US House 1983, 507)

Morris noted that the core problem in the civilian and commercial sector (which he defined as separate from the work done within the DOD and its associated contractors) was the fact that these computer users failed to implement the most elementary rule of computer security: they did not change the default passwords from the manufacturer.[2]

In contrast, Morris laid out the more tactical approach to cybersecurity adopted at Bell: over the course of two to three years and under special authorization to act as a "tiger team," he had been working to hack into some of the more sensitive personnel and financial records of the company. He detailed the system of safeguards and access restrictions that completely locked him out of sensitive systems and noted that he could not even get into the company's payroll records to change his salary. Thus, from a DOD point of view, much of the activity surrounding hacking and hackers as new high-tech villains was hyperbole, although the department was already adopting more sophisticated hacking techniques as a resource to probe its own system security. Here the boundary between state contractor, computer science researcher, hacker, and penetration specialist was fluid, much as it had been in the 1960s. In the defense sector, hacking had been incubating and developing through its functional relationship with technological innovation and technical development. In a few years it would become an important component of conventional war operations and planning.

The cultural and ideological work performed by the state in the 1980s and 1990s was largely undertaken by federal and local law enforcement. They aggressively pursued hackers, publicized BBS arrests and raids, and seized and destroyed their computer equipment but ultimately stopped short of significant prison sentences; often hackers were placed on probation and ordered to pay fines or a restitution. At the same time, the intense law enforcement attention during this period, as well as the ensuing media hysteria and cultural status occupied by hackers, helped make them a particularly visible group capable of being framed as dangerous (Halbert 1997). Sociologists of deviance have long noted that the investigation, prosecution, and punishment of criminal acts can be understood as powerful rituals of signification oriented toward the policing and maintenance of society's normative and moral boundaries (e.g., Lemert 1951; Erikson 1966). Such rituals and ceremonies become particularly salient in the context of social and technological change, where cultural, economic, or political structures and expectations are in flux or undergoing sustained transformation. Indeed, social change can generate what sociologist Kai Erikson has called "boundary crises" moments that "dramatize the issues at stake when a given boundary becomes blurred in the drift of passing events, and encounters which follow between the new deviants and the older agents of control provide a forum, as it were, in which the issue can be articulated more clearly, a stage on which it can be portrayed in sharper relief" (1966, 68–69). The boundary crisis of the 1980s and 1990s unfolded against the backdrop of hacking and the ongoing readjustment of law, economics, and democratic processes this activity would set in motion.

Sociologist Stanley Cohen ([1972] 2002) famously coined the term "moral panic" to describe a media-generated panic in 1960s Britain over clashing youth groups. Cohen's analysis emphasized the sensationalized and distorted news coverage that presented these groups as folk devils or outsiders, the amplification of deviant conduct that ensued when group members came to identify with these subcultural labels, as well as the disproportionate mobilization of law enforcement, moral entrepreneurs, and other agents of control to deal with the problem. Cohen argued that the nationwide panic gained traction because postwar social anxieties over changes in status, class, and consumption patterns generated a boundary crisis for which these youth groups readily served as scapegoats. In a similar vein, cultural studies scholar Stuart Hall and colleagues ([1978] 2013) analyzed a media generated moral panic concerning muggings in early 1970s Britain in the context of widespread anxiety over black immigration, sexual permissiveness, and youth counterculture. Hall et al. argue that the state seized on the panic to tackle its own crisis of authority linked to economic decline, open warfare with Northern Ireland, and increasing militancy among trade unions and student groups. Both books provide a window into the *ideological exploitation* of deviance (Cohen [1972] 2002, 116–117), whereby deviants become a resource in the pursuit of socially or politically defined ends with little or no regard of the consequences for the offenders themselves. Hackers are open to state ideological exploitation in Cohen and Hall's sense because they sit at the intersection of a complex set of cultural anxieties and state policy predicaments concerning the shifting role of technology and the internet in everyday life.

Finally, although the above discussion has focused on the US example, in the 1990s hacking clearly emerged as a law enforcement problematic for state governance more broadly. For example, according to Philippe Baumard (2017), the French Domestic Intelligence Service (DST) adopted an operation similar to the BBS stings of US law enforcement to identify French hackers in 1992. Under DST direction, the hacker Jean-Bernard Condat set up a false Chaos Computer Club France—named after the highly influential Chaos Computer Club formed in Berlin in 1981—in Lyons in 1989. Condat's Chaos Club featured its own online zine, the *Chaos Digest*, and was the subject of a live prime-time television program in which Condat hacked into the French Intelligence Service in real time. The sting blended intelligence work alongside a criminalization campaign: the DST managed to identify some 2,500 active hackers, but it also used the club and its digest as a technical resource to learn about the most up-to-date intrusion techniques. Finally, according to Baumard, the DST also used the club to recruit and identify new employees from the ranks of hackers (2017, 24–25). The French example further illustrates how the criminalization of hacking can function as a tool of state governance: it provides a pivot point from viewing hacking as a problematic activity to harnessing it as a resource. The DST sting operations and incursions mapped available resources and capacities in the community, generated detailed technical knowledge about exploits and intrusion techniques, and provided a cache of potentially compromised (and hence willing) intelligence workers.

Hacking as a State Resource

The above law enforcement boundary work culminated in a blunt and relatively coercive assemblage of tactics, practices, and modes of interagency collaboration meant to shore up the public image of a crime-fighting state capable of meeting the aporias of governance introduced by the advent and rapid diffusion of new networked technologies. Yet in other state domains (e.g., the defense or military sector), hacking was increasingly viewed not as a problem to be overcome but as a resource that could be harnessed. Indeed, around the same time the FBI and local law enforcement were targeting teenage hacking crews, the US Air Force was fielding some of the earliest state hacking units. The 609 Information Warfare Squadron (IWS) was established at Shaw Air Force Base in 1995 (US Air Force 1999; Klimburg 2017) with objectives such as "to develop IW [information warfare] strategies that support component and theater plans and objectives; to plan, integrate and orchestrate offensive IW capabilities and concepts into air component missions; and to plan and conduct Defensive Counter Information operations for the AFOR/CC [Air Forces Commander]" (US Air Force 1999, 8–9).

Already during the 1990 Gulf War, US forces had identified the strategic value of cutting off an enemy's command, control, and communication nodes (DOD 1992). Coalition forces heavily bombed "microwave relay towers, telephone exchanges, switching rooms, fiber optic nodes and bridges that carried coaxial communications" in an effort to wipe out Saddam Hussein's capacity to communicate with his troops and Iraqi citizens before US troops were on the ground (DOD 1992, 127). Yet a 1994 plan for the invasion of Haiti to restore President Jean-Bertrand Aristide after a military coup displayed how information warfare could function alongside conventional military operations, as well as illustrating the differential framing of hacking by state entities outside the law enforcement domain. Although Aristide was restored to power through diplomacy, the war plan involved a war-dialer-inspired strategy. The US Air Force would flood the country's phone lines with busy signals so that Haiti's air-defense system (which was connected to local phone lines) would be rendered inoperative, and American aircraft could fly over the country unimpeded. The plan was hatched by a junior air force officer (who would soon join the staff of the 609 IWS); he came up with the idea based on his experiences as a teenage hacker (Kaplan 2016, 58–59). A similar strategy was used in Belgrade in 1997 when it was discovered that Serbian air-defense systems were connected to civilian telecommunications systems; US Army tech crews hacked into the phone system to probe for operational data and vulnerabilities (Kaplan 2016, 111–113). These early examples underscore the hybrid nature of early state hacking within the military sector: hacking was operationalized as a complement or appendage to military operations but not as a unique modality of attack in its own right.

At the same time, the potential of information warfare as a distinctive attack technology was illustrated in that year's Eligible Receiver exercises—a yearly war simulation organized by the Pentagon's Joint Chiefs of Staff and designed to explore a new threat or line of attack (Klimburg 2017, 163). In 1997 the simulation focused on cyber defense and involved using an NSA elite hacking unit, Red Team, to perform systems penetration tests on the whole DOD network (Kaplan 2016, 66–67). Over the course of six months before the start of the exercise, the Red Team performed reconnaissance on the DOD's classified and unclassified networks, looking for points of access and vulnerabilities. The only restriction placed on the NSA team was that they could only use commercially available hardware and software and could not rely on insider information. The second part of the exercise, which involved the Red Team posing as a state hacking unit, penetrating the networks and wreaking as much havoc as possible, was scheduled to last two weeks. The Red Team took over the entire DOD network in four days (Kaplan 2016, 68). As Colonel Walter "Dusty" Rhoads (the 609 IWS commander at the time) recalled:

> So they were in PACOM [US Pacific Command] networks and built a series of world events which involved social engineering and rolling blackouts and, you know, social unrest. One of the most interesting parts of the exercise was, every

evening in the afternoon session there was a very professionally produced news summary—like the evening news except it was the ER '97 events of the day. And it was really pretty attention-getting . . . frankly it scared the hell out of—out of a lot of folks, because the implications of what this team had been able to do were pretty—were pretty far-reaching. (Atlantic Council 2012)

Two events the following year drove the point home. The first, code-named Solar Sunrise, involved two California high school students coached by an Israeli hacker operating under the moniker The Analyzer. The three teenagers exploited a well-known Unix vulnerability and hacked into a score of military base computers at a time of renewed tension between Saddam Hussein's Iraq and the United States. The incident was reminiscent of a breach in 1990, during the first Gulf War, when Dutch teenagers penetrated thirty-four DOD sites and downloaded or accessed sensitive information on weapons systems data, military personnel, and logistics (GAO 1991). The second major event was a penetration-testing and reconnaissance campaign of military networks by Russian hackers codenamed Moonlight Maze. The hackers did not just probe the networks but managed to exfiltrate some 5.5 gigabytes (GB) of nonclassified but sensitive data (Kaplan 2016, 86). The impact of both Solar Sunrise and Moonlight Maze were amplified by the media attention they garnered. *Newsweek* broke the Moonlight Maze story with the alarming headline: "We're in the Middle of a Cyber Attack."

That same year, the NSA (in partnership with the CIA) developed its elite hacking unit, Tailored Access Operations (TAO), which specializes in infiltrating, exploiting, monitoring, and gathering intelligence from computer networks. Finally, in the wake of the September 11 attacks, state-based hacking operations mushroomed and shifted from being primarily focused on foreign threats to engaging the domestic sphere as well. The Signals Intelligence (SIGINT) Directorate, which housed TAO, recruited several thousand personnel in the four years post-9/11 and became the fastest-growing part of the NSA, swelling to some six hundred personnel at its main headquarters in Fort Meade and another four hundred at NSA remote operations centers across the United States (Hayden 2017; Kaplan 2016, 135). And it was not just the national security sector that began to see hacking as a resource of governance, but law enforcement began creating their own computer crime hacking units as well.

The above examples illustrate the multiple trajectories that linked hacking practice and emergent forms of state cyber governance. Whether hacking was viewed as a problematic of governance, a resource for warfare, or an integral component of national security depends on the differing state domains within which it appeared and gained logistical traction. Yet these cases also represent hacking's prehistory, and although the United States and its allies enjoyed remarkable dominance in exploiting networked technology during the early days of the internet, the current situation has changed dramatically. The tactical field of state hacking has grown very crowded, and hacking has become a central state resource, not just for the United States but for all states. In step with this new technological realignment, the sort of cultural boundary work described in the context of US law enforcement efforts in the 1980s and 1990s has been broadened and significantly stepped up (as we will see in chapter 4). It now clearly serves various purposes. The criminalization of hacking and hacktivism shores up the image of the state as a credible actor capable of meeting a broad array of asymmetric and tactical digital threats, whether those be terrorism, state-sponsored disruption and influence, or cyber crime. This is increasingly important in light of the near-daily headlines concerning high-profile data breaches and leaks, political misinformation campaigns, and industrial espionage, as well as zero-day digital Armageddon. One aspect of this ideological effort is evident in the form of a new governmental transparency, which includes declassified investigations and reports on state hacking efforts, briefings and white papers from cybersecurity companies detailing persistent threats, and a public relations campaign by federal law enforcement focused on the indictment, extradition, and arrest of cyber criminals. Although these efforts originate from different state domains, respond to unique practical imperatives, and involve a complex assemblage of state agencies and actors, their public visibility promotes an image of dramatic and seamless state coordination.

Further, this portrait of the cyber state working to assert control over a lawless and deterritorialized frontier, where terrorists, malicious state actors, and cyber-criminal botnets roam (regardless of whether in practice this is actually the case) has helped further the collapse of the legal, categorical, and normative distinctions between crime control and national security already under way since 9/11 (Aas 2013; Bigo 2000). Indeed, as we will see in the sections that follow, drawing up criminal indictments against foreign operatives, issuing criminal charges against state hackers, and making formal requests for extradition have all become important tactical and symbolic fronts in the widening "code war" (Carlin and Graff 2018).

The Field of State Hacking

Thus far we have charted a partial genealogy of the different strategies the US state has adopted to govern hackers and hacking technologies. We have argued that these governance strategies can be understood as state *boundary work*. That is the selective and logistical redrawing of borders within the state and between state and society to bring certain material practices and processes into closer proximity (and hence alignment) with state objectives while selectively keeping those same practices at a distance in other domains of practice. We have argued that this work is central to the representation and image of the hacker state and have described this boundary work as it played out in the domains of national security, military war planning, and operations, as well as criminalization. In chapters 4 and 5 we track how these different governance strategies (i.e., hacking as a law enforcement problem and hacking as a state resource) develop in the contemporary period. In the following sections we apply the boundary work framework to survey the field of contemporary state hacking.

The field of state hacking is characterized by a tremendous heterogeneity in terms of the number and variety of actors that populate it as well as the scale at which they operate. Virtually all states hack other states. Some states hack corporations for trade espionage. Many hack foreigners for intelligence and their citizens for surveillance or censorship. But some states also enlist cyber criminals to perform digital heists or to disrupt rival state infrastructures; they encourage patriots and DIY enthusiasts to wage private hacking campaigns that target rivals, and states sometimes furnish exploits and attack packages. Many also retain the services of cybersecurity firms and professional intermediaries to perform the above work. Finally, states are also *hacked* by private citizens, hacktivists, or cyber vigilantes seeking transparency, accountability, revenge, or just amusement.

Large countries like the United States turn to hacking because, like drone warfare, the technology holds the promise of securing state interests without the deployment of physical troops and thus clearly carries less accountability to oversight committees, journalists, the international community, and the public—although this may be changing. Small countries like North Korea turn to hacking because online the power asymmetries between it and the rest of the world are greatly reduced. As we will see, state hackers are motivated by a shifting array of concrete aims, long-term goals, and immediate tactical initiatives. They are the product of disparate state genealogies and unique technoscientific infrastructures. They operate in a tactical field that seemingly levels traditional power asymmetries and furnishes smaller states and nondemocratic states with unique advantages.

The Chinese Hacking State

The Chinese hacker state provides an important counterpoint to our discussion of the United States. It possesses an impressive armada of state-based cyber capabilities, but it also harbors an equally sizable alliance of loosely knit "patriotic hackers," who sometimes hack on its behalf. For example, a nationalist collective of hackers called the Red Hacker Alliance (also known as the Honker Union) has been active since 1998 (Henderson 2007, 58–59; 2008). The alliance is a network of linked websites that share intrusion and attack techniques, as well as a loose grouping of 80,000–300,000 hackers who coordinate attacks on foreign governments and related agencies in response to real or perceived attacks on the Chinese nation.

These hackers flooded Indonesian government websites and mailboxes with email bombs (mass-mailed duplicate emails meant to overwhelm inboxes) and denial of service attacks in response to the 1998 riots in Jakarta, when the Chinese community was violently targeted by indigenous Javanese (Henderson 2007, 17). The following year the hackers attacked Taiwanese government websites and initiated a two-month-long cyber skirmish with Taiwanese hackers over the president's endorsement of a "two states" understanding of Sino-Taiwanese relations. In 2000 they attacked Japanese government websites after the denial of the Nanjing Massacre and struck Taiwan again after the election of a proindependence president (Henderson 2007, 24–25). Over time the attacks grew technically more sophisticated (e.g., employing Trojan software and malware) and more numerous, even as some factions within the network (e.g., The Green Army) professionalized and started cybersecurity companies. In 2001, in the aftermath of a collision between an American spy plane and a Chinese jet, a six-day cyber war broke out between the Red Alliance and American hackers, involving email bombs, denial of service attacks using zombie nets, and the hijacking of government websites. The official White House website went down for several hours, and the group claimed to have hacked one thousand American websites during its campaign (C. S. Smith 2001).

Chinese patriotic hackers continued to wage highly visible but ultimately noncritical attacks throughout the decade. Much of this activity was of low sophistication and gained visibility because of its concentrated scale and obvious political targeting, rather than because of the security threat it posed. Throughout this period, hacking outfits like the Red Hacker Alliance were essentially hacktivists whose relationship to the Chinese government was difficult to assess. Although there was clearly some degree of contact and communication between state officials and some members of these groups, their motivation appeared to be genuinely patriotic and indirectly aligned with the state.

Yet by 2010, the activities of these volunteer political activists were supplemented with a focus on penetrating economic targets. Many patriotic hackers began moonlighting as hackers for hire, setting their sights on acquiring and exfiltrating foreign technology and intellectual property (Klimburg 2017). A case in point is a 2009 joint investigation by the University of Toronto's Citizen Lab and the SecDev Group into a cyber-espionage GhostNet comprising 1,295 malware-infected computers in 103 countries. Although the report identifies China as the geographic source of the network and notes that one-third of the infected computers can be considered "high-value diplomatic, political, economic and military targets" (SecDev Group and Citizen Lab 2009, 6), it speculates that nonstate actors actually established and ran the espionage scheme. Similarly, a 2016 report tracking the activity of seventy-two unique China-based hacking groups over the course of three years by security firm FireEye identified 262 network compromises of government and corporate entities in the United States and the rest of the world (FireEye 2016). Although it is unlikely that all of these are freelance hackers, the report also explicitly notes the broad spectrum of actors (government, military, contractors, patriotic hackers, and cybercriminals) that can align themselves at any one time with state interests.

Thus the scale, frequency, and scope of Chinese state hacking has shifted, as has its logistical and structural coordination. Much of this activity can be understood within the framework of state governance strategies developed earlier in this chapter. Hacking in China emerges less as a law enforcement problem to be overcome and more as a broadly wielded political technology aligned with state interests. In this sense, hacking is framed against Chinese cultural and ideological representations of the state-society dichotomy within which the state is presented as an all-encompassing organization that promotes economic progress, social order, and nationalist spirit (Shue 2004; Pirie 2013). Within this view, independence from government control does not necessarily imply a clear separation from the state. Rather, citizens are posited as an integral component of national security, and the state includes them within its strategic planning (Henderson 2007, 102).

The use of unofficial forces (e.g., civilian militias) has a long history, can be traced back to Maoist thought, and was a key component of how the People's War was framed (Green 2016). Yet since 2006 efforts to better integrate and formalize civilian capabilities within the state's cyber-military infrastructure have also gathered pace: China's 2006 five-year plan outlines the merging of civilian and military capabilities, and the State Council's *Medium- and Long-Term Program for Science and Technology Development*, published in the same year, also highlights the integration of military and civilian technology (Inkster 2016, 104). Finally, according to the 2015 military white paper "The Science of Military Strategy," "nonstate," or "informal," forces are now specifically included as the third level in China's three-tiered state cybersecurity forces (Klimburg 2017, 281–282).

Alongside the structural rearrangement of its patriotic hacking cadre, the Chinese state has also introduced a raft of new laws that redefine the legal and cultural place occupied by hacking. In February 2009, China amended its antihacking law to criminalize the development and distribution of malicious software. Given that previously the law sanctioned only intrusions of government systems, this shift has been read by commentators as an overt restriction on the operating latitude once informally granted hacking groups (US-China Economic and Security Review Commission 2009, 175). The law was quickly put to use, and several high-profile and amateur hackers were arrested and convicted by security authorities (Krekel 2009, 39). Apart from sending a signal to patriotic hackers, this criminalization of hacking also targeted the exponential scale of cyber crime in the country, which, given the country's alleged synergistic relationship to hacking groups, it seems to have been slow to check. For example, according to the Ministry of Public Security, online fraud jumped by 30 percent every year between 2011 and 2014 (Inkster 2016, 43). More recently, in December 2015 China passed a counterterrorism law that requires internet service providers (ISPs) and telecommunications firms to hand over encryption details to Chinese law enforcement. Although omitted from the enacted law, the original draft of the bill went even further: it explicitly required these companies to install backdoors in their technology for state actors to exploit (Inkster 2016, 44–45).

Thus far we have focused on the impact of volunteer and nonstate hackers, but perhaps the most formidable elements within Chinese hacking efforts are state based. Indeed, by the time a US grand jury in the Western District of Pennsylvania indicted four People's Liberation Army (PLA) officers in 2014, state hackers had been engaging in intellectual property theft at an estimated cost of $300 billion a year for quite some time (Easton 2013). The four members of PLA Unit 61398 (the most prominent of multiple state hacking units) were charged with economic espionage, theft of trade secrets, identity theft, computer hacking, and other malicious acts. Their targets included critical infrastructure, solar industries, the United States' largest labor union, and many others. Among the terabytes of information harvested were seven hundred thousand pages of emails—including design plans from Westinghouse, a nuclear plant construction company, while the company was engaged in negotiations to build a nuclear plant in China (Talbot 2015). And evidence suggests that Unit 61398 hacked and stole intellectual property from nearly 150 companies in twenty different economic sectors (Mandiant 2013).

Yet even the above examples fail to capture the scale and breadth of Chinese efforts as well as their potential long-term consequences. For example, two breaches in 2014 of the US Office of Personnel Management (OPM) databases involved the personnel records and security-clearance reviews of 22.1 million Americans (Nakashima 2015a; Sanger and Myers 2018). The data included the exposure of every security-clearance background check performed by the office since 2000. In total the highly sensitive data of some 19.7 million applicants alongside the information of 1.8 million family members and contacts were exfiltrated. A smaller database included social security numbers, job assignments, and performance evaluations; the larger database also held the fingerprints, usernames, passwords, and detailed financial and health information of 1.1 million individuals who had filled out their applications online (Nakashima 2015a). As former FBI director James Comey noted in a press briefing at the time: "If you have my SF 86 [Standard Form 86 for security clearance], you know every place I've lived since I was 18, contact people at those addresses, neighbors at those addresses, all of my family, every place I've traveled outside the United States. . . . Just imagine if you were a foreign intelligence service and you had that data" (Nakashima 2015a).

Alongside the penetration of OPM servers and databases, officials now suspect that Chinese hackers were also responsible for the massive hack of Marriott International's Starwood guest reservations database. Although the hotel company only discovered the breach in 2018 as a result of installing new security software, the hack took place in 2014 and involved a trove of 5.25 million unencrypted passport numbers and another 20.3 million encrypted passport numbers, as well as 8.6 million encrypted credit cards. In total the breach is estimated to have affected 383 million guests, making it the largest such breach to date (Holley 2018).

According to US authorities, China's hacking efforts are multipronged. On the one hand, these hackers seek the technological and economic templates for market dominance: blueprints, patents, manufacturing work flows, contact lists, emails, and other processual paradigms for the global commodity chain are favored targets (Easton 2013). On the other, the recent focus of activity appears to be a multiyear project to dox the American state. The theft of OPM data alongside the Marriott hack provides a trove of data that complements well-known (and others still to be discovered) breaches of the sensitive and personally identifying information of US federal workers.

Although these efforts have been described as "passive surveillance" rather than "disruption" (Hackett 2016) and have been identified as in line with wider Chinese military strategy and philosophy prioritizing "active defense" (Inkster 2016, 87), this view is itself a representation of the state for cultural consumption. The line between passive surveillance and active disruption or attack is clearly very fine, since all the necessary prerequisites (e.g., penetration of systems and infrastructures, installation of backdoors, possession of admin privileges) are already there: in many of the 2014 breaches, hackers took their time, exploring and monitoring the databases they had pilfered for many months. Finally, the scale and breadth of data harvested provides a window into a new computational front in cyber war: the use of big-data analytical techniques to amplify the profiling and predictive spoils of cyber espionage. Indeed, in many ways, these efforts reflect the elevation of the hacker/security researcher methodology to state practice: aggregate datasets and password databases, probe for weaknesses and vulnerabilities, and assemble schematics and logistical information, not necessarily because they are useful in the present but because they will continue to be relevant in the future.

China represents a unique case not only because it hacks both foreign state institutions and private businesses, but also because its foreign activities are an extension of its domestic cybersecurity and surveillance practices. China's "networked authoritarianism" operates in conjunction with a corporate sector willing to provide political surveillance and censorship in return for access to the lucrative investment opportunity represented by the country's rapidly expanding internet-based market (MacKinnon 2012, 32–36). In this sense, China's firewalled, deterritorialized intranet forms the strategic base from which the PLA and others can stage their incursions.

Yet the Chinese effort is also singular with respect to the United States. In the latter, as we have seen, the governance of hacking technologies has been historically premised on drawing boundaries and erecting categories of difference between various state-based forms of hacking (grounded as they are on the disparate practical imperatives and legitimation criteria available in the state domains within which they emerged), as well as between state-based efforts more broadly and nonstate (and hence on their face illegitimate and illegal) forms of hacking. In contrast, China's practices have shaped an altogether different representation of the hacker state, one that systematically blurs the categories of difference and the boundaries that separate state-based and nonstate hacking practices (i.e., political hacktivism, do-it-yourself cyber espionage, state-sponsored exfiltration, and contracted trade secrets theft). The result has helped reify a cultural view of the Chinese state as a well-coordinated monolith, which interpenetrates society rather than standing strictly apart from it.

This predicament has affected questions of attribution and legality (e.g., was this an incursion by the Chinese state?), strategic motivation (e.g., what is the end game?), the state of Sino-American relations (e.g., are we in an undeclared cyber war?), and scale (i.e., what is the actual scope, capability, and size of the Chinese cyber forces?), greatly confounding the capacity of the United States and its allies to respond in an effective, timely, and responsive fashion. The US response, besides conducting its own surveillance and penetration of Chinese systems (activities that one suspects have been going on all along) has been to repurpose its well-articulated criminal justice system in the service of code diplomacy. Federal agencies have indicted government officials and PLA hackers, charged technological companies like Huawei, filed extradition requests, and encouraged strategic partners like Canada and the UK to follow suit.

The Russian Hacking State

While China has adopted a seemingly defensive hacking posture, the approach of the Russian state has been decidedly more aggressive. Whereas the former's stance flows directly from the state's own unique genealogy, the Russian hacker state has been shaped by decades of Cold War proxy battles and a long-term adversarial relationship with the United States. On April 27, 2007, Estonian workers in Talinn removed a Soviet war memorial from the capital's central district. The diplomatic controversy surrounding the removal of the 1947 monument (which commemorated the Soviet defeat of Nazi Germany) had been escalating in the preceding months and had featured Russian officials angrily condemning the government's plans, as well as pro-Russian protests and social unrest that at times turned bloody.

On the day the statue was removed, Russian aggression moved online: Estonia suffered a three-week cyber campaign, which targeted government and media websites, as well as the private sector and banks. Distributed denial of service (DDoS) attacks carried out by a botnet of eighty-five thousand computers effectively paralyzed and shut down Estonian networks, forcing the government to block international web traffic to domestic sites to keep services running for citizens (Landler and Markoff 2007). Estonia has long prided itself as one of the most extensive adopters of networked technology; many government services are provided through electronic means, and the state is increasingly shedding its physical presence in favor of online delivery: citizens vote, file taxes, fill medical prescriptions, and get test results online. As such, despite the attacks' widespread depiction as the "first cyberwar," they disproportionately affected the country because of its level of digitalization but did little critical damage.

Yet the attacks also illustrated a midway point between American and Chinese hacking efforts. There was significant evidence of state coordination. Experts have pointed to the involvement of the now-defunct Russian

Business Network (RBN), which at the time of the attacks was responsible for a reported 60 percent of cyber crimes worldwide (Klimburg 2017, 229). The attacks themselves were relatively unsophisticated and have been attributed to Russian hacktivists or patriotic hackers, as well as to pro-Kremlin youth group Nashi. Indeed, as early as mid-April, Estonian and European security researchers monitoring Russian-language internet forums noticed recruitment chatter describing a forthcoming cyber attack. On the eve of the attacks, these forums also hosted information on how to target Estonian servers, as well as providing Windows command shell scripts and instructions on the most opportune time to use them for maximum effect (Schmidt 2013).

Just a year later, fighting broke out in another former Soviet satellite, the Republic of Georgia. The war concerned two Russian-supported autonomous provinces (South Ossetia and Abkhazia) that had been in conflict with the Georgian state since its declaration of independence in 1991. Over the course of five days, Russia captured the South Ossetian capital of Tskhinvali and marched through Ossetia toward Tbilisi, the Georgian capital. Throughout this conflict, Georgia was the subject of cyberattacks similar in nature and staging to the Estonian experience. DDoS attacks, website hijacking, and vandalism peaked during August 8–10, when Russia invaded the country. Fifty-four news, government, and financial websites were affected, and the functionality of 35 percent of Georgia's internet networks was compromised during this period. The National Bank of Georgia even had to suspend its electronic banking services for ten days during the campaign (White 2018, 1).

Much as in Estonia, and later in Ukraine, patriotic hacktivists and cybercriminals played an important role in the campaign. On the day hostilities started, Russian hacker forums like xaker.ru and StopGeorgia.ru began publishing target lists, identifying vulnerabilities, and distributing downloadable malware packs—these sites also published reports on the efficacy of ongoing and completed attacks (Connell and Vogler 2017, 17; White 2018, 6). Moreover, many if not most of the servers from which the attacks were staged were known to have been owned or associated with the RBN—as they had been identified in previous DDoS activity and attacks on commercial websites.

The effect of the attacks was mixed. On the one hand, these agents effectively blocked a central communication channel between the Georgian government and its citizenry, as well as between the former and the outside world. Yet on the other, given that the degree of penetration of the internet was not as pervasive as in Estonia, there was little lasting damage. What is important to note here is the adoption of hybrid warfare, very much in the same spirit as the United States in the Gulf War and other engagements, where cyberattacks are blended into conventional war operations and complement them. According to commentators, the goal of the cyberattacks was not only to disable domestic communication channels but also to generate a discursive vacuum in the international blogosphere so that the Russian government could shape the narrative of the war (Deibert, Rohozinski, and Crete-Nishihata 2012). In contrast to Estonia, which has its own internet exchange point (IXP) and was thus able to block the full scale of malicious attacks while still keeping its sites up, the Georgian government did not have this option. A significant proportion of the country's network pathways are routed through Russian networked infrastructure, which made them particularly vulnerable (White 2018, 15; Healey 2013, 72).

In contrast to Estonia and Georgia, the Russian campaign in Ukraine was not concentrated and localized in time and space. Much as would be the case for Russian influence campaigns in the United States, Russian state and civilian actors operated on a broad scale, but with a diffuse program of staging and attacks. As in the two earlier cases, Russian hacktivists targeted Ukrainian websites with phishing attacks, malware, DDoS barrages, and telephone denial of service (TDoS) attacks. According to one study, a low-level harassment campaign was ongoing since at least 2009, and as the conflict between the two countries escalated, so did the scale and coordination of the attacks, which came at key junctures in the struggle (e.g., the Maidan protests, the Ukrainian parliamentary elections, and the Russian taking of Crimea).

For example, four days before the May 2014 Ukrainian presidential election, Russian hacktivist group CyberBerkut attacked the country's Central Election Commission and temporarily shut down software to monitor turnout and count votes. Shortly before the polls closed, the group hacked the commission's website and posted false election results, which were then rebroadcast by Russian Television's *Channel One* (Sprang 2018; Medvedev 2017; Peterson 2016). In December 2015, a series of coordinated cyberattacks attributed to Russian hackers targeted the Ukrainian electrical system, affecting 225,000 customers. Although service was restored after several hours, the affected distribution substations continued to function with constrained capacity (E-ISAC 2016, v). Finally, besides executing malware exploitation of Ukrainian government computers, disrupting telecommunications infrastructure, and jamming parliamentary cellphones, the Russian FSB also engaged in a lengthy cyber-espionage campaign (Operation Armageddon) targeting law enforcement, the military, and the government from 2013 onward (LookingGlass Cyber Threat Intelligence Group 2015; Sprang 2018).

In chapter 3 we discuss how these disparate operational proving grounds served as laboratories for cyber warfare, which culminated in the successful hacking of the US 2016 presidential election, but for the purposes of this chapter, it is important to situate Russian hacking operations within the boundary work frame developed earlier. First, note that the tactical field of state hacking is also an epistemological space. The vulnerabilities, code, exploits, and malware that states develop and mine are not the only objects that circulate between licit and illicit, state and nonstate, official and activist actors in this zone, as in the NSA's EternalBlue zero day. State hackers also learn from the successful tactics of adversaries and adopt these tactical positions within the realm of their own strategic capabilities. For example, the Russian state, and for that matter the Chinese as well, has watched closely the hybrid warfare plans adopted by the United States in Haiti, in Kosovo, and in the Gulf War. Russia has taken these operations one step further in both the Georgian war and its annexation of Crimea. Similarly, the potential of cyber attacks to carry a kinetic effect (i.e., obtain a real-life destructive impact), first pioneered by the United States' 2009 use of the Stuxnet worm to derail Iran's nuclear program, has been paralleled in the Russian attack on the Ukrainian electrical grid. And Russia is not the only emboldened actor: a 2015 blackout that affected 40 million people in Turkey has been attributed to Iranian hackers (Halpern 2015).

At the same time, China and Russia complicate the contention that proxy wars are now the primary way state hacking power is exercised (Maurer 2018). To be sure, states have strong incentives to use proxies (whether these are cybercriminals, patriotic hackers, or private security firms) because they make attribution difficult and thus undermine the legal status of hacking attacks. The more difficult it is to prove that any given cyberattack or hack is the work of a state government, the less likely the traditional pressure points of international diplomacy (sanctions, multilateral censure, embargos, and the like) will be deployed in retaliation. Proxies are also economically efficient in that they recruit, train, and develop cutting-edge tech relatively independently of government involvement (Maurer 2018). Yet given that many high-level sophisticated incursions are difficult to identify and even discover in the moment, and that the most visible proxied attacks are also of a relatively low level of sophistication, on many occasions these activities clearly provide a tactical smokescreen. They represent a chaos of multiple attack vectors, coordinated through a swarm of aggressive networked activity within which stealthier incursions often proceed unnoticed.

As with other hacker states, Russia has used its legal system to govern networked technology and curtail its use as a technology of dissent and protest. One of the most visible expressions of this has been the efforts of the Kremlin to hack the anonymity afforded by the Tor router—a popular tool for activists. In 2014, for example, Russia's interior minister offered a 3.9-million-ruble bounty for anyone who could find a technical means of identifying Tor users (Medvedev 2017, 37). Russia has framed the effort to crack anonymity, as have many other states (recall secretary of state Hillary Clinton's similar stance), under the larger rubric of fighting cyber crime. Yet these legal efforts ultimately seek to identify, locate, and expose the real-life identity of internet users. That is, they seek to establish a permanent link between one's online and offline identity, thereby collapsing the two into a single corporeal entity open to state strategies of interdiction and sanction (Fish and Follis 2016). For example, as in China, the majority of Russian internet users access the web through their mobile phones. The state tracks the identity of users through the SIM cards within the phones, which, like a physical internet connection through telecommunications carriers, require registration with a passport. Since August 2014, the same passport-based identification requirement applies to connect to state-funded and commercially provided public Wi-Fi. Additionally, again drawing similarities with China, content attribution is heavily policed: blogs that attract more than three thousand daily visitors must register with state agencies, and bloggers are legally and financially liable for any "inaccurate" claims they might make (Medvedev 2017, 39). Finally, since 2016, the state requires that any company collecting and retaining data about Russian citizens must physically store those data within Russian territory. Thus, like Chinese, the Russian hacking state complements its disruption efforts with a robust strategic stronghold on its digital landscape.

A final point should be made about the Russian hacking state: a core component of state hacking operations (since the Estonian attacks in 2007) has been the folding of domestic criminal networks into state hacking activities. Evgeniy M. Bogachev, the architect of an extensive and highly sophisticated global botnet, which siphoned millions of dollars from the infected computers of businesses and consumers, is a case in point. The FBI has offered a $3 million bounty for Bogachev, who also ran a ransomware scheme, which encrypted the hard drives of infected computers and then demanded payment to unlock a user's files. Cryptolocker, as the scheme was called, netted an estimated $27 million in ransom payments in its first two months of operation and infected some 234,000 computers (half of which were in the United States; US DOJ 2014).

Bogachev controls millions of computers, and the Russian state has grafted a sophisticated intelligence operation onto his network of compromised machines (Schwirtz and Goldstein 2017) by redeploying malware designed for mass larceny to further political disruption and espionage. According to the FBI, Russian authorities are unlikely to arrest Bogachev because he is working with or within the Russian state. Certainly he continues to live openly in Anapa (a resort town on the Black Sea) and enjoys a flamboyant and highly visible lifestyle (Symonds and Brooks 2017). Bogachev also developed the malware system GameOverZeus, which was exploited by a group of hackers called the Business Club.

In 2011, cybersecurity experts at Fox-IT monitoring GameOverZeus-infected machines began to notice requests outside the usual targets for cyber crime (e.g., bank accounts) but related to contemporary politics. For instance, in 2013 when former US president Barack Obama began sending arms to Syrian rebels, Turkish computers under Bogachev's sway were used to search for "arms delivery" and "weapon delivery" (Schwirtz and Goldstein 2017). Similarly, when FSB officers Igor Anatolyevich Sushchin and Dmitry Aleksandrovich were instructed to gather intelligence on American and Russian journalists, government representatives, and businesspeople in finance and transportation, they enlisted the services of two cyber criminals, Alexsey Alexseyevich Belan and Karim Baratov, to infiltrate networks and gather information on their targets. In keeping with the mutually beneficial terms the relationship depended on, the officers ignored the fact that while on official business, Belan and Baratov enriched themselves through the exfiltration of banking details (Maurer 2018, 104).

Bogachev, Belan, and Baratov underscore the ambiguous state of legality surrounding state-supported cyber operations. Russia enlisting cyber criminals in its espionage efforts is not as troubling from a legal perspective as is the seeming default position of *all* hacking states that (in terms of their own state practice) the cyber realm exists in a space where legal considerations can, at best, be legitimately bracketed or, at worst, do not apply. States (including the United States) routinely perform hacking activities, which would be illegal and prosecuted if performed by actors outside the state's protective mantle, and sometimes these activities are illegal for states to perform as well.

Earlier in this chapter we noted the gap between the representation of the state, as a central and unitary actor set apart from society, and the reality of state governance practices, whose multiple modalities betray not only competing and conflicting imperatives but also pose questions about the viability and success of state logistics and coordination in cyberspace. Yet Chinese and Russian efforts point to an altogether different model of boundary work: rather than make the state visible, real, and central—something that, given their totalitarian roots, it certainly is—these practical efforts work to make the state disappear. Analysts are unsure when and how the state is involved, state officials are unclear what constitutes successful attribution, and computer security firms track an ever-expanding list of threats that run the gamut between gifted DIY hobbyists, cyber criminals, and state spy agencies. Where is the state in Russian and Chinese hacking practices? Paradoxically, in ripping the mantle off its carapace and exposing its decentralized practical components, the state seems to vanish *into* society.

Indeed, in some important respects, this seems to be a deliberate, official policy. By folding into the work of the state the activities of patriotic hacktivists, civilians, cyber criminals, and computer security firms, Russian and Chinese state hacking systematically subverts the line between state and society. Thanks to the ubiquity of networked technology, the effects of this boundary work are not confined to the realm of geopolitics, but rather feed into a system that produces radical epistemological uncertainty with dramatic ideological effect (Aupers 2012). As we describe in chapter three, in the discussion of the 2016 US election, the ability to blur the distinctions between hacker activism, social media debate, and state action in the context of the election diffused this conspiratorial politics of suspicion more broadly. In these situations, who works within the state, for the state, or against the state can be intentionally blurry.

Boundary Workers for Hire

Thus far we have discussed hacking as a resource and a problem for state governance from the point of view of well-developed technological heavyweights like the United States, China, and Russia. Yet, as noted, networked technology levels power asymmetries and allows smaller states that may lack the resources or capabilities in conventional areas of military engagement (i.e., land, air, and sea) to assert themselves with impact in this new global arena of cyberwarfare. Fledgling democracies and authoritarian regimes both hack and produce malware, although their often-underdeveloped defenses may make them low-hanging fruit for larger states' hacking operations (Frenkel 2017). In this section we analyze the small states adapting to this open territory, and the boundary workers (cyber mercenaries, security contractors) that populate a burgeoning market for hacking services located at the threshold of state hacking practices.

Small states hack the press, citizens, and activists, but they are also sometimes willing to hack to financially benefit their regimes. In Latin America, Vietnam, the Islamic State in Syria (ISIS), and North Korea, the absence of transparency, the deterritorialization of the networked environment, and the willingness to disregard international scrutiny make investment in state hacking advantageous. Small states also underscore the apolitical nature of networked technology: it is a machinery of power that serves equally well Latin American political conservatives, Vietnamese socialists, North Korean authoritarians, and the fundamentalist propaganda of ISIS. Yet despite its potential use as an offensive weapon in these countries, the analysis of small states reveals a different, regional order of state hacking, in which efforts are directed not necessarily at the larger players but at immediate rivals, or they are concentrated within one's country. In the latter case, hacking technology becomes a core platform for the diffraction of ideological difference.

Observers of the ongoing cyber skirmishes and associated disruptions generated by the back and forth between countries like the United States, China, and Russia are increasingly aware that although networked technology provides the means for asymmetric engagement, it also increasingly carries significant risks. Thus for some regimes, the adoption and use of hacking is a more modest effort oriented toward the maintenance and enforcement of domestic control. Under these conditions hacking technology becomes both a state resource and a lucrative business opportunity.

For example, FinSpy, an intrusion and malware suite developed and sold by the well-known cybersecurity firm FinFisher, has been used to hack, monitor, and disrupt the activity of citizens in various states, including Ethiopia, Nigeria, Qatar, Turkmenistan, UAE, Vietnam, and Bahrain (Marczak et al. 2014). The Italian surveillance technology company Hacking Team similarly builds and retails intrusion and espionage tools, which it markets to a diverse client base. Hacking Team employs approximately forty people from offices in Milan, Annapolis, and Singapore. Within their portfolio of tools is DaVinci, a remote-control system that breaks encryption and provides law enforcement with the ability to collect communications by email, Skype, and chat on hundreds of thousands of computers at the same time. DaVinci and other "offensive" systems are used in approximately thirty countries. Hacking Team is an equal opportunity privateer, which provides computer security tools for corporate giants like the UK's Barclays Bank and British Telecom and Germany's Deutsche Bank but also intrusion software for state cyber-surveillance divisions in countries like Egypt, Italy, Russia, Ethiopia, Bahrain, and Sudan. The firm claimed that their tools were "sold exclusively to government agencies . . . and never sold to countries that international organizations including the European Union, NATO and the US have blacklisted" (Osborne 2015).

Yet in 2015, the activist Phineas Fisher hacked the company's servers; exfiltrated more than 400 GB of internal emails, documents, and source code; and made the entire data dump publicly available. Among the data leaked and later redistributed by WikiLeaks was Hacking Team's client list, which showed seventy active accounts belonging to a host of both national and provincial governments as well as military and police forces. Hacking Team's services are costly: licensing for its core espionage tool Remote Control System (RCS) is $200,000 per year (Schwartz 2017). And although some of the company's clients feature among the most egregious violators of human rights and online privacy—Azerbaijan, Morocco, United Arab Emirates, and Kazakhstan—the United States and Russia have also made use of their services, illustrating some of the lacuna generated by the state's own boundary mechanisms. For example, in 2011, the FBI paid the company more than $700,000, and the Drug Enforcement Agency appears to have used the company's software to target Colombian cartels, thereby outsourcing capacities that its own NSA surely had but that were not necessarily coordinated with domestic cybersecurity branches (Cox 2015). And the Russian FSB also paid Hacking Team 451,000 euros to license RCS between 2012 and 2014 (Schwartz 2017). US law enforcement's use of Hacking Team's services provides a window into the boundaries that develop within different state domains: highly developed hacking technologies in one area of state practice are not necessarily a resource available for coordination with other domains.

These practices have dramatic real-life consequences: for example, Ahmed Mansoor, a democratic activist working in the United Arab Emirates, was identified with Hacking Team's tools, apprehended by police forces, and tortured (Perlroth 2016; Maurer 2018, 79). And when these tools, as well as the zero days and exploits they rely on, are leaked, their capacity for mass network exploitation is dramatically broadened: just hours after Phineas Fisher released the exfiltrated Hacking Team source code and tools, the Adobe exploits and zero days it contained were already being used as a vector for the deployment of cryptoware by cybercriminals (Thomson 2015). By sitting at the threshold of state boundary practices, cyber mercenaries like Hacking Team provide a much-needed resource and service. Some smaller states can skip the costly development in human resources and infrastructure necessary to generate and maintain tools of digital violence by acquiring them in neatly priced software packages. Yet this form of contractual exfiltration is also more modest: the state's attention is not focused on the wider international field of tactics but rather on tightening the strategic bases of control domestically. And this business is clearly booming; even though as a result of the 2015 Phineas Fisher hack, Hacking Team hemorrhaged money and lost clients, it has since significantly bounced back (Franceschi-Bicchierai 2018).

A similar boundary worker is Columbian hacker Andrés Sepúlveda, who considers himself a defender of right-wing politicians fighting against the creep of Marxism in Latin America (Robertson, Riley, and Willis 2016). Sepúlveda claims to have hacked elections throughout Latin America: Panama, Honduras, El Salvador, Colombia, Mexico, Nicaragua, Guatemala, Costa Rica, and Venezuela. His team was assembled from a talented region for specific tasks: "Brazilians, in his view, develop the best malware.

Venezuelans and Ecuadorians are superb at scanning systems and software for vulnerabilities. Argentines are mobile intercept artists. Mexicans are masterly hackers in general but talk too much. Sepúlveda used them only in emergencies" (Robertson, Riley, and Willis 2016). Sepúlveda even encouraged Anonymous to join his group in attacking Hugo Chávez in the 2012 run-up to his fourth campaign for the Venezuelan presidency. His network was inclusive, embracing Latin authoritarians, hacktivists, and cyber criminals in illegal political surveillance.

When Chávez won and subsequently died five months later, triggering an emergency election won by Nicolás Maduro, Sepúlveda hacked Maduro's Twitter account and posted that the election was a fraud. Maduro fired back by shutting down the internet in Venezuela for twenty minutes. For a time, Sepúlveda and his team ran an efficient hacking subscription service: political opposition phones, campaign websites, and donor databases could be exfiltrated or tapped from between $12,000 and $20,000 per month. He is now serving ten years for criminal conspiracy, espionage, and hacking-related offenses associated with Colombia's 2014 presidential election. In Colombia he worked for the election of Enrique Peña Nieto, installing malware on opposition routers, tapping phones and computers. He bought $50,000 worth of Russian malware, which he used to tap the smartphones of oppositional candidates, and deployed 30,000 Twitter bots to plant pro-Peña stories; computers called voters at 3 a.m. with pro-opposition messages, angering would-be voters. Sepúlveda illustrates the breadth and effectiveness of the small state hacker's toolkit, combining in equal parts regime stabilization (e.g., surveillance) and political disruption activities.

Yet money was not Sepúlveda's sole motivation. In 2012, Colombian president Juan Manuel Santos began peace talks with the Revolutionary Armed Forces of Colombia (FARC), frustrating the right-wing Sepúlveda. He supported Santos's opponent, Óscar Iván Zuluaga, by hacking one hundred FARC accounts and then brazenly providing evidence to national television about the group's repression of peasant voting. A month later, forty commandos raided his office and arrested him. Sepúlveda pleaded guilty and is now serving a ten-year sentence in a Colombian prison. In a prison interview, he explained his motivation: "I worked with presidents, public figures with great power, and did many things with absolutely no regrets because I did it with full conviction and under a clear objective, to end dictatorship and socialist governments in Latin America. . . . I have always said that there are two types of politics—what people see and what really makes things happen. I worked in politics that are not seen" (Robertson, Riley, and Willis 2016). Sepúlveda continues to hack in prison, where he does progovernment work, such as identifying ISIS-linked Twitter accounts (Realpe and Peñarredonda 2016). Yet his work as an ideologically motivated for-profit hacker for hire, his use of Russian-made malware, and his eventual "rehabilitation" is evidence of how smaller states can exploit flexibility in the hacker-state space for political gain. Sepúlveda has been remade from a freelance tactician into an exclusive state resource through the justice system. His prosecution and incarceration became an occasion to neutralize a disruptive actor and secure a monopoly on his hacking services as well as an opportunity for a small state to expand its boundaries online.

Although the scale of ISIS's occupied territory and physical footprint is in a constant state of flux, the aspirational state in Iraq and Syria maintains a robust and highly effective digital presence. In addition to hacking, ISIS uses social media for recruitment, propaganda, and organization—which Twitter actively attempts to stop (Waddell 2016). The Islamic State Hacking Division, or United Cyber Caliphate, has hacked multiple websites, and several of these ISIS-related hackers have been prosecuted. Ardit Ferizi, who went by the Twitter handle @Th3Dir3ctory, was convicted of exfiltrating the personal data of around 100,000 US Service members and sending a list of 1,351 targets to Junaid Hussain—a British citizen and ISIS supporter. Hussain then posted the names as a "kill list" on Twitter with the statement: "soldiers . . . will strike at your necks in your own lands!"[3]

ISIS kill lists, both official and unofficial, are on the rise and are a new tactical deployment of a mainstay in the hacktivist toolkit: doxing (i.e., the release of personal identifying information on a target or targets online; Katz 2016). Indeed, Ferizi identifies himself as a hacktivist and supports Anonymous; he claims to support the efforts of Kosovo against the Serbs as well as other hackers from India, Pakistan, Bangladesh, and Algeria.

In 2012 his hacking crew, Kosova Hacker Security, claimed to take down Interpol's website for two days in retaliation for the anti-Islamic film *Innocence of Muslims* (Nakoula 2012). They participated in #OpIsrael, leaking the personal information of thirty-five thousand Israeli citizens, including seven thousand credit card numbers, as well as breaching the OTE-Greek Telecom Service and leaking ten thousand user credentials in #OperationGreek.

Corporations were also targets; for example, IBM's research website was hacked by this group through SQL injection (Turla 2013). Ferizi was eventually arrested in Kuala Lumpur (where he had been living) and extradited to the United States, where he was convicted of terrorism-related hacking charges and sentenced to a twenty-year prison term (Nakashima 2015b; Blake 2016).[4]

Ferizi's fellow boundary worker Junaid Hussain got his start hacking the email of a staffer of Tony Blair (then UK prime minister) in 2011. Behind Jihadi John, the hostage beheader, and Bakr al-Baghdadi, the leader of ISIS, Hussain became one of the Pentagon's most important targets because of his capacity to inspire lone wolf attackers via the internet (Gadher 2015; Coker, Schmitt, and Callimachi 2017). In addition to his aptitude for recruitment, he was also proficient at fund raising for ISIS by hacking banks (Almousa 2015). He developed malware to enable remote control of computers and encouraged ISIS commanders to abandon unsecure platforms, like Facebook and WhatsApp, for encrypted services. Hussain was accused of taking over the US Military's Central Command Twitter account for the Islamic State in January 2015; later he apparently usurped *Newsweek*'s handle (Mosendz 2015). He was also in communication with one of the gunmen who retaliated for "Draw Mohammed Day" in Garland, Texas. He was killed in a drone attack in Raqqa in August 2015. Ferizi remains incarcerated, and the physical territory of ISIS has been reduced by 98 percent (Ackerman, MacAskill, and Ross 2015). It appears that the threat of an Islamic State in Syria has waned, though some have warned that radical fundamentalist ideology continues to thrive where ISIS foreign troops have left, and that the group's online presence remains strong (Dopp 2018).

In ISIS we see the example of state hacking as pure tactical resource: a group with a contingent and unstable occupation of territory skillfully uses networked technology to expand its presence and draw new recruits to its global campaign. In North Korea, we see a similar tactical reworking of state hacking. North Korea has developed a massive cadre of hackers, numbering well over seven thousand employees, yet the bulk of these hackers are not operating from within the country but are living overseas in South Asia, China, or Europe (Mozur and Sang-Hun 2017). North Korean hackers follow the unexpected and nonlinear patterns observed in other smaller states.

The NSA attributes the 2014 hack of Sony Pictures as retaliation for the release of *The Interview* (2014), a political slapstick comedy that featured the assassination of North Korean leader Kim Jong-Un. North Korean hackers calling themselves the Guardians of the Peace inserted a server message block worm (SMB) tool to install a backdoor, listening implant, hard drive self-destruct tool, and destructive target-cleaning tool in Sony's system (Lennon 2014). The SMB connected to command-and-control servers located in Thailand, Poland, Italy, Bolivia, Singapore, and the United States. The data exfiltrated involved forty-seven thousand social security numbers, as well as a vast data dump of more than thirty thousand internal documents, which included embarrassing email correspondence between studio executives and talent (AFP 2014; Kilday 2014). US politicians immediately mobilized to defend Sony: Arizona Senator John McCain described it as an "act of war" (Mullen 2014), and President Barack Obama sanctioned North Korea for the hack (Miller 2015).

The NSA also claims that North Korean hackers spread malware using a watering-hole technique to hack several financial sites around the world, including banks in Poland, Bangladesh, Russia, Venezuela, Mexico, Chile, China, the United States, and the Czech Republic (Mozur and Sang-Hun 2017). Given the overwhelming scale of sanctions against North Korea at the time, hacking for foreign currency becomes an important tactic and resource for smaller states. North Korea's success in hacking foreign media corporations and banks indexes many unsuccessful attempts on not only private business but also governmental institutions.

Yet it should be pointed out that North Korea is by no means an outlier in terms of hacking corporations. For example, the NSA's Black Pearl program has hacked Brazilian oil giant Petrobras and the SWIFT banking system, among other private-sector networks (Watts 2013; Greenwald 2014). Thus the sort of boundary drawing we have seen in the context of US domestic law enforcement is replicated in the international sphere as well; although US hacking agencies engage in similar acts of corporate espionage and network exploitation, they label the actions of "rogue" states illegitimate (and potentially illegal), while categorizing their own efforts as legitimate extensions of the state's own prerogative for self-defense. The end result, though, is that states both large and small, democratic and authoritarian, routinely cross the categorical divide between state services and corporations in the pursuit of useful information and disruption. Likewise, states come to the defense of their businesses and make military threats for stifling corporate activity. These actions and responses are out of sync. They further blur the increasingly fine line between public institutions and private corporate interests and illustrate the ambiguity that characterizes this tactical space of online conflict.

Our analysis confirms Maurer's contention that coercive state power is executed in cyberspace not only through the operations of the state but as a result of the "dynamic interplay between the state and proxy actors detached from the state" (2018, 151). Yet, state and proxy motivation is never stable. State actors can be profiteers, cyber pirates, or hacktivists at any given moment (152). This fluidity challenges the rigidity, silophication, and independence of government institutions. Given the silence of international law and domestic regulations in this new terrain, it is open season for the networked state.

In this chapter we have reviewed the ways in which the state has adapted to the promise and potential provided by the internet for expansion. This observation required us to contribute to the sociological and STS-inspired theory of boundary work, examining how hacking has become one important resource for states intent on projecting their authority in cyberspace. Democratic, authoritarian, and "smaller" states have equally mobilized to transform the threat of hacking into an asset. Along with state hackers, proxies in cyber crime, hacktivism, and others work in the gray zone between legal and illegal state hacking. In the chapter that follows we continue our investigation into hacker states by focusing on the impact hacking and leaking has on democratic processes, such as the reporting, fact-checking, and public sphere functions of the press. Here the Russian hacking of the 2016 US presidential election provides an illustration of the new powers of the networked state in an era of fake, fast, and data-driven journalism.

3 When to Hack

Troll farms. Twitter bots. Dark posts. Fabricated Americans. Email dumps. Fake news. The multipronged, multiyear, and technologically varied nature of Russian interference in the 2016 US presidential election is difficult to map. As the declassified report released by the National Intelligence Council noted, the Russian strategy blended "covert intelligence operations—such as cyber activity—with overt efforts by Russian government agencies, state funded media, third-party intermediaries and paid social media users or 'trolls'" (2017, ii). The campaign drew extensively from the toolkit and tactical array of hackers, hacktivists, transparency activists, and resistance groups. It skillfully exploited democratic openness to critique and debate, the media and blogosphere's long-term cooperation with leakers and whistleblowers, and the emergent counterfactual politics of suspicion among citizens to disrupt the elections and paralyze the democratic process.

The disruption and disinformation campaign was deft in its manipulation of the public sphere and its deep penetration of the political system. Yet Russia was not the only actor waging an influence campaign during the 2016 election. Cambridge Analytica, using the scraped psychometric profiles of some 87 million Facebook users, also pursued an information and influence campaign during the US election. In this chapter, we chart the conditions of possibility for these hacks and argue that their success is bound up with the history and practice of leaking, whistleblowing, and hacktivism since 2010. These campaigns weaponized the media ecologies and pathways, cultural expectations, and collaborative work partnerships forged in the era of megaleaks and data dumps. But, the success of the Russian campaign also provided cover for the equally disruptive influence operations conducted by Cambridge Analytica, which, when revealed by whistleblower Chris Wylie, exposed a dramatic blind spot generated at the intersection of networked technology and democracy.

Chapter 2 introduces the concept of state boundary work as an analytical lens through which to understand how hacking became both a target of state governance and a core resource for the expression of state power. We argue that networked technology has a disruptive and leveling effect on both traditional power asymmetries and the field of international relations, where these inequalities have been most frequently asserted. One of the effects of this new situation is that it potentially expands the capacity of nonstate entities to act with impact on a global scale and, in this regard, we highlight the increasingly important role played by patriotic hacktivists and other boundary workers in the state's overall tactical embrace of networked technologies. Finally, chapter 2 primarily focuses on the exploitation of computer systems as the primary vector for state hacking efforts and destabilization campaigns.

In contrast, this chapter discusses the hacking of democratic systems by drawing on the 2016 US presidential campaign as a case study. As international relations theorists Thomas Rid and Ben Buchanan (2018, 8) have recently argued, when hacking operations turn their sights on democracies, they primarily target political and civil society institutions, not computer networks. The aim is to compromise the systems and relations of trust that form between these institutions and their constituents, thereby undermining democracy's building blocks. Certainly the more than eighty individual instances of document dumps and email leaks (Rid and Buchanan 2018, 9) during the presidential campaign targeted confidence in the system. They were successful in eroding public trust because the public sphere, domestic politics, and the news media had already been primed for the age of disinformation (and the richly speculative and doubt-laden terrain that nurtures it) by years of data dumps and disclosures by transparency activists and antistate hacktivists.

In what follows, we look at the tactics of these transparency activists and hacktivists in greater detail. We begin with Chelsea Manning's bulk disclosures to WikiLeaks and Edward Snowden's slow unmasking of the US hacker state in PowerPoint slides and documents leaked to Glenn Greenwald and the *Guardian*. Manning's and Snowden's differential impact can be understood in light of the divergent temporal and scalar tactics they used to make the scope of state boundary practices transparent. We contrast these approaches with the more radical and confrontational hacktivist program also at work during this period and exemplified by the campaigns of Anonymous, LulzSec, and Phineas Fisher. Unlike the above whistleblowers, these groups introduced new scalar and temporal tactics to weaponize information disclosures (i.e., confidential documents, email spools, and more recently, code weapons) and directly force confrontations with state law enforcement and their contractors rather than targeting the public sphere. Throughout this period, we argue, time and scale considerations were not contingent variables in the publication of information disclosures but rather formed core tactical resources manipulated by whistleblowers, hacktivists, and eventually state hackers to achieve particular strategic ends.

Megaleaks, Speed, and Responsible Disclosure

Chelsea Manning's 2010 leaks of raw Apache footage (later repackaged by WikiLeaks as the "Collateral Murder" video), army field reports comprising the Afghan and Iraq War logs, as well as US State Department cables (which would be known as Cablegate) represent a watershed in the era of transparency activism. The leaks were singular in size and unprecedented quality; the material they contained spanned several decades and involved an archive's worth of classified and confidential government records.[1]

Manning downloaded the reports and documents in her capacity as an all-sources intelligence analyst with unlimited access to the Iraq and Afghanistan databases of the DOD's Combined Information Data Network Exchange (CIDNE)—a computer system used to collect tactical information from troops (Manning 2013, 5). Yet the material was made up of unedited reports and footage as well as unredacted documents and cables, making it too technical and specialized for mass audiences without additional context and explication.[2] As Daniel Domscheit-Berg, then spokesman for WikiLeaks, noted, "No matter how explosive our revelations were, if no one presented them to the general public, they would languish neglected, on our website" (Domscheit-Berg 2011, 48). The character of the material and WikiLeaks' own hybrid position within the media ecosystem meant that publishing Manning's revelations required collaboration with press and broadcast media to craft stories and contextualize material, as well as to give the leaks wider exposure (Chadwick 2013, 108–109). In this way the Manning leaks became enmeshed in the temporalities of the industrial press.

The unprecedented size of the leaks also spoke to new problematics of scale: exceptionally large (in volumetric terms) or technically dense (in terms of specialist knowledge) leaks generate distinctive forms of obfuscation and opacity. Not only do large leaks make the minimization of highly sensitive or personally identifying information more difficult, but they also bring ethical and temporal imperatives to the fore. Raw data (i.e., nonanonymized) typically need to be checked and redacted before they are published in their full form. When faced with this time-intensive process, which can take months, publishers may hold back some or all of the data in the leak. This becomes more likely if sifting and anonymizing the raw data proves difficult to reconcile with temporal pressures because of excessive size or the sheer quantity of privacy concerns involved. Consider, for example, that both the Paradise and Panama Papers, leaks revealing financial offshoring by the world's elites, were 1.4 and 2.6 terabytes (TB) respectively, and that the raw data have not and will not be released.

But more generally, the promise of exclusivity (and hence of a scoop) is often premised on the publisher's assurance of timely publication. This is also related to the content of the leak and its impact: the aim of making the material public is to influence events that are in flux or to shift decision making about ongoing practices. Thus, although the size, condition, source, publisher, means of exfiltration, requirement for redaction, and content are all important factors that shape how and when the public receives the exfiltrated information, the overriding independent variable is time.

The above considerations are also important for a further reason. Whistleblowers and transparency activists frequently make public interest claims to justify their disclosures and to differentiate their activity from those of rogue groups performing intelligence or destabilization work. In the past these claims gained traction when activists were able to advance credible political and moral narratives about their activity and its associated risks. For example, although according to Manning the field reports that made up the Iraq and Afghan logs could not harm the United States and were not "very sensitive" (Manning 2013, 3), when WikiLeaks published the Afghan logs, it had to hold back 15,000 threat reports, which directly identified informants by name (Domscheit-Berg 2011, 157).[3] Yet it did make the remaining 76,911 unredacted documents available, including the one hundred Afghan names buried in the material that had not been excised from the data. In contrast, the *New York Times*, the *Guardian*, and *Der Spiegel* published and reported on a much more limited number of documents in which all personal and identifying information had been carefully expunged.

The ensuing reportage and debate over the possible harm generated by WikiLeaks's lapse shifted the discussion from the content of the leaks to the ethics of transparency (Domscheit-Berg 2011; Keller 2011). In a rush to generate new headlines, the press facilitated this shift from an analysis of content to a critique of the disclosure method, to the eventual and long-lasting character study of Manning and WikiLeaks editor Julian Assange—a ploy that has resulted in numerous articles, films, and other media, proving to have much more staying power than the actual content released (J. Smith 2016). Yet more broadly, the redaction issue mapped the contingencies and limits associated with "responsible" disclosures in the context of juggernaut-sized leaks and globally synchronized publication deadlines.

Manning's leaks set the template for the future publication of high-volume disclosures. For each leak, WikiLeaks (or another broker organization like the International Consortium of Investigative Journalists, which mediated the Panama Papers disclosure) granted exclusive access to a limited number of news media in different countries who collaborated on research and analysis, as well as generating relevant stories for their domestic markets. These activities were synced to a simultaneous international release date, which both maximized impact and potentially made it more difficult for governments to block publication or exert pressure on the publisher. With the Edward Snowden case we describe below, for example, the UK's GCHQ was able to pressure the *Guardian* into destroying their copy of the Snowden archive (Borger 2013).

In contrast to the above well-choreographed string of news dumps, Snowden's disclosures began with a slow and steady trickle on June 5, 2013.[4] Writing in the *Guardian*, Glenn Greenwald detailed a top-secret court order requiring Verizon (a major US telecom company) to provide the NSA with information on all telephone calls in its systems within the United States and between the United States and other countries. The following day, the *Washington Post* and the *Guardian* published the first stories detailing the NSA's bulk domestic surveillance program PRISM along with four internal PowerPoint presentation slides from the former NSA employee. Snowden's leaks were curated and accompanied by careful contextual reporting; in contrast to the relatively speedy publication of Manning's material, their dissemination was orchestrated over the course of multiple years to maximize their effect (Greenwald 2015). Indeed, apart from the tremendous political impact of his revelations, what remains striking today is the fact that the published and publicly disclosed documents represent a very small proportion of the full trove. The archive shared with news outlets contained about 50,000 documents, of which approximately 7,300 have been released since 2013. Further, although there is debate about the total number of sensitive documents Snowden downloaded from the NSA, conservative estimates put the figure at 1.5 million (Kloc 2014).

Snowden's exfiltration of documents was highly selective and targeted, an approach he complemented with a rigid disclosure framework. When publishing stories based on new revelations, journalists were expected to anonymize the documents and to provide the government advance notice in the event that the published material could put lives at risk (Greenwald 2016). Although these are routine practices for reporters covering sensitive leaks, they are not necessarily applied in a consistent fashion by transparency platforms like WikiLeaks. Some might argue that this is the result of the capricious and cavalier attitude of Assange; others could argue that different documents require different publishing tactics. Regardless of the overarching rationale, for leakers, hackers, journalists, and publishers, maximizing impact necessarily involves managing the temporality of publishing.

Daniel Ellsberg's (2002) account of leaking the forty-seven volume *United States–Vietnam Relations, 1945–1967* (also known as the Pentagon Papers) provides a useful contrast to the contemporary period and illustrates the extent to which the combination of networked technology and compact, high-volume storage equipment has transformed the reach and effect of data dumps. Over the course of one year (1969–70), Ellsberg smuggled the individual volumes of the top-secret study from his office safe at RAND to a nearby friend's ad agency, where he proceeded, night after sleepless night, to photocopy them (2002, 299–309). Not only was copying the material time consuming (it took him the better part of a year to make three "fairly complete" copies), but he also had to identify secure physical places for their storage and spend several thousands of dollars in reproducing the volumes (2002, 332). Ellsberg's account paints a vivid picture of trying to navigate the intersecting imperatives of time, speed, and scale. He documents how once he had successfully copied the volumes, he spent another two years trying to find an appropriate outlet (e.g., government hearings, newspapers, self-publication) to get the material to the public. According to Ellsberg, what further complicated the problem was the fact that the immediate applicability of the material was not necessarily self-evident; one had to read a substantial portion of the volumes (if not the whole collection) to glean its full significance for current events (2002, 375, 382).

Networked technology engenders unique forms of temporal and spatial compression, which transform time from a contingent force that must be reckoned with into a tactical resource that can be harnessed and manipulated for strategic advantage. If Ellsberg (2002, 289) were to release the seven thousand printed pages that make up the Pentagon Papers today as a pdf file, it would be no larger than 10 megabytes. It could easily, instantly, and anonymously be disseminated as an attachment to an email (McCurdy 2013, 139), posted publicly via a public messaging board, or mass distributed as a torrent. In contrast, media studies scholar Patrick McCurdy estimates that printing out Manning's State Department cables would require 503 reams of paper and forty hours at a rate of one hundred pages per minute (2013, 136). Yet the complete archive of the Manning leaks, which are just short of 3 GB, would fit on most USB flash drives. The differential impact of scale, portability, and networked technology on leaking is also evident in a recent point made by Snowden in an exchange on these issues with Ellsberg in the *Guardian*:

> The point between the period of Dan's activities and mine is the expansion of reach of a particular source who witnessed some wrongdoing. In Dan's case, what he had in his safe was the limitation of his reach. My reach was across a network rather than the confines of a safe. . . . And what this ultimately results in is a dynamic where a particular employee can plausibly . . . have more access at their fingertips than the director of an office or a unit or a group or an agency—or perhaps even the president. (MacAskill, Snowden, and Ellsberg 2018)

As McCurdy has noted, leaks in the digital age are a "function of the volume of data available and the ease with which it can be spread around and shared" (2013, 135). But leaks and data dumps are also the inevitable underside of the hacking state—a dynamic and interwoven assemblage of humans (e.g., security researchers, hackers, programmers, military cyber operatives, private security contractors), nonhumans (e.g., various forms of software, code, zero days, malware, exploits, and viruses), material infrastructures (terrestrial fiber optics, submarine cables, computer servers, and internet exchange points), and bureaucratic bodies—which generates, collects, stores, and makes instantly available an unprecedented amount of data. Ellsberg was one of only three individuals at RAND with physical access and clearance to the Pentagon Papers. In contrast Manning, who after all was a junior intelligence officer, enjoyed wide-ranging access across a vast network of databases and data exchange points—a level of access shared by an estimated 500,000–600,000 military and diplomatic personnel (Sifry 2011, 155). If the combination of highly compressible data packages, near-instant transmission systems, and strong encryption technologies provide novel means for whistleblowers, leakers, hacktivists, and state hackers to disrupt the operations of power, these vast and networked data repositories represent their idealized targets.

Doxing, Radical Transparency, and Hacktivism

As anthropologist Gabriella Coleman has noted, in the aftermath of Manning's revelations and arrest in 2010, a new modality of politics that drew on the material practices and technical proficiencies of geeks and hackers (i.e., the "weapons of the geek") became increasingly visible: "Anonymous (Chanology vs. AnonOps), Assange, Manning, the Pirate Bay, and others . . . [were] clearly part of a wellspring of hackers and geeks who were taking political matters into their own hands and making their voices heard" (2014, 106). Thus alongside the carefully curated insider disclosures described above, a wave of radical and insurgent hacktivist operations increasingly targeted nation-states, their associated proxies and boundary workers (i.e., security services and contractors), as well as law enforcement personnel. Although certainly not the only hacktivists at work during this period, Anonymous and affiliated hackers LulzSec were the most prominent. In 2011, for example, Anonymous targeted FBI contractors IRC Federal and ManTech corporation, DOD contractor Booz Allen Hamilton, global intelligence firm Stratfor, and government contractors HBGary and HBGary Federal. It and LulzSec also hacked US law enforcement institutions, including the Texas Police Chiefs Association, the California Department of Justice, the Bureau of Justice, and seventy-seven other US law enforcement institutions over the course of 2011 and 2012.

The motivations for these hacks were mixed. Certainly, to the extent that they unfolded against the backdrop of law enforcement investigations, arrests, and stepped-up criminalization campaigns, they represented a militant response to an escalation of state boundary practices (akin to those described in chapter 2 with respect to the 1980s and 1990s). Yet these disparate activities also invoked notions of justice and the public interest in their quest for politically sensitive and damning information (Coleman 2015, 286). Many of the operations described above came under the mantle of OpAntiSec, which, when announced on Pastebin by LulzSec on June 19, 2011, was explicitly characterized as transparency activism: "Your hat can be white, gray or black, your skin and race are not important. If you're aware of the corruption, expose it now, in the name of Anti-Security. Top priority is to steal and leak any classified government information, including email spools and documentation. Prime targets are banks and other high-ranking establishments" (LulzSec 2011).[5] Four days later, LulzSec announced the first installment of a 3.2 gigabyte data dump from the Arizona Department of Public Safety titled "Chinga La Migra" (Fuck the Immigration Police). The press release stated in part,

> We are releasing hundreds of private intelligence bulletins, training manuals, personal email correspondence, names, phone numbers, addresses and passwords belonging to Arizona law enforcement. We are targeting AZDPS specifically because we are against SB1070 and the racial profiling anti-immigrant police state that is Arizona. . . .
>
> Every week we plan on releasing more classified documents and embarassing [sic] personal details of military and law enforcement in an effort not just to reveal their racist and corrupt nature but to purposefully sabotage their efforts to terrorize communities fighting an unjust "war on drugs." (quoted in Tsotsis 2011)

Similarly, in Shooting Sheriffs Saturday—an Anonymous operation also conducted under the mantle of AntiSec, which involved hacking the websites of seventy local US law enforcement agencies—the group's goal was multipronged:

> Over 10GB of information was leaked including hundreds of private email spools, password information, address and social security numbers, credit card numbers, snitch information, training files, and more. We hope that not only will dropping this info demonstrate the inherently corrupt nature of law enforcement using their own words, as well as result in possibly humiliation, firings, and possible charges against several officers, but that it will also disrupt and sabotage their ability to communicate and terrorize communities. (Anonymous 2011)

These operations typically yielded highly compressed data dumps, which along with email spools and internal documents, often included databases of personally identifying information belonging to rank-and-file workers, clients, and upper management (including home addresses, private telephone numbers, internal logins, passwords, and credit card information). The content was not curated, anonymized, or redacted. Most of the data dumps and press releases were distributed quickly and without media intermediaries. The press releases often followed a well-established format. They began with a text-based piece of artwork (usually in the retro ASCII genre) that identified the group; the codename for the operation or attack, complete with ready-made Twitter handle; and a cleverly worded narrative that detailed the organization attacked, exploits used, data accessed and released, as well as the motivation or rationale for the incursion. Press releases were usually posted on public messaging boards like Pastebin and torrent sites like the Pirate Bay.

These dumps were equal parts acts of transparency, acts of provocation, and acts of retaliation that deployed doxing (i.e., the exposure of personal and previously private information about an individual online) as an explicitly political tactic. Digital media scholar Daniel Trottier (2017, 56) has argued that such actions are best understood as a form of "weaponized visibility," where the publicity generated is unwanted, intense (e.g., assorted content like posts, photos, and videos can circulate to thousands and more over the course of a few days), and enduring (i.e., the visibility campaign might be the first hit in searching an individual's name). Given that privacy is increasingly becoming a "luxury commodity" (Papacharissi 2010; Rainie and Anderson 2014; Hess 2017), weaponized visibility seeks to flatten power asymmetries by neutralizing the walls of anonymity that often characterize the upper echelons of corporate or political power.

More than any other act of weaponized visibility, the publication of email spools is a particularly potent signifier. Email has remained the dominant technological tool of the workplace since its introduction; it has weathered significant changes in communications platforms (e.g., social media, video chats, and texts) and security threats (e.g., hacks, spamming, phishing attacks; Purcell and Rainie 2014, 6–7). Given its status as the central communication artery in the office and a key forward-facing platform to interact with clients and the outside world, full email dumps can provide a detailed snapshot of the inner workings of a corporation, business, or government. The email dump finds fertile ground in a conspiratorial worldview in which state secrecy covers up injustices, nation-states are purveyors of violence and terror, and corporations are corrupt and criminal. In this view, the idea is that the incriminating information is there, just on the other side of a corporate or government firewall. And, as political philosopher Jodi Dean (2001) argues, the audience for this conspiratorial worldview continues to grow because the urge to reveal or expose secrets has now become a core driver of the networked flows of communicative content that compose our collective digital reality. In this sense, email dumps may contain an archive's worth of illegality, but they necessarily tend to obfuscate more than they reveal (Connor 2015, 43–44).

Thus one key difference between the hacktivism described above and the transparency work of Manning and Snowden is that the former favored disintermediated rather than mediated disclosure and dissemination tactics. The choice to adopt messaging boards or torrent sites as distribution vehicles rather than a platform like WikiLeaks or the news media itself represents a tactical trade-off. Certainly, it plays to the powerful logic of speed and "intensive time" (Virilio 1986, 46): the immediate and abrupt presence of both the breach's announcement and its dissemination compresses the symbolic and confrontational aspects of the hack and the dump into a powerful and an instantaneous act of political communication.

Yet in Manning's and Snowden's cases, the media had ample time to read through and research the material, as well as to craft the stories that would maximize their impact and give the leaks greater longevity. The spacing and syncing of releases was staggered to maximize clarity and provoke debate, whereas the breakneck pace of hacktivist operations (e.g., during the summer of 2011, LulzSec went on a fifty-day hacking rampage) worked against discussion and transparency. The sometimes daily announcement and release of a hack and its contents played to the sort of continuous, constantly updating and streaming real-time news logic media studies scholar Mimi Sheller describes as "news now" (2015). Here, the audience has become an important component in the news production cycle, and the line between producer and audience, as well as the line between the event and news reporting on the event, blurs (2015, 19).

Sheller argues that "news now" displaces the agenda setting, content filtration, and factual verification typical of past traditional news media, and that it opens new prominent opportunities for content like megaleaks and data dumps, which is caught between news production and consumption (2015, 20). Not surprisingly, then, the media outlets focused their coverage on the drama of the hack and the cyclical regularity with which targets were exposed but not the potentially damning content the leaks contained. This is striking given that two of the most notorious hacks and data dumps during this period, the hack of FBI contractors HBGary and HBGary Federal and global intelligence firm Stratfor, revealed important information about the hacker state and the associated security industry, which ballooned in scope and scale post-9/11. The seventy-five thousand HBGary Federal emails dumped by LulzSec revealed the efforts of Bank of America (BOA) to enlist the aid of the US Department of Justice in silencing WikiLeaks (which at the time had been threatening to release a series of damaging emails), and the DOJ's referral to lobbying firm Hunton Williams, which then put BOA in contact with Team Themis—a group made up of several private contractors and boundary workers, including Palantir Technologies, Berico Technologies, HBGary, and Endgame systems—which was tasked with discrediting WikiLeaks by undermining the credibility of journalist Glenn Greenwald. The emails also showed that the group was developing a system to manage multiple fake social media identities via *sock puppets* to manufacture and influence popular support (Chatterjee 2012; Ludlow 2013).

The 5 million Stratfor emails, covering the period from 2004 to 2011, exposed Stratfor's exaggerated marketing and general incompetence (Fisher 2012), but they also shed light on more analog variants of boundary work under way between private intelligence firms (which are government contractors) and corporate giants. For example, the emails documented how companies like Dow Chemical and Coca-Cola hired Stratfor to surveil and spy on activist and protest groups that targeted or threatened to tarnish their public image.

The near-daily breach-driven headlines shifted the visibility and prominence of hackers and hacking groups within Anonymous (which continued to be engaged in various different operations) and the public consciousness (Coleman 2013a, 223). In other words, despite the limited media effect of any individual hack or data dump, cumulatively these operations fed public anxieties and helped shape contemporary cultural tropes about hacktivist politics. But they were also demonstrative in the sense that they exposed the near ubiquitous state of cyber "insecurity" among a staggeringly diverse field of official actors responsible for safeguarding sensitive information for government, corporations, or private citizens. Indeed, the fact that so many of these supposedly competent security organizations were compromised using basic, well-documented vulnerabilities and techniques (e.g., publicly available exploits, well-known SQL injection vulnerabilities, etc.) certainly caught the attention of those seeking to exploit similar security holes to obtain state secrets, gain trade advantage, or engage in cyber crime.

They also indirectly contributed to the growth and expansion of insecurity markets. On the one hand, some of the personal and identifying information contained in these dumps was most certainly used as an entry point for phishing scams and malware by cyber criminals, as in the Stratfor case (Sengupta 2012). On the other, the breaches themselves effectively bolstered the computer security industry and the credentials of hacked companies that could now reframe their breach as "penetration testing" and as a demonstration that they were ahead of the security curve. In chapter 2 we describe the different strategies the US state has adopted to govern hackers and hacking technologies under the heading of *boundary work*. We defined this as the selective and logistical redrawing of borders within the state and between state and society to bring certain material practices and processes into closer proximity (and hence alignment) with state objectives while selectively keeping those same practices at a distance in other domains of practice. In the hacktivist prosecutions of 2012, we see the full spectrum of state boundary tactics on display. In the United States, a series of very public arrests followed by well-covered criminal trials and lengthy criminal sentences awaited Anons like Jeremy Hammond and Barrett Brown. In the UK and Ireland, where many of the remaining LulzSec members were located, the sentences proved significantly less severe but nonetheless deterrent.

Yet perhaps the greatest revelation of this period was the fact that Sabu (Hector Monsegur), charismatic leader of LulzSec, was actually a boundary worker. In a move reminiscent of the French Domestic Intelligence Service in 1992 or the law enforcement stings of BBS of the 1980s, the FBI raided Sabu's New York apartment on June 7, 2011, and turned him into a confidential informant well before LulzSec's AntiSec campaign began. Sabu was working in cooperation with federal authorities (and some argue under their explicit direction) all along, feeding them information on upcoming attacks and gathering intelligence on Anonymous, WikiLeaks, and LulzSec members (which would later prove crucial in identifying their offline identities and building material criminal cases against them). For example, in the wake of the Stratfor hack, he supplied an FBI-owned server to store the cache of 5 million exfiltrated emails (Ball 2012).

Finally, 2012 and 2013 also provide examples of how state boundary work has broadened internationally through the coupling of US criminal justice structures with international extradition frameworks and state mutual assistance partnerships (a development we describe in greater detail in chapter 4). Julian Assange, the embattled founder of WikiLeaks, found himself appealing extradition from the UK to Sweden on rape and sexual molestation charges, which many believed were linked to an open indictment against him in the United States. When Assange's last appeal before the UK Supreme Court failed in June 2012, he requested asylum at Ecuador's London embassy, where he remained until his arrest by the London Metropolitan Police on April 11, 2019. He is currently serving a fifty-week custodial sentence for violating his UK bail conditions by entering the Ecuadorian Embassy and awaiting the outcome of extradition proceedings to the US, where he faces federal conspiracy charges as well as seventeen counts under the espionage act.

The following year Edward Snowden (the former NSA boundary worker employed by contractor Booz Allen Hamilton) would reveal the breathtaking sweep and sprawl of the US hacker state, whose expansive global surveillance network included the collusion of major technology and telecommunications companies, the collection of data traffic from undersea fiber-optic cables, and the exploitation of scores of hacked computer networks. As the revelations became public, and the United States revoked his passport, Snowden found himself requesting temporary asylum from Russia, the only country that would not extradite him to the United States.

More broadly, the cumulative effect of these leaks, attacks, and operations is that they crystallized a new digital mode of civil disobedience, which combined both liberal and radical democratic elements. Snowden and Manning were insiders, operating under the sort of "conscientious" law breaking that scholars have identified with the liberal tradition of civil disobedience. Like its more analog counterpart, liberal digital civil disobedience targets public opinion and seeks to persuade the population or political elites that a particular set of laws or policies are unwarranted, illegitimate, or unjust (Scheuerman 2016; Brownlee 2016). In the most demanding and influential version of this view, civil disobedience is nonviolent law breaking that is committed openly and that displays a general belief in the legitimacy of the legal order and a willingness to accept the legal consequences of the act (Rawls 1991, 106–107). These acts are generally understood as *defensive* in scope, in that the goal is not to disrupt or bring down the democratic order but rather to spur policy change or interrupt systemic and serious incursions on basic rights and liberties so that democracy may sit on firmer foundations (Cohen and Arato 1999, 587–588; Scheuerman 2014). In other words, these are communicative acts that seek to reestablish the link between the public sphere and political society and are naturally aligned with traditional and emergent news media in their role as a networked fourth estate (Benkler 2013).

In contrast, hacktivist operations of the sort engaged in by Anonymous and LulzSec fit a more combative form of digital disobedience, which has been labeled radical democratic (Scheuerman 2014; Celikates 2016) or even "anti-legal" (Scheuerman 2015). Political philosopher Hannah Arendt, whose writings are often associated with this position, situated civil disobedience somewhere between criminality and outright revolution (Arendt 1966, 74–77; Cohen and Arato 1999, 595). Unlike the liberal tradition that insists on nonviolence, Arendt likens civil disobedient groups to the voluntary associations Alexis de Tocqueville described in *Democracy and America*: horizontal ad hoc organizations made up of private citizens who come together to pursue a limited number of goals and who disband once those are achieved ([1835] 2000, 489–492).

Expanding on Arendt, political theorist Robin Celikates argues that the dynamism of these acts is located between the opposing poles of symbolic politics and real confrontation (2016, 983). The tension between these two poles is important because civil disobedience—to a greater extent than other political practices—is dependent on the interplay between drama and contestation. It requires the staging of a crisis to force a confrontation but only gains political meaning (and hence success) if that confrontation transcends the particular moment and is invested with symbolism as it circulates through the mediated structures of the public sphere. Celikates writes, "It can function as a symbolic protest only if it involves moments of real confrontation, such as practices of blockade and occupation, which will sometimes contain elements of violence. . . . At the same time, it can function as real confrontation only if those practicing disobedience remain aware of its irreducible symbolic dimension" (2016, 988). The above account emphasizes the episodic and often anti-institutional character of civil disobedience, its expansive understanding of citizenship, and its centrality as a form of political action, which emerges in representative democracies where official channels of action and communication are closed or blocked by institutionalized political processes (Celikates 2016, 991).

We would expand both liberal and radical accounts by arguing that when these forms of civil disobedience take digital form, the difference between them is no longer clear cut. Rather, both become viable and complementary technological resources for exposing and resisting state power. Yet the fact that data dumps and other disclosures conducted by anonymous or confidential sources working in the public interest are increasingly framed as legitimate political acts should not blind us to the fact that the overall framing and visibility of such activities also provides a vector for more hostile attacks. Indeed, the tactics and justifications of transparency activists, whistleblowers, and hacktivists have become part of a disruptive smorgasbord of state hacking activity through which false flag operations, information warfare, and cyberwarfare mask as legitimate political dissent.

Transparency, Transnational News Media, and the Rise of the Hacker State

The events described above introduced the world to a historically distinctive experience of crime, which in the years since has become definitive of life in what we call *high breach societies*. Whereas even a few years before, the possibility of having one's computer hacked or one's information compromised in a large-scale breach seemed exceptional, far flung, and remote, in just a short number of years, people all over the world have been reeling from the effect of hacked consumer credit-reporting agency Equifax, as well as ransomware attacks affecting national health services, telecommunications companies, and government agencies. In this sense, this earlier set of operations normalized both the data breach and the data dump, thereby substantiating the sense that anyone, anything, and anywhere could be breached (it was no longer a matter of *if* but a matter of *when*).

Yet the normalization of vast repositories of exfiltrated data also fed the ascendance of big-data journalism and the transnational, collaborative news partnerships that emerged to analyze and report on data breaches and dumps. Beginning in 2013 with the Offshore Leaks, 2014 with LuxLeaks, continuing with Swiss Leaks and the Panama Papers in 2015, as well as the Paradise Papers in 2017, leaks and whistleblowing increasingly became central drivers of news reporting and coverage. The scale and size of the above revelations is astounding even when compared with Manning's megaleak of a half-dozen years before: as we note earlier, the entirety of Manning's leaks were just under 3 GB, and certainly some of the releases, like the Luxembourg Leaks (4.4 GB), were comparable in size. Yet others far eclipsed anything seen since: the Swiss Leaks were over 100 GB; the Offshore Leaks were 260 GB; the Panama Papers were 2.6 TB; and the Paradise Papers were 1.4 TB (Hamilton 2015; Obermaier et al. 2019; Hopkins and Bengtsson 2017).

The breadth of these collections is equally formidable. The Panama Papers contained 11.5 million documents—emails, pdfs, photos, and databases—spanning more than four decades (1970–2016); the Paradise Papers involved 13.4 million files and spanned six decades (1950–2016). Equally impressive is the scale of the investigations: the Panama Papers involved more than four hundred journalists from a dozen news organizations, working under the mantle of the International Consortium of Investigative Journalists (ICIJ 2016). The reporting and analysis of the files began in September 2015, and the articles were synchronized to be simultaneously published around the world on April 3, 2016. Similarly, the Paradise Papers involved ninety-six media organizations and a total of 381 journalists, again working under the mantle of the ICIJ for one year before once again synchronizing the publication of the first stories (ICIJ 2017).

Two developments are evident. First, mainstream news organizations have increasingly incorporated reporting on leaks and soliciting such sources as a component of their professional identity and everyday work routines. Virtually every major newspaper now has prominently figured on its web page and mobile applications instructions and multiple options for how to securely contact and provide data or material via encrypted technology. The advent of impressively large unstructured collections of data has also required the development of new collaborative practices as well as new technological solutions for analyzing heterogeneous datasets qualitatively (Baack 2011, 2016). The former in particular is a factor of scale. Leaks like the Panama Papers or the Paradise Papers are simply too large for single or even multiple news organizations to manage.

A second development speaks to the ethics of whistleblowing as civil disobedience. The tension between professional journalistic ethics and transparency platforms over harm minimization and how much of any data dump or cache to publish, already evident in the partnership between the

New York Times and WikiLeaks over the Manning files (Benkler 2011, 2013), has become more pronounced. Indeed, although the ICIJ curates a searchable database that integrates some of the documents from its copious leaks, it and its media collaborators are completely against releasing the raw data. The ICIJ director Gerard Ryle has taken an almost antidoxing stance, arguing that although the organization's reporting has exposed those public figures and politicians benefiting from the global tax evasion arrangements detailed in the papers, ICIJ is against releasing the sensitive information of private individuals: "We're not WikiLeaks. We're trying to show that journalism can be done responsibly" (Greenberg 2016). WikiLeaks, not surprisingly, has been extremely critical of this approach on Twitter: "#PanamaPapers: If you censor more than 99% of the documents you are engaged in 1% journalism by definition."[6] In other words, news organizations have also begun to crowd out and displace alternative publishers like WikiLeaks for leaked information. Not only do the more established media outlets have the circulation and digital footprint to ensure a certain measure of prominence and explication; they also provide ethical reassurance for would-be whistleblowers. Further, this wave of megaleaks initiated a novel pattern of media and government collaboration. While the raw data have not been made available to the public at large, they have been made available to various states so that taxation and internal revenue services can claw back unpaid taxes.

Two of the identities of the leakers are well known. Hervé Falciani, a former HSBC computer security specialist, leaked the Swiss Papers (a trove of secret Swiss bank accounts from the private HSBC Switzerland branch) to the French authorities and *Le Monde*. Antoine Deltour, a former employee of PricewaterhouseCoopers, leaked the tax rulings for more than three hundred multinationals based in Luxembourg between 2002 and 2010. And although the whistleblowers in the Paradise and Panama Papers have remained in the shadows, those who leaked the latter penned their own account of why they released the data:

> Historians can easily recount how issues involving taxation and imbalances of power have led to revolutions in ages past. Then, military might was necessary to subjugate peoples, whereas now, curtailing information access is just as effective or more so, since the act is often invisible. Yet we live in a time of inexpensive, limitless digital storage and fast internet connections that transcend national

boundaries. It doesn't take much to connect the dots: from start to finish, inception to global media distribution, the next revolution will be digitized. (Doe 2019)

Finally, the above is not to say that the visibility and impact of hacktivist modes of transparency activism were completely eclipsed by state arrests and prosecutions. On the contrary, the year 2014 witnessed a further radicalization of digital dissent. Alongside email spools and confidential documents, data dumps now increasingly feature the tech schematics and code for the hacking tools and weapons themselves. For example, in 2014, the hacktivist group Phineas Fisher hacked the Gamma Group, which sold the infamous FinFisher surveillance suite adopted by repressive governments like former Egyptian president Hosni Mubarak's regime. This yielded some 40 GB of data, including internal documents like brochures, product, and price lists, as well as the technical specifications for the group's merchandise—although a large portion of the data was encrypted. In July 2015 Phineas Fisher reappeared with the announcement that they had hacked the equally notorious cybersecurity mercenaries Hacking Team, which yielded some 400 GB of exfiltrated data, including its client list, email correspondence, internal documents, and the source code for its products. And just hours after Phineas Fisher released this source code, the Adobe exploits and zero days it contained were already being used as a vector for the deployment of cryptoware by cybercriminals (Zetter 2016).

Both hacks followed the familiar radical script. A link to the Gamma Group files first appeared on Reddit and was distributed via a torrent link to the data. The Hacking Team files were also distributed via a torrent link, this time contained in tweets from the Hacking Team's own hijacked Twitter account. Almost nine months later, Phineas Fisher followed up the hack and data dump with a Pastebin file (entitled "Hack Back!"), complete with the obligatory text-based artwork (a figure with the hashtag #antisec at its feet, urinating on the Hacking Team logo), which served as a step-by-step walkthrough of the hack—a do-it-yourself introduction to hacking and a political manifesto (Cox 2016). Finally, a month later, the same hacker posted a thirty-nine-minute YouTube video that detailed how to use the widely available Kali Linux penetration-testing suite to scan the site vulnerabilities of the Catalonian Police Union (Mossos d' Esquadra) website before launching an attack, exfiltrating personally identifying data, and posting it online.

Yet despite Phineas Fisher's inspired call to hacktivist arms, 2016 will largely be remembered for the disorienting and game-changing avalanche of email and document dumps that began in the summer of that US presidential election year. Hackers penetrated the US Democratic National Committee (DNC) computer network in the summer of 2015 and again in April 2016. Although the DNC hired a cybersecurity firm to deal with the hack, plug the vulnerabilities, and track those responsible, it did not make the hack public until June 14, 2016 (Nakashima 2016b). The next day, a self-proclaimed hacktivist, Guccifer 2.0, emerged. He took credit for the hack and provided several internal memos (including donor lists, a strategic briefing report on Donald Trump, and documents from Hillary Clinton's time as secretary of state) to prove he was the genuine article (Nakashima 2016a). He also announced passing thousands of emails and documents pilfered from the DNC to WikiLeaks and that they would be forthcoming. Seven days later and three days before the beginning of the Democratic National Convention in Philadelphia (July 25–28, 2016), WikiLeaks released a data dump of 20,000 internal emails, 891 documents, and 175 spreadsheets (Hamburger and Nakashima 2016; Vicens 2016). This first dump was notable because of its timing, sheer volume, and indiscriminate character: John Podesta's risotto tips absurdly sit alongside evidence of strong anti–Bernie Sanders bias among DNC staffers.

Yet even as the FBI launched an investigation into the DNC intrusion, another data release from a different hack emerged on August 12, 2016. Much like the DNC, the Democratic Congressional Campaign Committee (DCCC) was hacked by Guccifer 2.0 sometime in March or April 2016 (Lichtblau and Weiland 2016). Similarly, the August 12 release of an Excel spreadsheet with the cell phone numbers, identifying information, and personal emails of nearly every Democrat in the House of Representatives, several House Republicans, and DCCC staffers was but a prelude to a more sustained and disruptive—if less visible—effort (New York Times 2016). The attack also deployed a tactic that we have already seen in radical transparency actions: doxing. Indeed, Representative Nancy Pelosi's experience is typical. She was in flight between Florida and California when the news broke and was inundated by obscene texts, voicemails, and phone calls when she turned her phone back on after landing.

The August 12 disclosure was followed by a series of targeted leaks and dumps directed at House election races in at least six states (Pennsylvania,

New Hampshire, Ohio, Illinois, New Mexico, and North Carolina). Operating like a whistleblower or leaker providing a political scoop, Guccifer 2.0 baited journalists and political bloggers with often very candid background assessments, strategies, and evaluations of Democratic candidates and their rivals. Documents relating to the Florida primaries were released on August 15; Pennsylvania documents were released on August 21; Nancy Pelosi's personal documents were released on August 30; and on September 15, documents concerning races in New Hampshire, Ohio, Illinois, and North Carolina were also released. Finally, on September 23, New Mexico representative Ben Ray Luján's personal papers were released as well.

The DCCC dump was followed by two further hacks and dumps. In March 2016 (around the same time as the DCCC and the DNC were hacked), the email account of White House chief of staff and chairman of Clinton's US presidential campaign, John Podesta, was also hacked. The culled fifty-eight thousand emails were published by WikiLeaks over the course of October and November 2016, just a month before the presidential election. Alongside the Podesta emails, the email account of Capricia Penavic Marshall (the White House chief of protocol) was also hacked, and correspondence between Marshall, Hillary Clinton, and the Clinton Foundation appeared on the site DCLeaks as well.

For quite some time since the Snowden revelations, civil liberties groups and monitors have been apprehensive that the United States has developed a global, pervasive panoptic surveillance network capable of penetrating even the most robust security protocols. Indeed, the central thesis of this book is that despite the messy entanglement of technics, technologies, and technicians, nation-states are quickly adopting the tactics and tools of hacktivists and hackers to project their sovereign footprint into the digital realm. It should be evident that the state that has learned the most valuable lessons is Russia. This is in part because Russia is not a democracy. As we note in chapter 2, it maintains strong central control over dissent, media outlets, and its own cyberspace. It makes only a pro forma nod to playing by the rules of international diplomacy and transnational governance. It has developed a decentralized, nodal approach to cyber supremacy, largely drawing from the experience of dissident groups and loosely affiliated networks of information activists and cyber criminals. If democracy and the rule of law remains a barrier to the capacity of the United States to follow suit (notwithstanding its own deep experience in covert cyber operations), the dense nodal and decentralized approach pioneered by the Russian state also illustrates why individual acts of hacktivist disruption and radical transparency fall on fallow ground. The Russian case exposes the empty promise of transparency, openness, and debate inherent in democratic ideology while using these same "conventions" as vectors for disruption. In other words, hacking on the Russian scale overwhelms democratic processes and those certainties on which governance and its obedience are premised.

Russia succeeded because it brought together a multivectored approach. It skillfully exploited temporality and scale, scrambling liberal and radical transparency tactics to widen the already existent gulf between what Jodi Dean (2009) characterizes as contribution and critique. Breach-driven headlines once again dominated the press, overwhelming existent and emergent digital public spheres and setting the pace, content, and talking points of media discussions and press commentary. All the while, a less visible social media campaign sowed doubt among a speculative and distrustful electorate already primed for the revelatory insights and disclosures the leaks might bring. A disruptive data dump campaign would be difficult for American authorities and political processes to manage and grapple with on their own, but its real efficacy is linked to the way in which these leaks and dumps short circuited the political media cycle (Chadwick 2013) and exploited transnational media ecosystems.

Democracy and Paralysis

In this chapter we place significant emphasis on how the unique forms of temporal and spatial compression that networked technology engenders transform time into a tactical resource, which can be harnessed and manipulated by whistleblowers, hacktivists, and state hackers for specific strategic ends. In the sections that follow, we describe the challenges that the use of such tactics pose for democracy, a political system that struggles to cope with contemporary processes of social, economic, and technological acceleration.

As many scholars have recently noted, there appears to be a growing disjuncture between the pace of democratic politics and the accelerated tempo that increasingly characterizes our technologically driven social, cultural, and economic lives (Virilio 1986; Hassan 2008; Rosa 2013; Wolin 1997; Scheuerman 2004; Connolly 2009; Saward 2017). According to the above authors, there is a desynchronization effect between politics and these varied social processes, which affects the structural and procedural arrangements of liberal democracy and constrains the capacity of political bodies to respond to the speed of events in an efficient and timely manner. For example, political scientist William Scheuerman (2004, 50) argues that many of the procedures and attributes of legislatures are designed (or at least latently contribute) to slow down the pace of decision making, allowing for reasoned debate and circumspection as well as public consultation. In a similar vein, political philosopher Sheldon Wolin (1997) described the growing sense that

> political time is out of sync with the temporalities, rhythms, and pace governing economy and culture. Political time . . . requires an element of leisure . . . owing to the needs of political action to be preceded by deliberation[,] and [this] . . . occurs in a setting of competing or conflicting but legitimate considerations. Political time is conditioned by the presence of differences and the attempt to negotiate them.

Sociologist Hartmut Rosa (2013) also stresses the unique time requirements of democracy. In his view the acceleration of social processes—in particular the pace of scientific-technological innovation and the tempo of economic circulation—place pressure on the political system to deliver rapid, collectively binding decisions while introducing a series of paradoxes. First, as the speed of technical and social innovation increases, politicians have less time to make decisions and more "necessary" decisions to make. Second, as the pace of change grows and development in these areas accelerates, the amount of time needed to make decisions also grows because the ramifications that might flow from them are complex and potentially far reaching in scope (e.g., genetic editing or artificial intelligence; Rosa 2013, 262).

For Rosa and others, one important consequence emerges from the pressure to produce speedy legislative decisions: sound and rational decision making might be decentralized, privatized, or relocated to faster systems, such as the executive function of government. This last point is particularly salient in the context of state hacking in that it suggests that authoritarian models of government—without the lag of deliberation and the often delaying interaction with a free press—enjoy an advantage in managing the pace of technological change (and hence in adopting and governing through it) over liberal democratic models. But more generally the social acceleration literature identifies, as a routine feature of contemporary governance, a pronounced regulatory incapacity between slow-paced legislatures and the growing tempo and number of social processes that require regulation. Not only does this effectively leave significant technological domains with far-reaching social, political, and cultural influence essentially unregulated (to the celebrations of libertarian investors in social media companies such as Facebook), but it also makes legislatures structurally slow to respond to the sort of "information bombs" and disruptions (Virilio 2000) that unfold unchecked from these domains.

In contrast, Jodi Dean (2009, 2010) focuses on the novel ideological consolidation of democracy and capitalism under the auspices of what she calls "communicative capitalism." Unlike the above scholars, Dean's diagnosis of democracy is not one of slow, deliberative decision making out of sync with social and technological change, but one of deadlocked democracy captured by the market fundamentalism of neoliberalism (2009, 22). Networked technology has accelerated, intensified, and expanded the access and opportunity to communicate, but this has also helped to fracture and fragment the possibility for constructing strong counterhegemonic spaces for debate and action. According to Dean, this fragmentation of resistance is linked not to its suppression but to its augmentation and viral distribution through networks of communication technology always already embedded within market structures. Expanded and intensified global telecommunications materialize the core values and ideals of democratic politics (e.g., access, inclusion, participation, etc.), even as they function to secure neoliberalism's ideological infrastructure and its ongoing concentration of global inequalities. In this analysis, information is a commodity whose profitability and circulation increase along with greater speed.

A central component in the above dynamic is the unparalleled hegemony enjoyed by the ideal of publicity. Publicity is both intimately connected to democratic praxis (J. Dean 2001) and a core facet of technoculture's marketing machinery. In other words, the urge to reveal and expose is a trap: it allows individuals to feel politically or socially active even as their contributions reinforce the status quo and produce little effect on public policy or power (J. Dean 2009, 148). The supposed democratic potential of proliferating communication technologies—which is roundly endorsed across the political spectrum—promotes a distorted picture of what does and does not constitute political action because it prioritizes the volume and number of connections—the scale of contributions—over and against their content. The distinction between what is trite commentary and what is elegant critique does not matter to profit based on reductive quantification. Quality is elided as simple circulation is measured and monetized. In this calculation, the subject of critique (power) is freed from the need to answer for its deeds or account for itself (J. Dean 2009, 21). There is no content to address. In contrast to the social acceleration literature discussed above, the disconnect between the deluge of circulating political contributions within the digital public sphere and the politics of official policy is a result of too much discussion (or at least contribution that masks as discussion), not too little. Here the electorate may feel anesthetized by excessive information or condescended to by overly eloquent punditry reaching for answers and choose a representative who promises simple solutions, enemies, and "news" (Hedges 2002).

As we note in our discussion of leaking, whistleblowing, and hacktivist exfiltration, the drive to reveal or expose secrets is now deeply imbricated in the circulating flows of networked communicative content that animate our contemporary digital reality. According to Dean, its consequences is evident in three interrelated trends: (1) the banalization of publicity, (2) the collapse of symbolic efficiency, and (3) the production of suspicious and searching subjects. Dean argues that publicity as both act and ideal has become generalized to the point of banality (2010, 112). Revelation is uncoupled from action and becomes an end in itself or a stand-in for real action. Indeed, the strength and impact of a leak or data dump is tied to the extraordinary character of the material the disclosure contains. An influential leak is factual; it provides information or documents that offer incontrovertible legal-grade proof of a whistleblower's or leaker's claims about the state of reality. Such leaks can usually weather official denials and evasions. And in cases of serious criminal activity or malfeasance, they might prompt governmental action through investigations and prosecutions. The point is that in the ideal, revelation is closely tied to action. This might involve criminal investigations, job losses, or loss of public confidence. In short, revelation gains meaning not just from what is disclosed but also from the sort of action it sets into motion. Otherwise, it does barely more than confirm the preleak state of suspicion or conspiratorial thinking that inspired it. To say that the CIA or NSA engages in covert and often illicit activities that would be illegal if performed by a different law enforcement body or

that the very wealthy find a vast array of legal vehicles for avoiding or less-
ening their tax burden is a truism. Few people believe—other than the pro-
testations of the CIA, NSA, or the wealthy—that such situations are untrue
or even unlikely. It is an altogether different situation to be confronted with
the Snowden leaks or with the Panama Papers, that is, to be confronted
with legal-grade proof that the state of reality is much, much worse than
one's own capacity for skeptical or paranoid thinking.

Certainly, few would claim that Snowden's revelations or the Panama
Papers failed to spur individuals to understanding (the extent and efficacy
of those actions to change surveillance or offshoring practices is debatable,
however). The scale of the diplomatic fallout caused by Snowden's leaks is
matched by the extent to which Americans and the rest of the world are
now highly conscious of and vigilant against incursions on their privacy.
Similarly, the Panama Papers represented a tax windfall and unexpected
boon for nation-states under the grip of austerity policies (countries have
clawed back unpaid tax revenue as a result of the disclosures). Dean's point,
though, is that the abatement of the link between revelation and action
has helped further a collapse in "symbolic efficiency" (2010, 132, 112). This
results in an increasing inability to distinguish truth from lies and a dramatic decline in the existence of a politics in which truth matters. She gives
the example of the US government admitting to having engaged in torture
and yet still avoiding any significant repercussions. One could also cite the
increasing frequency with which politicians (including current US president Donald Trump) lie on the record about facts that are easily checked
and disproved. Finally, Dean argues that generalized publicity and untruth-
ful politics produce a new form of political subject that is "searching, suspicious" and "ever clicking for more information, ever drawn to uncover the
secret and find out for themselves" (2001, 625).

Both the social acceleration literature and Dean's discussion of communicative capitalism emphasize, in different ways, the synchronization gap
between political institutions, networked public spheres, and ongoing processes of transformative social and technological change. These accounts
also complicate the seemingly straightforward leaker or whistleblower
narrative, in which an important document or cache of documents spurs
public debate and outrage, ultimately culminating in a significant shift in
political thinking and government policy. From Dean's point of view the
audience to which these disclosures are addressed is seemingly caught in

a loop: it is primed to seek out these revelations but also unsure (or worse indifferent) about their truth value and thus compelled to seek out new caches of information to resolve this tension. The problem, however, is that feeding and maintaining this loop is a key component of how the monetization structures of communicative capitalism function. If Dean's appraisal of the contemporary state of reality is correct, then the social acceleration literature provides little comfort. Insofar as these effects are byproducts of social, economic, or technological change, government may find it increasingly difficult to regulate or intervene in a timely manner at all.

Democracy's Exposure and the Information Bomb

Russia's multiyear, multipronged information warfare campaign illustrates the point that like everything else in our high breach societies, democracy itself can be breached. Indeed, as a recent US Senate report on electoral interference during 2016 has noted, Russian actors targeted the electoral systems of at least eighteen states (although varying estimates in the intelligence community indicate that the number is almost certainly higher; US Senate Intelligence Committee 2018). Yet Russian efforts were not just confined to penetration testing and data dumps; they also involved the adept manipulation of existing racial, class, and political tensions and divisions via social media ads, fake Facebook accounts, and Twitter bot armies. Most certainly, the impact of such efforts would have been greatly reduced if Russian actors had been unable to weaponize social media platforms for their own ends. Yet, the lasting repercussions of this campaign are more difficult to assess. Certainly, it provides a successful example of how states can weaponize networked technology to attack one of the core facets of the democratic process, but it also brought into relief the extent to which that process is open to disruption and exposure by a host of nonstate actors as well. As we argue throughout this book, one characteristic of networked technology is that it has a temporary leveling effect on the exercise of power: individuals, groups, and private contractors now operate with impact on the global stage. Nowhere is this more evident than in the congressional hearings that have unfolded in the wake of the 2016 election.

According to the prepared statements of Facebook, Google, and Twitter, when the companies appeared before the House Intelligence Committee to testify concerning Russian meddling in the 2016 election, Russian agents reached 126 million Facebook users and 20 million Instagram users, tweeted 131,000 messages, and uploaded some one thousand videos to YouTube (Isaac and Wakabayashi 2017) in connection with their election meddling. In addition, Facebook identified 470 fake Russian accounts, as well as three thousand ads on its and Instagram's platforms, one hundred thousand dollars' worth between June 2015 and August 2017, paid for through accounts linked to the Internet Research Agency (IRA). The ads promoted 120 Facebook pages that had been set up by the IRA and that were responsible for generating eighty thousand pieces of content (Stretch 2017, 5).

Google's platform was also targeted: two Russian backed accounts bought $4,700 worth of political ads and uploaded eighteen channels of video content on YouTube (Salgado 2017, 3). Finally, Twitter identified 36,746 accounts associated with Russia, which generated 1.4 million automated election-related tweets over the course of 2016 (Salgado 2017, 9); it also—drawing on Facebook's data—connected the IRA with a further human-coordinated 2,752 accounts (Edgett 2017). Although the above numbers represent a drop in a very large bucket in terms of the total global scale of content traffic that moves through these sites and platforms daily, they also illustrate the scale of the interference. A figure whose full size remains elusive because much of the underlying data is from Facebook, which was surprisingly slow to admit even the possibility of meddling through its platform, and which has been known to regularly underestimate the scale of privacy and data breaches (cf. Thompson and Vogelstein 2018).

The aftermath of Russian interference places the normative and legal vacuum left by the de facto self-regulation of social media companies center stage. Russian actors did have a sophisticated understanding of how the automated technology that underpins social media could be exploited (e.g., how algorithms can be developed to organize and sort emotive content linked to anger or fear). But the hearings did not just expose strategic vulnerabilities; they also focused attention on the sort of systemic, regulatory incapacity connected with social acceleration. The expanding chasm between slow-paced legislatures and the growing independence, tempo, and number of networked processes and platforms that require regulation was evident in the lead-up to the House and Senate hearings on Russian meddling. It was also evident in the hearings themselves, beginning with the witnesses who appeared before Congress. In striking contrast to the congressional hearings on the 2007 financial crisis, when the CEOs from the major institutional players in the financial sector appeared in person to testify, Twitter, Facebook, and Google sent their lawyers in their CEOs' stead.

Improbably, the outcome of those November hearings was itself overshadowed just four months later, on March 17, 2018, when the *Observer* (the Sunday edition of the *Guardian*) and the *New York Times* published in-depth interviews with whistleblower Christopher Wylie, who had served as the director of research for SCL (a UK-based defense contractor for the US and UK governments) and Cambridge Analytica (the US data analytics firm that worked on the Trump presidential campaign and the Vote Leave campaign in Britain) until late 2014 (Cadwalladr and Graham-Harrison 2018b; Rosenberg, Confessore, and Cadwalladr 2018). Wylie had helped set up Cambridge Analytica and had created the software program it used to exploit "psychographic" profiles of Facebook users for right-wing microtargeted political advertising and influence campaigns (Cadwalladr 2018). Essentially, Cambridge Analytica took the military information operations (IO) framework developed by its parent company (SCL) in the defense and military sectors of the hacker state and operationalized them to influence political campaigns (initially in Asia and Africa and then in the West). To do so, in 2014 the firm teamed up with Aleksandr Kogan, a Cambridge University lecturer who developed a Facebook app (This Is Your Digital Life) that paid users between five and ten dollars to take a personality test and consent to their data being used for academic research (Cadwalladr and Graham-Harrison 2018a). The app recorded the results and paired them with the user's Facebook data to establish patterns that would ultimately help the firm build an algorithm to predict political leanings but also emotional and psychological trigger points. As Wylie told the *Observer*, "We exploited Facebook to harvest millions of people's profiles. And built models to exploit what we knew about them and target their inner demons. That was the basis the entire company was built on" (Cadwalladr and Graham-Harrison 2018b).

Only three hundred thousand users actually took the test, but the total number of Facebook accounts scraped by the app ballooned to 87 million users, because when individual users granted third-party apps access to their Facebook data to make the app work, they also ported into the app the data of all their friends (a feature of the app developer platform called Open Graph, which was operative from 2010 to 2014; Meredith 2018). Cambridge Analytica's harvesting of user data breached the terms under which

Facebook and its users had granted Kogan data access (academic research). Further, the military-style information campaign and influence activities that Cambridge Analytica undertook with the data were likely illegal. Yet, the use of apps to scrape the data of Facebook users and their friends using the functionality in Open Graph was hardly a secret. For example, the Obama presidential campaign in 2012 also collected millions of Facebook users' data through its own app, albeit in a transparent and open manner (Pilkington and Michel 2012).

Wylie became disenchanted with the firm's work after Donald Trump's successful presidential campaign, the company's newly awarded US State Department contracts, and an invitation to pitch to the Pentagon (Cadwalladr 2018). He also knew that throughout the period he worked for Cambridge Analytica, Kogan was also working on projects funded by the Russian state, where similar algorithms were being built drawing on Facebook data for psychometric profiling. Cambridge Analytica was also in close contact with Lukoil (the Russian oil giant) executives and had passed on a white paper by Wylie describing the firm's US operations to top management (Cadwalladr and Graham-Harrison 2018a). He worried that the company had become an intelligence target for Russian security services (and thus an unintended factor in Russia's 2016 US presidential influence campaign) because of its use of Russian researchers, its information-sharing practices with Russian FSB-linked companies, and its role in pro-Russian intelligence campaigns in Eastern Europe (UK Parliament 2018; Wylie 2018).

Wylie began steering the *Guardian* and UK authorities through a year-long investigation into the firm's activities in early 2017, based on his insider knowledge and the meticulous documentation (e.g., receipts, invoices, contracts, emails, legal correspondence, internal memos, strategy documents, etc.) he took when he left. One year later, he emerged as a fully formed public media figure with a persona and presentation that referenced the sort of liberal transparency activism we have associated with Snowden and Manning. Unlike them, though, he was able to broker protection from the authorities and break the confidentiality agreement he had signed with SCL by working with law enforcement on both sides of the Atlantic (i.e., the NCA in the UK and FBI in the United States) before the story broke. In this sense, Snowden and Manning represent a cautionary tale of the pitfalls and dangers associated with whistleblowing, even as their prominence and the aftermath of their revelations primed media ecosystems on how to time and frame such disclosures for maximum impact.

For once, the actual reporting of news events appeared to play catch-up to events on the ground: two investigations, one by the Information Commissioner's Office and the other by the Electoral Commission in the UK, were already under way before the scandal became public. Indeed, what characterized the *Guardian* and the *New York Times* reporting that broke the story was not necessarily the blitz of content, articles, and commentary that we have come to expect from such disclosures but a single inescapable revelation. Cambridge Analytica had waged an exfiltration and influence campaign designed to sway the US election and the UK Brexit vote, but Facebook had known about the breach since 2015 and had failed to inform law enforcement, the Federal Trade Commission (FTC), or the 87 million users whose data were harvested.

For a few days, this was considered to be the largest breach in history, until it was revealed as only the tip of multiple icebergs. The exploit Cambridge Analytica used was a functionality of the app developer platform, which meant there were likely more breaches out there to be discovered. Moreover, Facebook also revealed that over the course of several years, "malicious actors" had used a reverse search tool on its platform to scrape the public profiles of most of its 2 billion users (Timberg, Romm, and Dwoskin 2018). Facebook was soon reeling from the pace and gravity of the disclosures as well as the consumer outrage they generated. Brian Acton, a co-founder of WhatsApp (a company owned by Facebook) tweeted, "It is time. #deleteFacebook," and Elon Musk deleted both SpaceX and Tesla's Facebook pages; #deleteFacebook became a trending topic on Twitter.[7] Largely because of this sustained pressure, on April 10 and 11 Facebook's CEO, Mark Zuckerberg, agreed to testify before the US Senate and the House of Representatives.

Despite the combative and contentious atmosphere, the US Congress genuinely seemed as puzzled as the ordinary user over the revelations. Many members premised their remarks and questions with a statement praising Facebook and acknowledging their extensive use of it. Others marveled at its meteoric ascent and current monopolistic scale, but the majority of lawmakers expressed surprise at the current dearth of social media regulation. The Senate's questions illustrated how little the representatives knew about how Facebook actually worked, let alone its data practices, business model, or privacy standards. In comparison, the tone in the House of Representatives was decidedly more confrontational and inquisitorial. Representative Greg Walden (R-OR) began the hearings with a loaded question: "There are critical unanswered questions surrounding Facebook's business model and the entire digital ecosystem regarding online privacy and consumer protection. What exactly is Facebook? [A] Social platform? Data company? Advertising company? A media company? A common carrier in the information age? All of the above? Or something else?" (Washington Post 2018a).[8] Mark Zuckerberg's answer was characteristically elusive:

> I consider us to be a technology company, because the primary thing we do is have engineers who write code and build products and services for other people. . . . [W]e do pay to help produce content. We build enterprise software, although I don't consider us an enterprise software company. We build planes to help connect people, and I don't consider ourselves to be an aerospace company. (Washington Post 2018a)

Walden's question sought to penetrate the anticategorization strategy that Facebook and other "disruptive" Silicon Valley companies have consistently adopted in a bid to escape existent industry-specific regulatory frameworks and oversight: knowing the *type* of company is the first step in knowing which framework is applicable.

Similarly, Representative Marsha Blackburn (R-TN) expressed dismay that unlike the other three industry sectors that routinely generated, handled, and managed the most sensitive American consumer data (finance, healthcare, and credit reporting), which are bound by compliance legislation designed to safeguard and protect consumer privacy (Gramm-Leach-Bliley, HIPAA, and the Fair Credit Reporting Act, respectively), no privacy documents apply to social media (Washington Post 2018a). Besides an absence of compliance legislation, the representatives were also concerned that the sole existing oversight mechanism for Facebook (a twenty-year consent decree with the FTC, signed in 2011) had seemingly been sidestepped and ineffectual. As representative Tony Cardenas (D-CA) put it, "I'm of the opinion that, basically, we're hearing from one of the leaders—the CEO of one of the biggest corporations in the world—but yet almost entirely in an environment that is unregulated, or, for basic terms, that—the lanes in which you're supposed to operate in are very wide and broad, unlike other industries" (Washington Post 2018a). Indeed, the representatives continually returned to the specifics of Facebook's 2011 consent agreement with the FTC, a settlement precipitated by joint legal complaints filed by the Electronic Privacy Information Center and a host of consumer advocacy groups. The allegations, reminiscent of the current controversy, shine a light on Facebook's privacy practices: Facebook claimed that it restricted the amount of user data accessed by third-party apps; that users could restrict their sharing to "friends only"; that it would not share user data with advertisers; that the data contained in deactivated or deleted accounts would be inaccessible; and that it verified and certified the security of apps in its "verified apps" program. All these claims were shown to be misleading or patently false, resulting in extensive exposure of the data and profiles of the company's users. Essentially, the settlement bars "Facebook from making any further deceptive privacy claims, requires that the company get consumers' approval before it changes the way it shares their data, and requires that it obtain periodic assessments of its privacy practices by independent, third-party auditors for the next 20 years" (US FTC 2011).

Although the consent decree is not a legal admission of guilt, it does force Facebook to commission biennial audits of its privacy practices by third-party auditors, as well as to report the findings of those audits to the FTC. If it violates the agreement, it could face penalties of up to $40,000 per user per day. Although on the face of it, the agreement appears to have significant punitive teeth, it is actually indicative of the hands-off approach that has animated Congress's engagement with networked technology more generally (Reardon 2018). For example, despite spending weeks with a group of external consultants (including a former special assistant to George W. Bush) prepping for the testimony and rehearsing talking points, Zuckerberg did not seem to know even the basic facts surrounding the agreement (Roose, Kang, and Frenkel 2018). He appeared not to be familiar with the specifics of the legal complaint, including what Facebook was accused of doing with the data of its users, as well as the enforcement powers of the FTC.

Indeed, when asked directly by representative Paul Ruiz (D-CA) whether Facebook's failure to notify the FTC about the Cambridge Analytica breach indicated that "the rules were kind of lax, that you were sort of debating whether you needed to or something?" (Washington Post 2018a). Zuckerberg confirmed that in Facebook's opinion, it did not have a legal obligation to notify the agency. Ruiz then, in laying out the scale of the problem and the necessity for regulation, also pointed to a secondary theme that pervaded the hearings—the wider regulatory incapacity of Congress:

> Well, one of the things that we're realizing is that there's a lot of holes in the system . . . you know, we don't have the toolbox, you don't have the toolbox to monitor 9 million apps, and tens of thousands . . . of data collectors, and there's no specific mechanism for you to collaborate with those that can help you prevent these things from happening. And . . . if we started having these discussions about what would have been helpful for you to build your toolbox, and for us to build our toolbox, so that we can prevent things like Cambridge Analytica, things like identity thefts, things like . . . what we've heard today. (Washington Post 2018a)

Ruiz's statement perfectly captured the mood. The hearing was largely symbolic and performative; it allowed Congress to air the grievances of their constituents and to express their awareness of the scale of social media influence, as well as its perils. Yet for all his adversarial posture, Ruiz evidently viewed the hearings as a "discussion," or a conversation between what were framed as equal partners. Indeed, much of the questioning chimed with this view: representatives oscillated between asking Zuckerberg for his thoughts on how social media should be regulated, on whether Facebook would agree to be regulated, and threatening that if the company failed to self-regulate, it would be regulated. This last point was captured most eloquently by Representative Billy Long (R-MO): "[A] little bit of advice—Congress is good at two things: doing nothing and overreacting. So far we have done nothing on Facebook. Since your inception in that Harvard dorm room, many years ago, we've done nothing on Facebook. We're getting ready to overreact. So take that as just a shot across the bow, warning to you" (Washington Post 2018a).

Yet all this fell short of a decisive and clear push to regulate. This sense of incapacity was only accentuated by the fact that several representatives took the opportunity to ask the Facebook CEO to read their individual bills or to help them draft new bills that they hoped would be passed, which could provide a framework for regulating the company. Others seemed to hope that the coming European Union's General Data Protection Regulation could be extended to include American users. Above all, after a total of almost ten hours of testimony spread over two days, there was little by way of a joint conclusion or resolution about the next steps forward, save the sense that an open-ended discussion and deliberation would continue in Congress and between some members and Facebook.

Yet this left unanswered two intractable questions that hung over proceedings and inflected the hearings with a sense of foreboding. The first
concerned the wider privacy implications of the Cambridge Analytica
scandal itself. The second involved the automated technology Facebook
proposed to ensure that breaches like this would never happen again. The
Analytica data have clearly been sold to other parties, who presumably still
have possession of them and have potentially marketed them to others
(during the testimony Zuckerberg confirmed that Kogan had sold the data
to at least "a handful" of other parties). But more worrying was the scale
of the potential breach, made possible by the four years Open Graph was
operative. As Zuckerberg noted when repeatedly pressed about the number
of applications that could have scraped user data during these years: "There
are tens of thousands of apps that had access to a large amount of people's
information before we locked down the platform in 2014. So we're doing
an investigation that first involves looking at their patterns of API access
and what those companies were doing" (Washington Post 2018a). Representative Jan Schakowsky (D-IL) pressed Zuckerberg further: "In response to
the questions about the apps and the investigation you're going to do, you
said you don't necessarily know how long. Have you set a deadline for that?
Because we know, as my colleague said . . . there's actually 9 million apps.
How long do we have to wait for that kind of investigation?" (Washington
Post 2018a). Zuckerberg was vague, saying that he expected it would take
many months, although when Schakowsky followed up, he conceded that
he hoped it wouldn't take "years." Facebook was also pressed about the
recent disclosures of yet another breach—this one of 2 billion users' public
profile information—via a reverse search tool, which the company turned
off only weeks before the hearings, but which it had been publicly warned
about in 2013 and in 2015.

Thus, one important facet of the hearings was the disquieting sense that
a series of information bombs had detonated years ago and that, although
we are still unsure of the number or even of the radius of their blast sites,
we are just beginning to see the dark and still-expanding fallout clouds
from those explosions. This calls to mind Paul Virilio's argument that we
currently exist at the nexus of a blast site, at the center of an unfolding
data explosion that is no longer localized in space and time: "To invent
the electronic superhighway is to invent a major risk which is not easily
spotted because it does not produce fatalities like a shipwreck or a mid-air

explosion. The information accident is, sadly, not very visible. It is imma-
terial like the waves that carry information" (1999, 3). It is unclear when
the bomb detonated or will detonate, but according to Virilio, the "information bomb" is a product of the information age. The acceleration of telecommunications and computer processing power, as well as the new and
pervasive *interactivity* that such technology permits, renders the accident
a truly global phenomenon capable of being experienced in devastating
simultaneity.

This sense of global scale and simultaneous communication is the second foreboding theme that emerged from the hearings. With 2 billion users
and billions of pieces of content uploaded daily, the magnitude of the Facebook operation is so large that humans have difficulty keeping up with
it—a tangled hyperobject (Morton 2013)—something beyond easy concep-
tualization. Indeed, Zuckerberg's answer to the long-term problematic that
emerges at the intersection of scale and time—"there are tens of billions or
100 billion pieces of content that are shared every day, even 20,000 people reviewing it can't look at everything" (Washington Post 2018a)—was
the need to build more sophisticated artificial intelligence (AI) tools and
deploy them more broadly across the platform. At another point in the
hearings, when he was questioned about illegal ads for opioids and cyber-
bullying (both of which seem to have proliferated on Facebook), he struck
an analogous chord: "I think the same solution to the opioid question
that you raised earlier, of doing more with automated tools, will lead to
both faster response times, and more accurate enforcement of the policies"
(Washington Post 2018a). And AI tools were also trumpeted as the new
"proactive" enforcement mechanism to deal with electoral tampering and
future influence campaigns. In other words, the long-term solution to the
exposure generated by the massive scale of content circulation enabled by
networked technology does not involve more user controls or greater governmental regulation, but requires a more aggressive deployment of automated technology.

It is difficult in evaluating Zuckerberg's testimony to assess whether
Congress will be able to close or at least bridge the gap between its slow-
paced, deliberative lawmaking process and the galloping pace of technological change companies like Facebook embody. Throughout Zuckerberg's
testimony, it seemed as if what the Senators and Representatives were oriented toward regulating and restricting was already a thing of the past (user

data scraping and identity exposure) and not necessarily the present (AI) or the future. Certainly, if the market's reaction was any indication, Zuckerberg struck exactly the right chord: the company's stock climbed steadily throughout the last day of hearings, growing in value by 5 percent.

Breaches, leaks, and data dumps have become normalized, even routine elements of our collective experience. Not a day goes by without a story based on some leaked report, document, or embarrassing piece of information about politicians, government policies, or cultural figures finding its way on to our news feeds. These transparency practices are now embedded in the very fabric of reportage on current and political events. In this chapter, we chart the prehistory of this era of forced transparency by examining the conditions of its possibility. We distinguish between two variants of transparency activism and associate them with differing political, normative, and temporal imperatives. We contrast the liberal democratic activism of Edward Snowden and Chelsea Manning with the radical digital disobedience of LulzSec and Anonymous. Whereas the latter weaponized visibility by embarking on a breakneck pace of data exfiltration and document dumps designed to embarrass, harass, and incriminate those in power, the former managed the temporality of their releases to ensure that they enjoyed the broadest possible reception and that public discussion might flow from them.

Both forms of transparency activism also target two disjunctures that emerge at the intersection of democracy and networked technology. On the one hand, there is a structural disconnect between the pace of deliberative decision making in Western democratic legislatures and the ongoing (almost runaway) acceleration of social processes connected with technologies that require some degree of oversight and regulation. On the other there is the normative and ideological capture of core democratic ideals (publicity, openness, transparency, deliberation, etc.) by communicative capitalism, which has fractured resistance and critical dissent by rendering political acts as banal content contributions circulating in a swarm of political and cultural commentary. This situation has generated enduring blind spots that leave our democratic systems open to disruption, tampering, and manipulation.

We argue that this is exactly what happened in the 2016 US presidential election, when Russian actors targeted the electoral process by adopting a multivectored information campaign that scrambled liberal and radical

democratic tactics and justifications for subversive effect. Cambridge Analytica's influence operations also benefited from the success of Russian
interference and, much like Russia, the disjunctures generated by the gap
between democratic deregulation and technological self-regulation. More
generally, both were successful in part because the ideological dominance
of publicity means that the system is structurally open to transparency acts,
and that political actors and citizens are practiced in debating and discuss-
ing them. But also, because of ongoing transformations in the temporal
life cycle of news events, the agenda-setting capacities of traditional media
and their effect on the shape of reporting on events themselves have made
traditional news media more open to data dumps and leaks.

Indeed, traditional news media have moved from being in a position of
quasi-collaborators and erstwhile partners in breaking and framing leaks
and data dumps to one in which the frequency, size, and scope of leaks
eclipses the capacity of transnational journalism to keep pace. In this newly
minted mediascape, Russian and private contractor efforts to weaponize
transparency find traction; they piggyback on the networked media ecosystem constructed by communicative capitalism, all the while exploiting the
newfound symbiosis among leaks, data dumps, and the press.

Starting with the leaks of the Pentagon Papers by Daniel Ellsberg and
ending with the US legislature's attempts to manage Facebook as a vector for the diffusion of misleading news and disruptive content, in this
chapter, we have investigated how networked public spheres—and the
political debate that supports them—are transformed by leaks, dumps, and
breaches. Online rogue publishers like WikiLeaks, online publications like
the *Guardian*, and personalization algorithms like those used by Facebook
and other social media remain important in determining the effects that
the release of secrets will have on public deliberation. Yet we also argue
that the size and timing of the revelation are increasingly important drivers
of its potentially transformative nature: the moment selected by Russian
operatives and WikiLeaks to dump hacked emails from DNC servers, for
instance, was coordinated for maximum impact. Other than timing, the
megavolume of leaked information can also carry a value that goes beyond
the content being leaked. The Panama Papers, at a whopping 2.6 TB, expose
not only offshore tax havens but also the fact that the near ubiquity of
dense data volumes requires new forms of reporting, analysis, security, and
deliberation.

We are living in a high breach society. Our democratic institutions—which now include the social media platforms that make possible the circulation of political content and ideas—are under threat from an excess of data, an opulence in computing power, and a proliferation of networks. The future of the networked public sphere appears to be big-data journalism filtered by AI. The defense against leaks and hacks? More computers. How can we make sense of the deluge of data? More computers. We are now living in an age whose problem and salvation appears to be one and the same. Will this computer-automated future no longer require state hackers to target marks, to defend institutions, and to guard the borders of the state? In the next chapter we bring this discussion back to the present, returning to the hackers themselves and how the state seeks to govern the bodies and minds of hacker activists.

4 Prosecuting a Hacker

> The judge says, "this is a court of law, not a theater!" but what's the difference?
> —Lauri Love, February 5, 2018

Court 1 at Westminster Magistrates' Court in London is the largest courtroom in the building. Although it is reserved for cases that pique the public interest, the décor is uninspired: dark modular furniture rests on office gray carpet, framed by unadorned white walls. The mood evokes the quiet churn of bureaucracy rather than the suspense of television courtroom dramas. Standing behind their desks, defense and prosecution speak in slow and deliberate tones; behind them aides generate an incessant click-clack of keyboard background noise. At the back of the room, journalists from the BBC, the *Guardian*, the *Associated Press*, *Russia Today*, and other media outlets chat breezily about the case.

The hacktivist Lauri Love sits in the glass dock reserved for the accused—a long narrow Plexiglas chamber with a clear door that opens in to the courtroom. He is wearing a dark rumpled suit and looks absorbed in the growing origami-like structure emerging from a small pile of colored paper next to him. Love's complexion is deep red, with dark blotches on his face from eczema and a thin line of blood running from his cheek to his shirt collar.

We are seated in the public gallery, a glass rectangle much like the dock but significantly larger. Although the court is well equipped with microphones, events from the courtroom are piped into the gallery through speakers that distort and muffle the voices of witnesses, lawyers, and the judge. The gallery is filled with Love supporters, family, and friends—including former LulzSec hackers Jake Davis and Mustafa al-Bassam, Love's lawyer in the United States

Tor Ekland, and Naomi Colvin from the Courage Foundation—a nonprofit that defends whistleblowers. Colvin in particular would play a central role in advocating against Love's extradition: throughout his ordeal, she tirelessly fund-raised for his defense, managed public relations and interviews, and provided emotional and pastoral care during his demanding extradition trial. This heterogeneous group is glued to their phones and computers; they will be live tweeting the events of the next two days.

Today and tomorrow represent a critical phase in the extradition hearings that began on July 15, 2015, when Love was arrested by the Metropolitan Police's extradition unit. The stakes are tremendous. Love is under indictment in three US jurisdictions for serious hacking offenses (including hacking into the US Missile Defense Agency, NASA, and the Environmental Protection Agency), and US authorities are treating his alleged crimes as offenses involving national security. In New Jersey and Virginia alone, he faces a sentencing range between 99–151 and 151–198 months, respectively.

The Biggest Military Hack of All Time

Lauri Love is not the first UK hacker sought for extradition by the United States. Richard O'Dwyer and Gary McKinnon were both subject to extradition requests, as was Usman Ahzaz—a Pakistani citizen studying in the UK at the time of his arrest. Davis and al-Bassam have also remarked that American authorities dangled the possibility of extradition at the time of their arrest, although both were ultimately tried in the UK. Gary McKinnon's case in particular provides a unique window into Love's situation. Much like McKinnon, Love has been diagnosed with Asperger syndrome and contests his extradition on human rights grounds—(i.e., imprisoning a person with this condition who requires specialized medical treatment would constitute inhumane treatment). His legal team, as well as many of the doctors and experts he will call as witnesses, also figured prominently in McKinnon's hearings. Finally, although McKinnon successfully resisted his extradition after a ten-year legal battle, the political and legal controversy that flowed from his case significantly shifted the legal basis on which Love's challenge to extradition ultimately stands. In what follows, we discuss McKinnon's case in some detail before comparing his situation with that of Love.

On March 19, 2002, in response to a US request for mutual legal assistance, McKinnon was arrested in London for violating the Computer

Misuse Act of 1990 and released on bail the following day. His computers were seized, and he was interviewed twice in connection with the arrest (on March 19, 2002, and on August 8, 2002). Seven months later, based in part on forensic analysis of the seized devices, two US grand juries (in the District of New Jersey and in the Eastern District of Virginia) returned indictments against him, and US authorities notified their counterparts that they were considering extraditing McKinnon to face charges associated with hacking into ninety-seven US government computers. Between November 2002 and April 2003, McKinnon's legal team took part in plea-bargaining negotiations with US prosecutors over what deal he might receive if he willingly went to the United States and pleaded guilty.[1]

The centrality of plea bargains to American criminal court practices is well known. More than 90 percent of all state and federal criminal cases are resolved through this method (Goode 2012), which allows prosecutors to systematically manipulate charges, incentives, and privileges as a way to ratchet up the costs of going to trial and induce cooperation from the accused (Davis 2007; Lynch 2016). Plea-bargaining agreements have also featured prominently in the prosecution and sentencing of US-based hacktivists. For example, Anonymous-affiliated Jeremy Hammond and Barrett Brown were both threatened with lengthy prison sentences (30 years and 105 years, respectively) before their plea deals. Similarly, it is widely believed that the suicide of internet activist Aaron Swartz (whose death occasioned Anonymous's Operation Last Resort, which Love allegedly participated in) was linked to the US attorney's decision to threaten him with thirty-five years in prison and a $1 million fine for downloading four million articles from JSTOR—an academic journal database. In McKinnon's case prosecutors offered a three- to four-year sentence in a minimum security prison if he agreed to plead guilty to two counts of computer fraud. To further sweeten the deal, they pledged to expedite his repatriation after six to twelve months—a development that would have shortened his sentence significantly because in the UK, prisoners can be released at the halfway point under parole board discretion.[2]

In the above deal, McKinnon would have served somewhere between eighteen and twenty-four months in total. If he chose to resist his extradition, however, prosecutors told him to expect an eight- to ten-year sentence (and possibly longer) served in a high-security prison with no chance of repatriation. The gap between these two offers also illustrates the black box of prosecutorial discretion in charging decisions and the effect of high dollar sums on the points system used to calculate criminal sentences in the US federal system. McKinnon's cooperation would have entailed placing the damage resulting from the crime in a lower points bracket ($400,000–$1,000,000) by calculating only the time it took employees to perform an assessment of the damage and fix it. Authorities agreed not to pursue sentencing "enhancements" based on national security concerns and on the monetary loss incurred by the government's inability to access the compromised computers while they were being repaired.[3]

McKinnon's hack was described by US authorities as "the biggest military hack of all time" (Broadbridge 2009, 12) and involved directly accessing ninety-seven US government computers, including fifty-three US Army computers responsible for the army's military network in Washington, DC; twenty-six US Navy computers (including the naval weapons station Earle, responsible for resupplying munitions for the Atlantic fleet), and sixteen NASA computers. McKinnon did not just access the machines but also deleted files and user accounts, as well as copying documents with logins and passwords along with other sensitive material. His actions shut down the army's entire DC network of two thousand computers for twenty-four hours and rendered the three hundred computers in Earle's computer network inoperable. The latter was used to monitor the identity, location, and battle readiness of navy ships on heightened alert after the September 11 attacks.[4]

The damage inflicted by the infiltration was exacerbated by the apparent ease with which McKinnon gained access. He ran an automated search of seventy-three thousand US government computers that had an open Microsoft Windows connection and identified a surprisingly large number of administrative accounts whose owners had failed to change their passwords from the default setting ("password"). Once he gained control of these accounts, McKinnon used them to escalate his administrative privileges and leveraged his control over these accounts to move from network to network.[5] When he was interviewed by UK authorities after his arrest, McKinnon admitted responsibility for the hack and explained that he had deleted and downloaded government files from the computers he had compromised in an effort to cover up his tracks. His motivation was informed by a conspiracy theory of government, a drive to expose that conspiracy, and the visceral thrill of hacking a US military classified network. McKinnon believed the US government was withholding viable information on clean energy and documentation on the existence of UFOs; he understood his hacking and the revelations that would flow from it as being ethical and in the public interest.[6]

After he rejected the plea deal, the District of New Jersey and the Eastern District of Virginia issued arrest warrants and submitted extradition requests on October 7, 2004. Eight months later, McKinnon was arrested, and an extradition hearing was scheduled for July 27, 2005, and then continued on February 14–15, 2006, and on April 4, 2006. On May 10, 2006, the district judge overseeing the hearings sent the case to the home secretary for the final say on extradition, which she scheduled for July 4, 2006. McKinnon then appealed the decision before the divisional court on April 3, 2007, but that appeal—and a subsequent one made to the House of Lords on July 30, 2008—was denied. Only in August 2008, after all domestic avenues had been exhausted, did McKinnon's lawyers have their client tested for autism spectrum disorder.

McKinnon's lawyers argued that a protracted trial in a foreign jurisdiction and an eight- to ten-year term of imprisonment in a US maximum or supermax facility represented cruel and inhumane treatment for a prisoner with Asperger syndrome. Yet the European Court of Human Rights declined to block the extradition, and even after his attorneys wrote the home secretary about his mental condition and McKinnon offered to plead guilty to section 2 of the UK Computer Misuse Act, the extradition was upheld. Undeterred, in December 2008, McKinnon's attorneys brought the offer of a plea to the Director of Public Prosecutions (DPP) in an effort to have him prosecuted in the UK. By June 5, 2009, McKinnon had also offered to plead guilty to section 3 of the same act, which carried stiffer penalties (unauthorized acts with intent to impair the operation of a computer), but it too was rejected. The home secretary's decision and the decision not to prosecute in the UK by the DPP were jointly appealed in hearings before the high court in June and July 2009.[7]

Both appeals were rejected, and McKinnon's fate hung in the balance for another two years, as the UK home secretary ordered further medical reports and awaited the recommendations of two parliamentary reviews of the new US-UK Extradition Treaty. Finally, on October 16, 2012, then home secretary Theresa May promised that she would be seeking to amend the extradition treaty and announced that McKinnon's extradition would be blocked on human rights grounds. On December 14, 2012, the DPP announced that it would not prosecute McKinnon in the UK for the crimes he was accused of.

A few key points can be gleaned from the above consideration of McKinnon's case. First, and perhaps most important, McKinnon's legal appeals, medical arguments, and attempts to plead guilty to violating the Computer Misuse Act in the UK were all roundly rejected by the courts. Indeed, at the time the United States had expected McKinnon's extradition to be imminent, and May's decision to reject the request generated significant hostility between the home secretary and then US attorney general Eric Holder (Hope and Coughlin 2012). In this sense, May's decision needs to be understood as a last-minute exercise of the executive pardon rather than as a triumph of the adversary process. Even a cursory glance at the legal decisions reveals the extent to which, from a legal point of view, McKinnon's extradition and its seeming inevitability were never in doubt. Second, the amendments made to the extradition process under the Crime and Courts Act of 2013 eliminated the powers of the home secretary to consider human rights–based appeals, so the very executive pardoning power that saved McKinnon no longer exists.

Finally, in comparing the McKinnon case to Love's situation, we should emphasize the unique facets of the former that made him a particularly sympathetic media story and political cause. Three factors in particular stand out: McKinnon was looking for evidence of extraterrestrials and clean technology, the repercussions of his hack were amplified by the failure of many US computer administrators to change their default passwords, and the unique nature of the case suggested that official embarrassment might be one motivation behind his aggressive prosecution. In contrast, Love is accused of participating with Anonymous—a notorious hacktivist collective whose members US officials had been targeting for some time. Perhaps most importantly, Love's overall goal is unclear. We know its precipitating cause (the suicide of Aaron Swartz), but we do not know if the goal was to raise awareness, exfiltrate important and embarrassing details about US policies, or simply generate chaos and havoc.

Extraditing Digital Fugitives

Extraditions are among the earliest and most common legal vehicle for cross-border cooperation in rendering fugitives (Sadoff 2016, 129). The current 2003 US-UK Extradition Treaty was introduced after the September 11 attacks as an effort to streamline the process and facilitate fugitive transfers in a world increasingly characterized by transnational and multi-jurisdictional criminal activity (Heard 2009). Indeed, the UK and US governments explicitly understand extradition as a critical law enforcement tool to tackle cyber crime, international terrorism, and organized crime (House of Commons 2012). Yet despite its enthusiastic adoption by the United States (between 2004 and 2011, the United States made 130 extradition requests to the UK), the treaty has been the source of significant political controversy and public debate in the UK almost from its inception (Baker 2011, 472).

One important source of critique centers on the evidentiary requirements needed to support an extradition request. In the past, these requests were subject to a fairly high evidentiary burden in that the United States would have to meet a prima facie test (i.e., presenting evidence that would be enough to justify a person's trial under UK criminal law) as part of the process. Under the new instrument, this requirement has been significantly reduced: it is no longer necessary to produce evidence of the accused's guilt, but rather the United States must produce *information*—which can include hearsay that would be inadmissible in a criminal trial—sufficient to pass either a *reasonable suspicion* (for UK to US transfers) or a *probable cause* (for US to UK transfers) test. There remains some debate surrounding whether the two legal terms are equivalent, or whether the treaty sets up a lower evidentiary threshold that is advantageous to the United States. The key point is that both tests shift the burden of legal proof to what might be sufficient grounds for arresting a suspect or searching a car during a traffic stop but short of what would be needed to prosecute a criminal trial. Indeed, some commentators have noted that the lower evidentiary threshold also sets up extradition as a possible form of preventive detention: authorities can have suspects detained before securing sufficient evidence to initiate the criminal justice process (Duffy 2005, 135). And a key contention throughout the McKinnon hearings was the allegation that the United States had waited two years to submit an extradition request because it wanted the 2003 treaty to enter into force and hence to benefit from the lower evidentiary thresholds.[8]

A second area of controversy involves the effect of a *forum* (i.e., the most appropriate or convenient place to hear a legal proceeding) bar to extradition. The forum bar was originally introduced into UK law by the 2006

Police and Justice Act but was never brought into force until its appearance in the 2013 Crime and Courts Act. The 2013 act allows a judge to consider whether extradition is in the interests of justice if a "substantial measure" of the accused's activity (which is central to the commission of the crime) was committed in the UK. It lays out seven considerations a judge should weigh, including whether most of the loss or harm generated by the crime took place in the UK; the interests of crime victims; the availability of evidence for a UK prosecution; the practicality of prosecuting all offenses connected with the request in the same jurisdiction; and the connections between the accused and the UK. Finally, the 2013 act also changes the right of an individual subject to extradition to raise human rights issues with the home secretary after the end of judicial proceedings but before actual extradition. The home secretary is now barred from considering the compatibility of extradition with the Human Rights Charter, although such issues can still be raised on appeal with the courts (Arnell 2013). This is an important point, as we saw in the case of McKinnon, because the change forecloses one of the few successful avenues through which suspects have successfully challenged their extradition.

The depiction of extradition proceedings as modern, streamlined, and efficient can be contrasted with the ten years McKinnon spent in court fighting extradition. For most of that time he was caught in the snare of legal imbroglios bundled with fugitive or outlaw status. This presents its own unique disability, as sociologist Alice Goffman (2014) observed in her ethnography of fugitive life in Philadelphia. She notes that to be "on the run" is an odd turn of phrase to describe the situation of legally compromised people because being on the run also means being "at a standstill":

> These young men are also at a standstill in the sense . . . that they cannot proceed with school or work until their legal issues are cleared up. . . . [T]he number of meetings, court dates, and other appointments [they] must keep up with to continue in good standing with the legal system can feel like a full-time job or at least a part-time job with unpredictable hours that undermine regular attendance at school or work. In this sense, living on the run is akin to treading water—continual motion without getting anywhere. (2014, 198–199)

Although the circumstances that surround the lives of Goffman's informants and those of hacktivists facing extradition are significantly different, both are enmeshed in a legal process that is actively working to withdraw its protection. The terms *fugitive* and *outlaw* were originally associated with the medieval practice of withdrawing the law's protection from criminals who were on the run or in hiding (Follis 2013b; Tabarrok 2012). Outlaws were declared "friendless men," considered dangerous, and allowed to be killed with impunity by fellow citizens (Follis 2013a, 174). Those subject to extradition hearings are clearly not outside the law in this sense, but the extradition process can be characterized as a progressive unwinding of the protective legal bond between sovereign and subject. Effectively, the multi-tiered hearing process, complete with its appeals and challenges, leads to a situation where one state surrenders its citizen-subject to the justice system of another.

Clearly for the accused, this is legally fraught terrain. Globalization and the emergence of networked technologies empowers individuals and non-state collectives to tread on ground that had previously been reserved only for states. In this sense, networked technology has had a leveling effect on traditional asymmetries of force between states but also and more importantly between states and political activists. The extradition process allows us to glean the legal impact of this new capacity. The international sphere is one in which sovereign claims are at a stalemate, and states exist in an uneasy balance between stability, cooperation, and conflict. Historically this also the zone of primordial state boundary work: boundaries and borders have expanded and contracted; citizens have been claimed while others have been rendered stateless. To operate in this space, in this zone of predominantly state action, also means that one is acting in the space between laws, where domestic laws and international prerogatives compete for jurisdiction: it is a space where bodies can be forcefully claimed and legally surrendered.

If, as sociologist John Torpey (2000, 10–12) has argued, the most apt metaphor for understanding the extent to which states are able to steer and cage the social activity of their citizens is an "embrace" or a "grasp," then the extradition process represents the slackening or the progressive unwinding of this grasp. It is the slackening of the state's hold on its citizen to give him over to another state. At the same time, this process of unwinding, or slackening, is performed on a grand stage that is equal parts punishment and spectacle. In legal scholar Malcolm Feeley's (1992) seminal analysis of sentencing patterns in New Haven, Connecticut, he argued that in the misdemeanor cases and low-level arrests he observed, much (if not all) of the punishment that a suspect ultimately received flowed from his or her interactions with the police and the courts prior to a determination of guilt or innocence.

For Feeley, the "process is the punishment" because the costs (e.g., pretrial detention, financial burdens, and time delays) for defendants accumulate in the pretrial process, when the charges leveled against defendants are contested; these burdens generate incentives for defendants to accept plea agreements to speed up the resolution of their case and receive substantially reduced sentences. Part of these unregulated "front-end punishments" (Geller 2016, 1041) involves a shift in the locus of sanctioning from a judge ruling on a case to the police and prosecutors: the former arrange the conditions and likelihood of bail, while the latter determine the shape of the plea agreement itself. Although extradition hearings are not criminal trials, and the criminal charges an accused will face once extradited are certainly not misdemeanors, the process of extradition is shaped by a similar logic: a set of pretrial hearings that stretch multiple years and carry forms of duress that are simply incidental, unquantified, and unrecognized in the overall assessment of criminal trial.

Finally, as we saw in McKinnon's case and will see in Love's extradition proceedings, the theatricality that surrounds extradition hearings calls to mind other criminal justice "spectacles" that have historically served to manifest power and to police the boundaries of belonging. Philosopher Michel Foucault famously described the absolutist spectacle of the scaffold as a "penal liturgy" (1977, 47), in which the condemned's public torture and death formed the focal point for a political and juridical ritual designed to reactivate or reaffirm the sovereign's power. In Foucault's analysis, the most spectacular and anticipated facet of the ceremony was neither the torture nor the execution but the possibility of its interruption by a letter of pardon. The pardon represented the sovereign's supreme capacity to suspend both law and vengeance (1977, 53).

This tension between the presence and absence of not just one sovereign (as in Foucault's case) but multiple sovereigns, as well as the ceremonial cast that proceedings take, informs extradition hearings and gives them a particular dynamism. We have proceedings in one sovereign jurisdiction (the UK), which are staged for the benefit of another sovereign (the United States), who appears in the form of indictments and sworn affidavits but does not actually appear in person (the Crown Prosecution Service represents American prosecutors). At the same time, much as in the above account of the gallows, the underlying suspense that pervades the hearings flows from the possibility that events might stray from an expected and largely predetermined narrative. For Foucault, the most unstable component in the penal liturgy of absolutist France was the condemned and whether he or she would subvert the narrative when asked to express contrition. Within extradition hearings, the instability centers on the domestic sovereign (in this case, the UK) and whether the proceedings might form the setting for an emphatic reassertion of its authority.

Hacking Civil Law: Lauri Love v. National Crime Agency

Lauri Love's case, much like that of McKinnon, illustrates the powerful offline resources that remain available to states when projecting authority through mutual assistance frameworks and claims of extraterritorial jurisdiction. On Friday, October 25, 2013, the NCA executed a search warrant at Love's home in Suffolk, in connection with violations of sections 1(1) and 1(3) of the Computer Misuse Act. In a ruse designed to get him out of the house before he could trigger the encryption on his computer, an agent posed as a UPS courier and insisted that Love come to the door to sign for a package. Once Love's identity was confirmed, he was handcuffed and left on the porch as fourteen officers invaded the home and spent the next five hours searching the house. The officers seized twenty-nine items of computer equipment and arrested Love. On Saturday afternoon, after a brief morning interview with police during which he was asked (and declined) to provide the encryption keys to the protected devices, he was released on bail with the condition that he surrender his passport and avoid connecting to the internet via "third parties" (e.g., encryption, VPN, etc.).

Although the District of New Jersey had issued a sealed criminal complaint against Love as early as May 16, 2013, Love's arrest flowed directly from an ongoing investigation by the UK's NCA and was followed two days later by a series of joint press announcements from the US Attorney's Offices in the District of New Jersey and the Eastern District of Virginia (US Attorney's Office 2014a, 2014b). The NCA wrote to the US Department of Justice before the press releases were issued asking that Love not be identified, as this could taint the case and complicate a UK-based prosecution. US authorities singled out the NCA for its bilateral support in apprehending Love, but the UK investigation formed part of a larger, sprawling list of parallel investigations, including those of the Computer Crime Unit of the US Army's Criminal Investigation Division, FBI field offices in Washington and Newark, and the Offices of Inspector General for NASA, the Department of Energy, the Environmental Protection Agency, and the Department of Health and Human Services.

Commenting on the arrest, the director of the US Army's Computer Crime Unit, Daniel Andrews, emphasized the national security and military risks posed by computer intrusions and argued that "the borderless nature of internet-based crime underscores the need for robust law enforcement alliances across the globe" (New Jersey US Attorney's Office 2013, 2). The existence of three parallel investigations in the United States, an investigation in the UK, and one in Australia (where two alleged co-conspirators were located) illustrates the hybrid, swarmlike tactics of cross-national law enforcement cases. Significant jurisdictional ambiguity also surrounds these cases, since despite appearing to be jointly pursued investigations, local law enforcement serve as proxies for US interests and investigative priorities.

Although most of the computer equipment seized was returned to the Love family, six items of computer hardware remained in the custody of authorities. In November, the NCA offered to "forensically wipe" the data on the devices to expedite their return.[9] Love refused, and in February 2014 he was served with notice that the NCA had invoked the disclosure requirement in section 49 of the Regulatory Investigatory Powers Act (RIPA). Effectively, under the legislation, law enforcement can request that the owner of an encrypted device seized by the police provide the key or password to decrypt it. Love was given twenty-eight days to decrypt the devices or face severe consequences. Under section 53 of RIPA, the maximum penalty for ignoring a notice in cases involving national security or child indecency is five years, and in all other cases, two years or an unlimited fine (or both). Although Love refused to comply, the NCA failed to follow up the request: it did not arrest or charge him. Instead, in July 2014, the NCA decided that they did not have enough evidence to pursue a criminal case against him, and he was released from bail.

At this point Love decided to sue the NCA to get his property back under the Police Property Act of 1897 (PPA), which empowers a magistrates' court to release seized or retained property in the possession of the police to its owner. His first application was in 2015, before Bury St. Edmunds Magistrates' Court: that court directed Love to provide the decryption keys for the devices. He objected, and when his objection failed, he withdrew his application. On March 2, 2016, Love initiated a second application under the PPA before Judge N. Tempia at Westminster Magistrates' Court. By this time, he had been arrested by the London Met's Extradition Unit, and extradition hearings presided over by the same judge had been scheduled. In this context, the encrypted contents of Love's hard drives gained new relevance as potential evidence in a future criminal trial in the United States. In the preliminary hearing, Tempia directed Love to provide a witness statement as to the contents of the files on those devices in support of his application for their return. Love provided an unsigned witness statement, which did not supply any of the requested information.

The NCA then asked that Tempia direct Love to provide the encryption keys in the interest of "good case management."[10] Essentially the agency argued that, in lieu of Love's description of the contents of the devices and in the context of what they could see on the devices before the encryption kicked in (i.e., data from the Police Oracle website, US Senate, and US Department of Energy, as well as some pirated films), the court needed to know everything that was on the devices before it could properly rule on who owned them. Drawing on the cumbersome metaphor of a safe, it made the case that just because Love owned the safe (i.e., the devices) he did not necessarily own the files that were in the safe (i.e., the encrypted data) and had not provided any documentation as to what was on them. Ultimately, Tempia ruled that she would not grant the NCA motion because the agency was attempting to circumvent the legitimate legal process for securing the decryption of those files. That process, which should have been followed two years earlier, would have entailed following up on Love's refusal to comply with the RIPA decryption order with the commencement of formal proceedings to secure his compliance.

Love's victory in the civil hearing was short lived. Although he was successful in fending off a decryption order from the NCA, his property remained with the UK government, and the final hearing on his civil action was suspended pending the outcome of the extradition proceedings. Yet this incident also underscores the ambiguous nature of mutual assistance frameworks and sheds light on the proxy arrangements that support them. On the one hand, if the NCA had followed through with RIPA procedure, Love's case would have been bound up in the UK criminal justice system, and this would have potentially complicated the US government's pending

extradition plans. On the other, given that the NCA and the Crown Prosecution Service (CPS) had already decided that they would not prosecute
Love, the attempt to circumvent RIPA and force a decryption order under
the court's discretionary powers could appear as evidence gathering for
Love's future criminal trials in the United States.

The Mind and Body of Lauri Love

There is a clear sense of inevitability to much of what transpires within
extradition hearings. Indeed, the presumption is that the accused should
be extradited based solely on the claims made by US authorities (as formalized in the 2003 extradition treaty). Incriminating or exculpatory evidence, indeed criminal evidence of any kind, although constituting the
backdrop and context for the proceedings is never explicitly presented or
discussed. Rather, accusations of criminality and allegations of conspiracy
and malfeasance assert themselves unchallenged in the evidentiary vacuum
produced by the hearings themselves. This lends an almost pro forma, or
ceremonial, cast to proceedings, where the burden is on the accused to
show that he is unfit for extradition without recourse to any conventional
legal means (most notably contesting the state's evidence) to assert mitigation or innocence.

Yet this is not the case for authorities who are in possession of the evidence and deploy it liberally to score strategic points. On the first day of
proceedings, Peter Caldwell (the CPS prosecutor representing the United
States) spoke at length and in considerable detail about Love's alleged
criminal activity, because "opening the facts" in the case was in the public
interest.[11] He quoted incriminating IRC chat room conversations with FBI
confidential informants and drew on evidence from computers seized in
the NCA raid discussed earlier. Caldwell presented Love's impressive list of
crimes, charges, motives, and victims with iron certainty—as if there were
no factual doubt about his interpretation of events, and Love's guilt had
already been determined. Love protested against Caldwell's characterization
even as it became evident that the deck was stacked against him, saying,

> The government has made its case which is accusation based on unproven alle-
> gations and assertions which I have never been provided the evidence in support
> of. The treaty doesn't require evidence from the US but a lot of very serious alle-
> gations have been made about me in open court today and there is no way for

me to substantively respond to these allegations because of the nature of how this process operates.[12]

Although Caldwell opened proceedings with the "facts" concerning Love's criminality, the hearings quickly became an inquest focused exclusively on Love's character, as well as on his psychological and physical state. Indeed, it is ironic that Love's alleged collaboration with Anonymous led to a legal process premised on the deep psychological and physical health documentation of the most personal facets of his identity. Alongside the testimony of his parents (the Reverend Alexander and Sirkka Love), the court heard from three psychopathology and neuropsychiatry experts, three experts on US prisons and federal criminal sentencing, as well as fellow activists and Love's employer at Hacker House—a cybersecurity and ethical hacking start-up.

The first witness, Baron Cohen (a Cambridge professor of psychiatry who also figured prominently in McKinnon's case) began by addressing Love's symptoms and Love's regular declaration in the media that if convicted he would commit suicide rather than face jail in the United States: "I think his depression is extremely serious, extremely dangerous, in terms of his risk of suicide. He hears voices in his head telling him to kill himself. . . . During [an] assessment, Lauri made no eye contact, which is a sign of Asperger's Syndrome. He sat in my office making paper models of origami." Baron Cohen then gestured across the room to Love, saying, "The court may have noticed that in the last 2 hours he's been doing the same thing. One of his repetitive interests is making these beautiful pieces of art."[13]

An important component of Love's legal strategy presented him as a misunderstood cybersecurity specialist rather than the callous criminal described in Caldwell's opening statement. Yet as much as the two sides drew on competing interpretive frames (medical vs. criminal justice), they also reinforced and referenced popular tropes. Criminologist David Wall has argued that the Victorian figure of the "savant"—a person possessing "profound knowledge who could utilize technology to his or her . . . advantage for good or bad" (2012, 12)—informs society's view of hackers. Criminologist Kevin Steinmetz (2016) and others (Coleman 2014; Thomas 2002) have similarly noted that over time, popular accounts have increasingly emphasized the sinister menace and technological danger that lurks at the fingertips of the computer savvy. Baron Cohen's testimony similarly drew a clear connection between Love's alleged criminal acts (which "involved

evading detection"), his technical and raw intelligence, and his capacity for
committing suicide:

> I was thinking that when it comes to suicidal plans, [Love] has thought through
> how to evade detection and the method he would deploy to commit suicide. . . .
> [M]y estimation of his technical understanding of what kinds of methods could
> lead to a fatal outcome, he's got all the knowledge and intelligence to have
> researched how to do that without being detected. . . . He's spent hundreds or
> thousands of hours researching not only around the case but around the methods
> of suicide.[14]

Love's lawyers sought to portray him as a deeply vulnerable and psycho-
logically fraught savant capable of turning his considerable gifts against
himself. In contrast, Caldwell mobilized an alternate reading of Love as
a cyber criminal adept at manipulation and cold opportunism. Love was
exaggerating both his symptoms and his capacity to commit suicide to
evoke sympathy from the court: "He is bright and has spent time on the
internet, but isn't there an element of fantasy in that aspect of what he
says? . . . Maybe putting him in the care of his parents isn't going to manage
the kind of risk you refer to. . . . His parents might not be able to detect it
either."[15] Although Love blurted out that he wouldn't kill himself at home
from the other side of the room, Caldwell continued with this theme in his
questioning of Professor Michael Kopelman (a neuropsychiatrist): "Is that
[paranoid thoughts] a manifestation of a tendency to dramatize a situation?
To be an actor in an important play?"[16] And later: "Is he clever enough to
make it up?" In response Kopelman reaffirmed Cohen's clinical opinion
given earlier in the day: "I don't think so. Obviously whenever one does
a forensic mental health assessment you have to bear that in mind. But
the consistency, the pattern of his symptoms, and indeed what his father
and others have said, make me think that this is not a fantasy as you put it
this morning."[17] When Love took the stand on the second day of hearings,
Caldwell's skeptical line of questioning became even more pronounced:

> My suggestion to you is you have in the public eye and in preparing your case
> made prominent your features of your circumstances such as Asperger's syndrome
> and have exaggerated your symptoms to medical professionals who have made
> those reports. . . . [Y]ou're a vulnerable person who has disadvantages but they're
> manageable disadvantages that you prefer to use as a shield in these proceedings
> rather than try to seek actual relief.[18]

This statement was met with audible gasps in the gallery, and behind us
someone whispered doxing threats directed against the prosecutor. It was

quickly followed by laughs when Love joked back, "What is your medical advice?" and continued, "It is up to you if you want to call into question the veracity of medical experts. If the thrust of the argument is that we collaborated to create misleading medical reports—that is disappointing." Undaunted Caldwell continued, "That is my suggestion to you. You do seek to promote your personal difficulties as a shield to extradition."[19]

What can be gleaned from these examples about how the state attempts to exercise control through the framing of subjectivity? Both the prosecution and defense are struggling to define Love's subjectivity. They present testimony and fact in an effort to reveal some kind of deeper, stable truth about Love. For one, it is embodied illness; for another, it is theatricality to avoid extradition; for both, the mutability of hacktivist identity needs to be fixed into a specific and immutable subject. It is this fixed subject that the state can then prosecute and potentially imprison. But for hackers, subjectivity is fluid—and they do not want to get caught. They rely on pseudonyms and seed ambiguity. Their discussions often take place among individuals who may have never met face to face, who guard their offline personas, and who deploy multiple versions of themselves contemporaneously. We adopt the term *versioning* to describe this process-oriented and performative mode of online identity management. Versioning targets the strategies of self-presentation and "face work" (E. Goffman 1959, 1967) that dominate actor performances in the offline world. In contrast, social media platforms like Facebook seek to extend these interaction structures. They use processes of replication, correlation, personalization, and indexing to chart an actor's offline associations so that they can be directly ported into digital form. Though the end product is more scalable, nuanced, and actor directed, the effect is to reify and confirm a singular "actual" social identity that is already categorically fixed in the offline world.

According to authorities, Love adopted a rotating set of monikers, including nsh, peace, shift, route, and Smedley Butler, but ultimately he was caught because of the digital trail of breadcrumbs he left behind. Indeed, the process of uncovering one's offline identity can sometimes be a straightforward combination of requesting subscriber information for social media accounts and open source intelligence gathering. In Love's case, authorities traced the attack on the US Army's Engineering Corps servers to a Romanian IP address associated with the domain name ch0wn.dyndns.org; the ch0wn domain was paid for by a Lauri Love who used the email address lauri.love@gmail.com as the PayPal address for the payment. Subscriber records for that account also listed the English IP address for the subscriber, and after some financial investigation, authorities determined that the physical location associated with this IP address was the home of Love's parents.

Further investigation of Google subscriber records revealed that nsh was the nickname associated with Love's Gmail account, and that Smedley Butler was the owner of a Gmail account (anonops31337@gmail.com) also linked to the ch0wn domain. Additionally, in an article in the *Observer* profiling the group Anonymous, the reporter interviewed an activist known only as nsh who was described as a British male studying at a prestigious university (thereby confirming nsh's location as the UK). In several IRC chats between 2005 and 2011, nsh and n5h gave their email addresses as lauri.love@gmail.com and stated Lauri Love as their legal name. Finally, the Twitter account @laurilove was named Smedley Butler, and lauri.love@gmail.com was listed as the email address on the account (the account also used the hashtag #nshmarks).[20]

None of this evidence was presented or made available for Love's rebuttal during the extradition trial, but the sealed US grand jury indictments (from New Jersey, Eastern Virginia, and New York) that described this identification process were unsealed and released to the public after his arrest in October 2013. Since then, he has appeared as a technical expert on a series of television programs, including BBC's *Newsnight* to comment on the 2015 TalkTalk security breach and *Channel 4 News* to discuss the Investigatory Powers bill. In the lead-up to his extradition hearings, *Russia Today*, the BBC's *Victoria Derbyshire Show*, and Channel 4 all featured specials with Love or his US attorney Tor Ekland. Finally, Love was extensively interviewed by print and online media in the long period between his initial arrest and the extradition hearings.

When hacktivists are doxed by authorities and find themselves threatened with long prison sentences, they may embrace the publicity and decide to "come out" (Fish and Follis 2016) to tell their version of events and galvanize public opinion. Indeed, the extensive media coverage of the McKinnon trial and the sympathetic portrayal he received in both conservative and liberal news sources significantly increased the political pressure on Secretary Theresa May to deny the US extradition request. Caldwell suggested that Love and his supporters had consciously crafted a media strategy designed to elicit public support against extradition. For example, at one point he noted, "Your referred to cases like McKinnon as situations where media had a positive bearing on the case. . . . With the assistance of advisors consciously seeking to put yourself in the imprint of someone like Mr. McKinnon: 'I'm like him, you should look at my case.'" Which Love adamantly denied:

> Are you asking me if I'm trying to appear more like McKinnon? I've engaged with the medical principles and the legal team have formulated their arguments around that. The way I think, I would have wanted this case to revolve around due process without reference to my personal mental health difficulties which are apposite. I would like to protect any person in this position whether they have a particular diagnosis or not.[21]

Some hacktivists willingly disclose their identities while in pursuit of information they find germane to the public interest. Whether they label their actions as investigative journalism or whistleblowing, the rationale for self-exposure flows from the motivation to bring to light the illicit, illegal, or unethical practices committed by governments or corporate institutions. At times, self-identification is an inevitable part of the process of information liberation since information about the data's provenance is necessary to legitimate and authenticate it, but at other times the decision to cross the threshold between offline and online social identity is deliberate and calculated. Coming out involves reclaiming political responsibility and legitimacy through self-disclosure and revelation. It is an attempt to shape social identity in the court of media or public opinion and outside the stigmatizing narratives of the state.

In this sense, the mainstream media play an important role in manifesting hacktivists' goals of bringing attention to political causes. Love is accused of collecting personal information for the purposes of doxing. But the courts that sentence hackers inflate the years in jail and fines based on financial and not intended political impact. This is because although the CFAA penalizes what are effectively trespass offenses (unauthorized access to a computer is a kind of trespass), when a defendant is convicted of violating CFAA statutes, the sentencing court then uses section 2B1.1 of the Federal Sentencing Guidelines, which refers to economic crimes, to calculate the criminal sentence (Kerr 2016, 1554). In so doing, the sentencing court applies a sentencing framework that produces proportionate sentencing outcomes for economic crimes like fraud or theft, but that are intuitively draconian or disproportionate for many computer crimes. Under 2B1.1 the loss incurred by a hack is broadly conceived:

> Under 18 USC § 1030, actual loss includes the following pecuniary harm, regardless of whether such pecuniary harm was reasonably foreseeable: any reasonable cost to any victim, including the cost of responding to an offense, conducting a damage assessment, and restoring the data, program, system, or information to its condition prior to the offense, and any revenue lost, cost incurred, or other damages incurred because of interruption of service. (US Sentencing Commission 2015, 90)

Section 2B1.1 includes special adjustments (i.e., calculation increases) for certain CFAA violations, including if the offense involved (a) the intent to obtain personal information, (b) the unauthorized dissemination of personal information, and (c) "a computer system used to maintain or operate critical infrastructure, or used by or for a government entity in furtherance of the administration of justice, national defense or national security" (US Sentencing Commission 2015, 85). A sentencing court will also consult a loss chart, which, depending on the losses claimed by the victims, will yield further calculation increases. Finally, section 2B1.1 contains sentencing enhancements if a crime is committed using "sophisticated means" (e.g., the complex or intricate mode of accomplishing the crime) or "special skills" (e.g., skills that might require a high level of education, professional certification, or licensing). Although these enhancements make sense in the world of white collar crime, in hacking cases, the use of a computer in the commission of the crime has routinely been used to trigger these enhancements (Kerr 2016, 1561).

The disproportionate consequences of conceptualizing computer trespass violations in terms of fraud or theft is evident in the case of notorious internet troll Andrew "weev" Auernheimer. He was sentenced to forty-one months (3.4 years) in prison for publicly disclosing a security exploit in AT&T's servers in 2010 that could reveal the email addresses of iPad users. At sentencing, the court applied enhancements for using sophisticated means, special skills, and obtaining personal information. At that point a sentence at the top end of the sentencing range would have been sixteen months. Then the court made further adjustments for the loss sustained by AT&T. According to the company the sole loss it sustained was the $73,000 it cost to print and mail a confirmation to its one hundred thousand customers that their data was safe and their accounts secure. This sum increased weev's sentencing range to thirty-one to forty-one months and the court applied the high end of the scale. But AT&T also emailed its one hundred thousand customers a duplicate of that letter. Effectively, if AT&T had decided not to mail a postal letter but just to email its customers, weev's sentence would have been reduced by two years (Fakhoury 2013; Kerr 2016, 1558).

A similar process was at work in the plea-bargaining negotiations concerning McKinnon's case. The rationale between the prosecution's plea offer of a three- to four-year minimum sentence and the threat of eight to ten years if McKinnon contested his extradition relied on similar calculations. US prosecutors would put the damage resulting from the crime in a lower points bracket ($400,000–$1,000,000) by calculating only the hours it took employees to perform an assessment of the damage and fix it; prosecutors would then multiply those hours by the worker's hourly wage. Authorities would also overlook the monetary loss incurred by the government's inability to access the compromised computers while they were being repaired and not pursue sentencing enhancements based on the national security threat and nonmonetary harm generated by the infiltration. Both cases emphasize the centrality of the prosecutor's discretion in assembling charges under the CFAA and the wide latitude authorities have in increasing the burdens associated with challenging the government's case.

As can be gleaned from the last five or six years of global data breaches, cybersecurity remains an under-resourced and neglected facet of many corporate and government digital environments. Often security protocols are outdated or nominal, exploits are well-known and widely available, and passwords require little effort to circumvent. Yet in the overall assessment of criminal damages, the figure that appears is not the cost of restoring the hacked system to its preexisting state of (in)security but rather the cost of upgrading the system's security features to the level they should have been at all along. Effectively, not only are CFAA charging decisions disproportionate in the sense described above, but they also create no incentive for at-risk digital entities to update their security practices until they have been breached.

Harsh Justice on Trial

Lauri Love arrives with his own theme music. It is a heavy, thumping dub-driven sound presided over by a soft high-pitched singer reminiscent of

Blondie. The music blares out of a massive speaker strapped to the purple Maclaren stroller he is pushing. Today and tomorrow the high court will hear Love's appeal against Judge Tempia's decision to grant the United States' extradition request. Although the hearing starts at 9:30 a.m., a large group of supporters have been here for some time, draping the building's wrought-iron fencing with mosaics and handmade signs, distributing fliers and "freelauri" t-shirts, as well as inflating almost a dozen massive heart-shaped red balloons. The mood is anxious but also carnivalesque. Activists are scattered among the supporters as well as bystanders, camera operators, microphone technicians, and reporters. People mill about talking on their phones, technicians check their equipment, and journalists conduct interviews.

If the aesthetic of Westminster Magistrates' Courts was characterized by a spartan modernism, the Royal Courts of Justice evoke all the Romantic-era spiritualism that animates neogothic architecture. The building, a sprawling Victorian complex of courtrooms, offices, and meeting rooms facing the Strand, is located on the boundary line between Westminster and London. Inside, it opens up on a cathedral-like scale: a lofty rib-vaulted lobby with a mosaic floor pattern in Italian marble and alcove staircases that lead to upper floor courtrooms. Much like the whole building, the lord chief justice's courtroom is a study in the power and majesty of law. It is small but richly adorned, with carved oak panels covering the walls and ceiling; three rows of oak benches sit in front of the judge's panel, and there is a row of benches for the press on the left between the two areas. The public gallery is in the back of the room and is lined with overflowing bookshelves and floor stacks of bound law reports and journals dating back to the eighteenth and nineteenth centuries. The room is high ceilinged since it must accommodate a larger viewing balcony upstairs.

Lord Burnett of Maldon (the lord chief justice) began the hearing by introducing his colleague, the Honorable Mr. Justice Ouseley, who would also hear the case. He also confirmed to reporters that they could tweet courtroom events and reminded members of the public that social media posts and recordings were prohibited in court. After these short announcements, he asked the defense to begin laying out its case.

Edward Fitzgerald—a distinguished lawyer who counts the radical cleric Abu Hamza, the author of the Moors murders Myra Hindley, and more recently former Italian PM Silvio Berlusconi as clients (he also defended

Gary McKinnon)—presented Love's appeal. The defense's case rested on three legal points: that district judge Tempia wrongly did not uphold the forum bar as a barrier to extradition; that under the 2003 Human Rights Act, Love's extradition would be oppressive and unjust given his physical and mental condition; and that extradition would breach articles 3 and 8 of the European Convention on Human Rights. Importantly, the above challenges gain their force from the contention that Love is not seeking to escape legal judgment but rather welcomes the chance to confront the criminal allegations against him in an English courtroom.

Fitzgerald sought to introduce several new pieces of evidence. For example, he provided the court with a statement from a former DPP (Lord Macdonald) outlining a series of cases involving UK-based hackers where both the victims and the bulk of criminal damage were abroad. He did this to make the point that established prosecutorial practice in these cases was to try criminal defendants domestically rather than sending them abroad. These, along with Fitzgerald's own additional tally, covered over a decade of hacking-related cases, including recent cases such as that of an unnamed teenager convicted in Plymouth of breaking into several international servers, including SeaWorld in Florida, China's Security Ministry, and the Thai Department of Agriculture, who received a two-year Youth Rehabilitation Order in June 2016; Sean Caffrey, who pleaded guilty to hacking the US DOD and received a suspended sentence of eighteen months from the Birmingham Crown Court in September 2017; and Kane Gamble (the founder of Crackas with Attitude), who pleaded guilty in Leicester Crown Court of ten charges involving hacking the computers of the US government, the CIA, and the FBI. Gamble was fifteen at the time of the offenses and was recently sentenced at London Central Criminal Court to two years' detention.

Although these documents were ultimately considered not relevant and hence did not form part of the judges' deliberation in deciding on a judgment, they offer stark contrasts. Not only do they illustrate the capacity of British courts to try hacking offenses with an extrajurisdictional component, but they also evidence the gulf between the severity of US sentencing practices and those of the UK. The most emblematic of these is Gamble, who used social engineering tactics to impersonate former CIA director John Brennan, homeland security secretary Jeh Johnson, deputy director of the FBI Mark Giuliano, national intelligence director James Clapper, and other Obama-era top officials. His group, Crackas with Attitude, was responsible for doxing several law enforcement officials (including some twenty thousand FBI agents) as well as releasing multiple sensitive and high-level documents. At his sentencing, the judge noted that Gamble had conducted "an extremely nasty campaign of politically motivated cyberterrorism" and sentenced him to two years' detention in a young offenders institution. In contrast, in the opinion of the court and Love's lawyers, if extradited Love would likely receive a custodial sentence between ten and fifteen years.

The admission into the record of the above cases was refused by the court, but a series of other documents was successfully introduced. These concerned the conditions of detention within the US Bureau of Prisons (BOP) and, more specifically, the two New York jails where Love would likely be held throughout his arraignment and trial. Given that Love would first be tried in the Southern District of New York, he would likely be held in one of two federally contracted jails: the Metropolitan Detention Center (MDC) in Brooklyn or the Metropolitan Correctional Center (MCC) in Manhattan. The former has been the subject of controversy for several years, starting with its role housing eighty-four suspects detained on immigration charges as part of the sprawling immigration roundup of Muslim, South Asian, and Arab men in the aftermath of the September 11 attacks (OIG 2003, 4). Allegations of physical and verbal abuse, twenty-four-hour restrictive confinement (in the specially built Administrative Maximum Special Housing Unit), and sleep deprivation culminated in an ongoing civil lawsuit filed by the Center for Constitutional Rights against former attorney general John Ashcroft, MDC staff, the BOP, and others on behalf of the detainees—as well as a $1.26 million settlement in 2009 with five detainees who were part of the suit.[22]

The court gave significant weight to two audits performed by the Women in Prison Committee of the National Association of Women Judges (NAWJ) in 2015 and 2016. Both reports labeled the conditions of confinement for women "unconscionable" since December 2013 and contended that the "absence of fresh, clean air, the complete absence of sunlight, and the absence of ANY [sic] outdoor time and activities," as well as substandard food and medical treatment, violated American Bar Association Standards on Treatment of Prisoners and the UN Standard Minimum Rules for the Treatment of Prisoners (NAWJ 2016, 3). According to the reports, the facility holds its population of approximately 161 women in two large windowless rooms twenty-four hours a day. Indeed, conditions were so deplorable that a Brooklyn judge refused to remand any more prisoners to the facility until she was satisfied that the US BOP had a clear plan in place to remedy the conditions (Marzulli 2016).

Additionally, the judges drew on a class-action lawsuit filed by MDC male inmates against the Justice Department and the BOP in 2016.[23] The allegations contained in the legal complaint corroborated the observations of the two NAWJ audits and made the point that conditions for the approximately 1,700 male prisoners there did not dramatically deviate from those for women. As the judges noted, "There is no reason in our view, to suppose that the conditions attributable to the state of the building are better on the men's floors or that men would be better treated in other respects."[24] Finally, they also considered the BOP's use of "restrictive housing" to manage prisoners with mental illness more broadly and a scathing report from the Office of Inspector General, which concluded that such confinement, "even for short periods of time, can have a significant impact on inmates' mental health and can be particularly harmful for inmates with mental illness" (OIG 2017, 63).

At every step, the gap between the officially stated BOP policies and the practical evidence (in the form of reports and expert testimony) of conditions on the ground within federal facilities militated against the US government's request. The court found Thomas Kucharski's three written statements particularly persuasive. Kucharski is an experienced forensic psychologist based in New York. He has worked as chief psychologist at the MCC and regularly visits both facilities. In his October 29, 2017, memo, Kucharski noted:

[T]here are multiple risks that would be associated with Mr. Love's extradition to the United States, his incarceration in a United States facility, and his standing trial there. . . . His eczema, his asthma, gastrointestinal symptoms, and palpitations, would certainly become far worse, and he might lose his hair again (alopecia). . . . [He] would not be able to cope with separation from his family and friends, nor would he be able to cope with the likely isolation in a United States facility. His depression would become far worse. . . . His suicide risk would become very high as a result of the exacerbation of his clinical depression and a deterioration in his physical health . . . his ability to cope with the proceedings in the trial. To make rational decisions, and to give evidence in a satisfactory manner, would be severely compromised in such circumstances.[25]

Not only did Kucharski unpack the reassurances of the BOP's Psychology Branch and the US Marshals Service, but he also drew a vivid picture of the impact of chronic staff shortages on mental health treatment in both institutions—as well as the incapacity of BOP policy and protocols to address the debilitating spiral to Love's mental and physical well-being that an extradition would initiate. Love's declared intention to commit suicide (if the request were granted) would likely have him placed on suicide watch immediately on his arrival at MDC or MCC. Yet, though this might prevent Love from carrying out the physical act, it would likely also exacerbate his depressive state and increase his suicide risk. As the court noted in its analysis of the evidence:

> If he were kept on suicide watch . . . [a]ll evidence is that this would be very harmful for his difficult mental conditions, Asperger Syndrome and depression, linked as they are; and for his physical conditions, notabl[y] eczema, which would be exacerbated by stress. That in turn would add to his worsening mental condition, which in turn would worsen his physical conditions. . . . [T]here is no evidence treatment would or could be made available on suicide watch of the very conditions which suicide watch itself exacerbates.[26]

Further, the judges anticipated that Love's multiple conditions would initiate a revolving door between segregation (either on suicide watch or administrative segregation) and the general population. Segregation worsened Love's depression and suicide risk, but the general population—even in a relatively low-security federal prison—would feature the twin standbys of the American penal experience: overcrowding and violence. Love would be a target for bullying and harassment because his other conditions (Asperger's, eczema) would make him extremely vulnerable and place him under "unrelenting stress."[27] The only way to address this would be to place him in segregation, but this would also close the causal loop that would accelerate the worsening of his condition.

The paucity of mental health services and treatment programs in the American federal prison system, as well as the general conditions of confinement, figured prominently in Love's appeal. Yet throughout the original hearings in Westminster Magistrates' Court, the key facts under contention also concerned Love's Asperger diagnosis, as well as his physical and psychological state. For the most part, Judge Tempia considered the same reports and evidence the high court reviewed; she interviewed many of the key witnesses (including Kucharski), yet her assessment was neutral and significantly influenced by a willingness to accept the assurances of BOP and US Marshals representatives against defense expert witnesses. In the appeal, rather unexpectedly, the routine operation of American justice in all its mundane dysfunctionality and austerity would itself became a barrier to extradition. On the first day of the appeal hearings, the judges interrupted and rebuked the CPS representative Peter Caldwell, citing the reports discussed above (and other extradition cases involving high-profile defendants) to make the point that the assurances of American justice officials provided no guarantees as to where Love might ultimately wind up or how he might be treated.

The judges disagreed with district judge Tempia on the applicability of the forum bar, including the weight that should be accorded to Love's connection to the UK (which involved a protracted discussion of what *connection* means on day two) and the capability of UK authorities to try the case domestically. Yet ultimately, the decisive factor appears to have been the actual conditions of confinement and treatment in the US federal justice system: the judges found that extradition would be "oppressive" as defined under section 91 of the 2003 extradition act and therefore should be barred.

In this sense, the same punitive logic that animated the dogged multi-year pursuit of Love's extradition by American authorities also contained the seeds of its rejection. Those seeds were evident leaving the courtroom on day two, when we heard Ben Cooper (one of Love's lawyers) comment to a reporter: "It's looking good." Earlier we described the theatrical staging and sense of inevitability that animates extradition hearings. We argued that notwithstanding their often mundane setting (they frequently take place in spare magistrates' courtrooms), such hearings perform important cultural work. A central element in political show trials is that they seek to resituate abstract, contingent, or contested political motivations and acts within the framework of law and justice (Allo and Tesfaye 2015; Prusak 2010). Although extradition hearings are not political show trials or even legal trials in the traditional sense, they are performative legal contests charged with political symbolism. Even before Love's arrest, and certainly in the years since, the cultural tropes and expectations we have come to associate with hacking, hacktivism, cybersecurity, and state hacking have been undergoing a sustained period of flux. Extradition hearings represent one facet of the ongoing state-driven interpretive work aimed at mapping the validity of state-generated categories of culpability, accountability, and criminality onto this shifting transjurisdictional terrain.

At the same time, extradition hearings have a spectacular quality not just because their presumed inevitability and diminished evidentiary requirements facilitate the "degradation" (Garfinkel 1956) of the accused and his or her public shaming. They are also, as we describe above, political rituals that involve the unwinding or slackening of one state's grasp (Torpey 2000) over an individual and their surrender to the justice system of another state. Thus, much like the "spectacular" punishments of the ancien régime described by Foucault (1977, 47), extradition hearings are riven with suspense and a measure of unpredictability. In Foucault's ancien régime analysis, the suspense was twofold: (1) the condemned or the crowd could refuse to play their part in the ritual and use the opportunity to try to subvert proceedings; and (2) there was always, until the very last moment, the possibility that the sovereign might make an appearance (via a letter) and pardon the condemned. In contrast, within extradition hearings, the suspense and possibility for disruption flows not from anything the accused might say, nor from potential clemency, but from the possibility that the request might be refused, that the hearings themselves might become a stage for the reaffirmation of a different sovereign and justice system over and against that of the requesting state.

When we returned to the Royal Courts of Justice some three months later to hear the judges' decision, the mood was palpably brighter. It was a sunny, crisp February morning in 2018, and there seemed to be a genuine feeling among supporters that the judgment would go Love's way. Law has its own unique temporality: after years of slow-moving hearings and legal limbo, the machinery of justice can also move with astonishing abruptness. Everything was over in a matter of minutes.

The lawyers, Love's family, and his supporters barely had time to settle in their seats before the judge read out the court's decision to block the extradition. Love was free. The courtroom erupted in cheers and applause. Someone shouted, "No love for US gov!" and the judge angrily told everyone to settle down: "This is a court of law not a theater!" Outside, the assembled crowd of supporters chanted and cheered, while film crews and photographers elbowed one another to get a clear shot of Love; his girlfriend, Sylvia Mann; and his family. Mann, who had become increasingly prominent in the final days of hearings after she penned an eloquent letter of support in the *Independent*, appeared dutifully by his side in the reaction interviews and news briefs (Mann 2017). Later, after the cordon of television cameras parted, and Love's group of supporters reassembled, the crowd walked in an impromptu parade along Fleet Street to Temple Chambers (where Love's legal team was based) like some postmodern inversion of a medieval march to the gallows. Love's dub-driven Maclaren stroller was out in front, setting the pace.

When Lauri Love began his ordeal in October 2013, the Obama administration had just begun its second term. Edward Snowden's revelations setting out the scale of NSA bulk surveillance were only five months old. Earlier that year, four LulzSec members (among them regular courtroom attendees and Love's friends Jake Davis and Mustafa al-Bassam) had been sentenced in London. Other than al-Bassam, who was sixteen at the time of the crimes and thus received a suspended sentence, the others were handed custodial sentences ranging from two to two and a half years. In November, US authorities would sentence another Anonymous- and LulzSec-affiliated hacktivist, Jeremy Hammond, to ten years in prison and three years of supervised release. As we discuss in chapter 3, Love's arrest came in the context of a remarkably fertile period (2010–13) of hacktivist transparency actions and the inevitable law enforcement blowback that they engendered. Throughout Obama's second term, authorities aggressively targeted leakers, whistleblowers, and transparency activists, but they also focused on the primary outlets for leaks and data dumps, such as newspapers and publication platforms like WikiLeaks.

It is no small measure of the transformative pace of networked technology that in 2020, some seven years later, security breaches and data leaks dominate the news—even if politicized hacktivism focused around the exfiltration of data and its disclosure has morphed into the sort of source code dumps and cyber weapon releases attributed to Phineas Fisher and the Shadow Brokers (discussed in the two final chapters of this book). The Trump administration has continued former President Obama's aggressive prosecution policy. For example, former NSA contractor Reality Winner was sentenced to five years and three months for leaking a top-secret document alleging Russian interference in the 2016 election to online news site the *Intercept* (Maass 2018). Reports have also surfaced that President Donald

Trump made his senior staff sign lifetime nondisclosure agreements in the early days of his administration as an added deterrent to leaking (Marcus 2018; Bennett 2019).

Despite this, the insider leaks continued: in the first six months of the Trump administration, the Justice Department received as many criminal referrals as it had over the previous three years combined (Woodruff 2017). At the time, then Attorney General Jeff Sessions testified that the Department of Justice had twenty-seven open investigations involving the unlawful release of classified information to reporters. A 2017 report by the Senate Homeland Security and Governmental Affairs Committee examined the scale of media leaks during the Trump administration's first 126 days in office and found 125 news stories based on leaks (literally an average of one leak per day), containing information potentially damaging to national security. A more targeted search of the *Associated Press* and the five major newspapers yielded 62 stories—an estimated seven times as many stories as under former presidents Obama or Bush (US Senate Committee on Homeland Security and Governmental Affairs 2017, 8).

Besides the above leaks, which have become quasi-routine components of journalistic sourcing for news stories, recent headlines are dominated by incidents of state hacking and cyber crime. Indeed, although Love escaped extradition, the use of extradition and mutual assistance frameworks in cyber-crime cases remains a powerful offline resource for projecting authority. US investigations are now coordinated with global partners, multijurisdictional, and routinely involve extradition. These routine practices can be understood as an escalation and refinement of the sort of state boundary work practices described in chapter 2. For example, in 2018, Russian spam entrepreneur Peter Yuryevich Levashov (responsible for the global spam botnets Waledac and Kelihos) was extradited from Spain to the United States to face federal hacking and spamming charges (US DOJ 2018a). Yevgeniy Nikulin, a Russian hacker indicted for the 2012 LinkedIn, Dropbox, and Formspring hacks, was extradited from the Czech Republic to the United States. And the Department of Justice announced that it had arrested thirteen individuals in a coordinated operation involving European, Asian, American, and Australian authorities, aimed at disrupting the Infraud Organization, a global internet-based criminal organization that specialized in large-scale acquisition and sale of identities (including personally identifiable information as well as banking and financial information), debit and credit cards, as well as computer malware (US DOJ 2018b). Five were arrested in the United States, but the remaining eight are all awaiting extradition (Whittaker 2018).

In 2017, Latvian hacker Peteris Sahurovs, or Sagade, was extradited from Poland to the United States to face charges connected with a *scareware* scheme, and Fabio Gasperini was extradited from Italy to the United States to face charges connected with a global botnet he created to perpetrate "click fraud" (US DOJ 2017a, 2017b). Finally, Eric Donys Simeu was extradited from France and charged for carrying out several phishing campaigns against Global Distribution System (a company that does the majority of airline bookings for travel agencies and travel-related sites) customers (US DOJ 2016a).

The above list is obviously not exhaustive, but it illustrates well a core adaptive response the state brings to this new digital era. Yet one is struck when reading headlines or news articles announcing the capture or extradition of wanted cyber criminals by the extraordinary amount of time law enforcement investigations take. Extraditions, as we have seen, can also take an inordinate amount of time and trials—which in the United States might involve criminal charges in multiple states and are complicated, detail-driven affairs that may stretch years. This is all to say that even as state investigators become more proficient in marshaling offline and online resources to prosecute cyber crime, they remain well behind the pace of events. The eighteenth-century penal theorist Cesare Beccaria (2010) once argued that deterrence (of the accused and of society more generally) was a factor of the certainty of apprehension and the speed with which punishment was meted out. Authorities may well be able to leverage metadata and other forms of "selfie-incrimination" (Fish and Follis 2016) to track down online criminals—networked technology has, after all, created an incredibly inexpensive and efficient surveillance apparatus—but their timely capacity to respond to the pace of criminal events remains a challenge. In the next chapter, we explore the assemblage of government strategies, corporate practices, and private-sector actors (e.g., ethical hackers and security professionals and researchers) that seek to shift security capabilities in a more proactive and reactive direction.

5   Hacking for Profit

I feel like I'm on the Titanic. . . . [P]eople are rearranging the deck chairs and the chairs are on fire. The iceberg is on fire. Everything is on fire.
—Lauri Love

A Looming Security Apocalypse

During his extradition hearings, accused hacker Lauri Love was asked on the stand whether his current line of work (as a security specialist for the computer security start-up Hacker House) could be described as "ethical hacking":

> No one who's a hacker likes that term. I now work as one of the good guys. I help people fix security problems, important people like banks, people looking after military installations, important university buildings. . . . I want things to be more secure. We're facing quite a big threat from computer insecurity. . . . Our eagerness to have shiny things has outpaced our risk aversion.[1]

In his public statements, testimony, and interviews with us, the theme of a looming cyber crisis figured prominently. This theme references a deep critique of the logic of what Jodi Dean calls communicative capitalism (J. Dean 2009). According to Dean, the term, at its core, depicts the ongoing expansion and intensification of global telecommunications as a materialization of core democratic values and ideals (e.g., access, inclusion, participation, etc.), all the while undercutting those ideals by securing neoliberalism's ideological infrastructure and its ongoing concentration of global inequalities.

A seemingly apolitical corollary of this program—which recent Russian activity has barely tempered—is the notion that more connections and more interactions are an unassailable good. What is problematic about this unfolding project is that it generates a digital economy where product innovations and transformations in connectivity between individuals and things routinely occur without reference to questions of security. As Love put it later on the same day of testimony:

> One of my fears as someone who's informed and paying attention is that we're heading for chaos because everything being more deeply integrated and closely connected and all it takes is for someone to take a shoe controller and to think about it long enough with enough determination and this greatly empowers people who we don't want to empower. Sometimes we get 15-year-old kids getting in arguments over video games which results in ruining Christmas by issuing DDoS attacks on Playstation.[2]

A case in point of the sort of potential crisis he had in mind unfolded on a Friday afternoon in October 2016, when the internet in the eastern United States slowed to a crawl, and among other disruptions, services like Netflix, Twitter, and Facebook went completely offline throughout Europe. The cause was a massive botnet constructed from Wi-Fi-connected but low-security IOT (Internet of Things) devices staging a DDoS (distributed denial of service) attack against internet switchboard company DYN. As court documents indicate, the botnet was originally constructed by three college students seeking to gain an advantage in the lucrative server-hosting business for online computer game Minecraft.[3]

The group created a fearsome botnet by designing new powerful malware (known as Mirai), which infected sixty-five thousand devices in the first twenty hours and doubled in size every seventy-six minutes, to reach an operating size of two hundred thousand to three hundred thousand infections (Antonakakis et al. 2017). The Mirai malware scanned for IOT devices that still had the manufacturer's security settings (i.e., many users failed to change the default username and password) and hijacked those devices it found vulnerable. It also enjoyed unique economies of scale. Up until Mirai, the largest botnets recorded struggled to break one hundred thousand infections, and Mirai's size meant that it could also generate an overwhelming amount of firepower to deploy across a targeted network's full array of IP addresses at the same time—not just a single website or server. These two factors effectively neutralized the most common methods for mitigating DDoS attacks.[4]

According to the FBI, the botnet creators used Mirai to launch DDoS attacks against business competitors (e.g., other Minecraft server-hosting services) and people they had grudges with, as well as renting their attack services to third parties and running an extortion racket, where hosting companies would pay the defendants protection money in exchange for not being targeted by DDoS attacks.[5] Finally, as investigators closed in on the group, it released the source code for Mirai on Hackforums, at the end of September 2016. Apart from spawning several copycat versions, releasing the source code also dramatically increased the number of infections: within weeks of its release, the number of infections doubled, reaching a peak of six hundred thousand. According to investigators, the creators of the Mirai botnet—which is Japanese for "future"—did not initially realize how powerful it was, yet its success at knocking out key nodes of the internet's infrastructure (a modified version of Mirai bounced 1 million German Telecom customers offline in November 2016) quickly escalated the existential threat posed by future botnets (Graff 2017).

The unintended scale of what Mirai's creators unleashed provides a useful illustration of Paul Virilio's (2007) contention that the "accident" is an increasingly central facet of our technological way of life. Within systems of technology broadly defined, accidents are the irreducible underside of progress, where technical and scientific advancements drive the expansion and augmentation of human capacities. In this sense, accidents are not exceptional or unexpected occurrences but rather foreseeable and constituent components of technological objects and progress ("every technical object contains its own negativity"; Crosthwaite 2013, 18). Yet Virilio also argues that the character and scale of accidents have changed dramatically since the advent of the nuclear bomb. During the industrial age and the world wars, accidents were localized events, contained by particular times and places (e.g., the derailment of a train or the crash of an airliner), but the advent of the nuclear bomb brought with it the possibility of a wholly different experience of the accident. The detonation of a nuclear bomb—much like the meltdown at Chernobyl—not only obliterates its ground zero but also offers the specter of a deadly fog that could traverse borders and boundaries leaving radioactive contagion in its wake.

The above shift parallels a transition from a global historical period shaped by the nuclear bomb to one that is shaped by what Virilio—

channeling Albert Einstein—calls the information bomb. It is unclear when the information bomb detonated or will detonate—it is likened to an unfolding process or a process of becoming reality—but we clearly entered the age of the information bomb with the emergence of the internet (Virilio 1998; Virilio and Kittler 1999). As Virilio sees it, the ultimate (or integral) accident is made up of the accumulation of fragmentary accidents that prefigure and pave the way for a new global environment. Hugh Davies has noted in this context that this accumulation increasingly appears as an "unfolding wreckage" birthed by the speed of progress and the rapidity of innovation: "Crashes of cars, planes, stock markets and computers, disasters and catastrophes of all types have become so commonplace and naturalized that it is no longer possible to tell genuine accidents, simulated crash tests and acts of war apart" (2011, 43). This chapter explores what it means to be an ethical hacker in the context of this unfolding wreckage. We map three models of ethical hacking in crisis times. In the next section, we briefly outline the WannaCry bug outbreak to showcase one antihegemonic model of ethical hacking represented by the actions of two "cyber volunteers": Lauri Love and Marcus Hutchins. We contrast this with a discussion of the professional side of ethical hacking by examining a hands-on-hacking training course we attended shortly after the WannaCry outbreak. Finally, we describe state-driven boundary work efforts to grow new cyber recruits and rehabilitate cyber outlaws to work in its service. Among other examples, we describe how this dynamic unfolds at DEF CON, the biggest hacker conference in the world. In this manner, we illustrate the entanglement between state structures and co-opted markets for talent and code.

Volunteer Firefighting

The hacktivist/cyber criminal outfit Shadow Brokers appeared on August 13, 2016, famously claiming to have stolen the NSA's stockpile of cyber weapons and inviting interested parties to bid on the arsenal at auction. Although the auction eventually fell through, either because of insufficient interest or because it was a hoax, the group began releasing 1 GB of the weapons and exploits for free between November and January. On April 14, 2017, they released a 300 MB dump of premier hacking tools, including five zero-day vulnerabilities, affecting most versions of Microsoft Windows operating system and Fuzzbunch—the Equation Group's version of Metasploit—a software suite of different complementary hacking tools (Goodin 2017a, 2017b). One of the exploits loaded into Fuzzbunch was EternalBlue, a remote code-execution vulnerability that targeted Microsoft's SMB protocol—allowing attackers to gain administrator access to Windows machines.

It is now well known that the bulk of the zero days and exploits released on April 14 had already been patched by Microsoft with little fanfare and visibility in a series of security releases (MS17-010, CVE-2017-0146, and CVE-2017-0147) exactly one month before (March 14, 2017; Franceschi-Bicchierai 2017). Although Microsoft did not disclose how the vulnerability came to its attention, it is now confirmed that the NSA alerted Microsoft of the exploits, given that the security patches covered bugs that had been teased by the Shadow Brokers in January (Nakashima and Timberg 2017). This meant that users running more up-to-date versions of Windows (i.e., Windows 8 and above) were not vulnerable to the exploits, and that those running versions of Windows 7 and signed up for automatic updates were covered by Microsoft's security update. Yet, apart from disclosing the vulnerabilities to Microsoft, neither the NSA nor any other US government agency notified the world about the seriousness of the situation.

Microsoft effectively normalized the situation by issuing a critical security patch without escalating the severity of the situation or indicating the elevated degree of risk for users more broadly than its usual internal protocol for critical security updates. Indeed, it is no accident that on the day the Shadow Brokers dump went public, several tech and news publications worldwide (e.g., Franceschi-Bicchierai 2017; Goodin 2017b) erroneously reported that the five zero days contained in the dump worked on fully up-to-date Microsoft systems. Apparently the security researchers who analyzed the release for the news outlets had not penetration tested the up-to-date Windows systems because they had no indication that Microsoft had actually patched the bugs (Thomson 2017b; Goodin 2017a).

From the standpoint of established corporate security practice, it is perhaps difficult to criticize Microsoft's actions. Microsoft did exactly what it was supposed to do: once it was notified of the zero-day exploits, it immediately set to work creating a patch and then released it as a critical security update one month prior to the Shadow Brokers' release. It took another four weeks for cyber criminals to configure EternalBlue to deliver the WannaCry payload, at which point, the update had been available for more than two months and most of the computers that could have been patched should have been. Indeed, in a blog post on Microsoft's official blog two days after the WannaCry ransomware attacks began making headlines, Brad Smith (Microsoft's president and chief legal officer) set out the details and timeline of the company's response to the bug while strongly criticizing the NSA for stockpiling vulnerabilities in the first place: "An equivalent scenario with conventional weapons would be the US military having some of its Tomahàwk missiles stolen. . . . [T]his most recent attack represents a completely unintended but disconcerting link between the two most serious forms of cybersecurity threats in the world today—nation-state action and organized criminal action" (B. Smith 2017).

Smith argued that the same rules that govern a state's use of conventional weapons should govern cyber weapons, and that a new international regulatory framework (a Digital Geneva Convention) should regulate such issues and impose requirements on states to report vulnerabilities rather than stockpiling or using them. Although the blog post provided a much-needed critique of the ubiquity of state hacking and its foreseeable repercussions on structures of risk, security, and anxiety, it also represented an elegant elision of Microsoft's responsibility for the attack and the broader ways in which Microsoft's actions informed the structural and systemic ecologies of risk and security that fed off the attack. It is to this question we now turn.

Smith's blog post contained a hard and a soft target. The NSA received the bulk of criticism, but the consumer and Microsoft user also came under significant attack. The fact that several computers remained vulnerable despite the availability of a security patch up to two months before the attack, confirmed, according to Smith, the extent to which cybersecurity was now "a shared responsibility between tech companies and customers." He further argued that customers could only protect themselves from the increasing sophistication of cyber-criminal attacks by making sure their "computers were current and patched" (B. Smith 2017). In making his argument, Smith drew on the trope of responsibilization, a central pillar in the way that the cybersecurity industry and digital capitalism frames cyber crime.

Responsibilization strategies have played an important role in the management of crime-control anxieties within Western democracies since the latter part of the twentieth century. Introduced as a way to address the seeming intractability of persistently high and rising crime rates, it involved shifting from an exclusively vertical, direct, and formal (i.e., police, courts, prisons) way of dealing with the crime problem to a more horizontal, networked, and indirect model. Instead of the state monopolizing sole responsibility for the crime problem and social control, nonstate actors like businesses, private contractors, neighborhood groups, and individual citizens were shaped into a loosely aggregated crime prevention network steered by the state. A key point is the fact that such strategies by definition challenge the assumption that crime control is a specialist task that should be concentrated within the specialist institutions of the state (Garland 2001, 126). Responsibilization strategies also ingrain shared responsibility within the system of crime control and thus, when things inevitably go wrong, shared blame. Criminologist David Garland summarizes these changes:

> The state's new strategy is not to command and control but rather to persuade and align, to organize, to ensure that other actors play their part. Property owners, residents, retailers, manufacturers . . . employers, parents, individual citizens . . . must be persuaded to exert their informal powers of social control, and if necessary, to modify their usual practices, in order to help reduce criminal opportunities and enhance crime control. (2001, 125)

The most visible, emblematic, and readily identifiable components of such efforts are publicity campaigns, which target the public as a whole through television ads, neighborhood watch leaflets, and billboards aimed at raising public consciousness and awareness of crime rates and potential victimization, as well as connecting the public with crime-control agencies. In other words, a central facet of state responsibilization strategies is that they have a public campaignlike character designed to leverage visibility and publicity into hardening the vulnerability of targets. Finally, responsibilization strategies in the world of conventional criminality are not just about weaving individual actors (i.e., citizens, community leaders, businesspeople) into the crime prevention net, but they are also part of a wider neoliberal shift involving the increasing prominence of nonstate and private organizations in the management of risk, security, and justice. Similarly, in the field of cybersecurity, responsibilization strategies combine with neoliberal rationalities and boundary work practices to shape competitive markets for outsourcing core state services through cyber proxies or intermediaries (Maurer 2018).

When the Shadow Brokers dumped their cache of Equation Group exploits and weapons on April 14, 2017, a clock began counting down. Despite Microsoft's software patches, many security researchers and analysts knew it was only a matter of time before those tools were repurposed for criminal or other clandestine purposes. That weekend, Lauri Love and a group of technology researchers (including ex-LulzSec members Jake Davis, Mustafa al-Bassam, and Darren Martyn) opened a #shadowbrokers channel on IRC, invited every security researcher they knew, and began pouring over the released code and exploits to document functionalities and capabilities. The goal was to distribute and crowdsource the task of understanding the exploits to mitigate the risk involved, understand the potential scope of the threat, and convince at-risk individuals and organizations to patch their systems before the inevitable broader deployment of those weapons against an unsuspecting public.

One month later, on May 12, 2017, the world woke up to reports of the first WannaCry infections in India, Hong Kong, and the Philippines (Brenner 2017). It did not take long for reports to start trickling in from Europe in the early morning: Spain's Telefonica (a multinational telecommunication company) was among the first large firms to report infection, and it was quickly followed by England's National Health Service (NHS) later that morning. By early afternoon, the worm had spread all over Europe and the rest of the globe, affecting French car manufacturer Renault, the German rail network (Deutsche Bahn), Russia's Interior Ministry, Megafon (the second-largest mobile provider and third-largest telecom provider in Russia), and Sberbank, among others (C. Graham 2017).

The crisis was contained late on Friday afternoon when Marcus Hutchins, a UK-based malware researcher examining the worm's code, noticed that one of the first things the program did when it infected computers was to ping (i.e., try to connect to) an unregistered web domain. He promptly registered the domain and inadvertently triggered a kill switch in the program. When the program pinged the unregistered domain, it was unsuccessful in making a connection and proceeded to encrypt the host computer's files with ransomware. Once the domain was registered by Hutchins, the connection was successful, and this told the worm to exit the system, preventing further infections.

Hutchins's actions have been well documented, as has the fact that he was arrested in Las Vegas by the FBI while attempting to board a flight back to the UK after attending the security conference DEF CON. He was charged with creating, distributing, and selling the Kronos banking trojan between July 2014 and June 2015 and has since pleaded guilty to two counts of entering a conspiracy to create and distribute the malware under the Computer Fraud and Abuse Act and the Wiretap Act.[6] GCHQ (the UK's equivalent of the NSA), with whom Hutchins had collaborated in a volunteer capacity during the WannaCry outbreak, knew that American authorities planned to arrest Hutchins and did not warn him. An agency source told the Sunday *Times*, "Our US partners aren't impressed that some people who they believe to have cases against [them] for computer-related offences have managed to avoid extradition. Hutchins's arrest freed the British government and intelligence agencies from yet another headache of an extradition battle" (quoted in Kerbaj and Wheeler 2017). Although Hutchins had effectively stopped the further spread of the WannaCry strain of the worm, hundreds of thousands of computers remained encrypted, and many more likely remained unpatched. This was further exacerbated by the fact that there was nothing preventing the authors of the worm from removing the kill switch and trying again, or for others to develop a new strain. Finally, given the scale and speed of the outbreak, most organizations and users remained in triage mode throughout Friday and into the following week. As with the original release of the exploits on April 14, a Friday release also meant that many security researchers would not be at work over the weekend.

Throughout this period, Love and his colleagues continued working within the IRC research group they had set up (at one point the number of those involved reached 250 researchers), analyzing the code and aggregating their observations to produce a definitive fact sheet of the bug's technical specifications (Goodwin 2017). This grassroots collaboration was nonhierarchical and had a low barrier to entry; researchers contributed what they discovered about the worm in the chat room; others would tweet these updates; and still others would aggregate that information into the fact sheet and more than a dozen released advisories. The fact sheet was accessed heavily over that weekend, and Love appeared on various news programs to comment on the attacks and to urge users to patch their systems.

The core group involved in this effort are now a part of LizardHQ—a group of researchers that puts out security advisories and alerts about systems vulnerabilities. In a talk at the annual Byline Festival in 2017, Love argued that this crowdsourced model is the only viable way to build cumulative, collaborative results and insights quickly and in the time window when they might generate the greatest harm minimization (see Goodwin 2017 for a link to the talk). He argues that this is part of the responsibility individuals literate in computer technology have: they should help find solutions to such critical events and help explain the situation to journalists and the public. Or, as he put it in an interview just a day after his extradition appeal was sustained, "People are constantly putting out small fires on the internet, and sometimes there's a big conflagration. At the moment there's no civic response to that, having volunteer firefighters. That's something I can contribute to. . . . If I can help find those hands to put out those 'fires' I can make a contribution" (quoted in Gregory and Ladefoged 2018).

Love's "volunteer firefighting" should be understood in the context of the tremendous skills gap that has emerged between the pace of technological change and the wider availability of specialists and experts with the technical capacity to understand those changes and respond to the inevitable emergencies or accidents that change makes possible. In 2015, a global survey of information security professionals predicted that by 2020, there would be a worldwide shortage of 1.5 million cyber professionals (Vogel 2016). More recently ISACA, a nonprofit advocacy group for information security, has raised this projected shortfall to two million by 2019 (ISACA 2016). Between 2010 and 2014, cybersecurity posts grew by 91 percent, eclipsing the rate of IT posts more generally (Burning Glass 2015, 3). Indeed, a 2016 survey noted that security professional demand grew 3.5 times faster than other IT jobs and 12 times faster than the rest of the labor market (Vogel 2016). According to *Forbes*, the size of the cybersecurity market is expected to more than double, going from $75 billion in 2015 to a projected $170 billion in 2020 (Morgan 2016).

It is a striking illustration of just how significant the security gap is that the above grassroots WannaCry mitigation team was initiated by former members of the notorious LulzSec hacktivist group (who are, after all, convicted criminals) and Lauri Love—who at the time of the outbreak was awaiting a high court appeal hearing to contest his likely extradition to the United States for hacking crimes. In this situation, capitalism, the state, and criminality are knotted together.

"Hacking, Like in the Movies"

The smell of cannabis and percolating coffee hangs in the air. A tight entranceway flows into a long open space with bikes on wall racks, personal lockers, two bathrooms, and a small kitchenette. The ground floor also features a large multipurpose room, with expansive storefront-style windows, where meetups and courses are held. The second floor is a large coworking space: a half-dozen tenants are scattered around the room, pensively absorbed by their screens. We climb to the top floor landing via the glass-encased, yellow-walled staircase and are greeted, welcome packet in hand, by Jennifer Arcuri. A table in the back of the airy attic room is stocked with coffee, croissants, and fruit. Four desk rows on either side of the room are surrounded by extension cords and surge-protectors. About a dozen would-be "ethical hackers" are already here, chatting, getting refreshments, or setting up their laptops.

We are here for day one of Hacker House's Hands-on Hacking workshop in Manchester city center. It is 9:30 a.m. and just five days after the breakout and containment of the WannaCry bug. The news has been reporting North Korea's involvement in the ransomware attacks and that Adylkuzz, a piece of malware that installs a mining program for the cryptocurrency Monero, has been quietly infecting computers by exploiting the same vulnerabilities (Mozur and Perlez 2017; McMillan 2017). We originally became interested in Hacker House because the cybersecurity start-up employed Lauri Love throughout his extradition proceedings. Its cofounder Jennifer Arcuri served as a character witness during the hearings and had described the firm's mission as quasi-rehabilitative: "My vision is to bring together law enforcement with cyber criminals—harness hackers' raw talent and bring them inside the entrepreneur ecosystem. . . . Law enforcement and hacking should not be two separate entities, instead my goal is to harmonize the two" (Young 2015).

For a time, the company was quite literally a house full of hackers. Arcuri purchased a property outside Manchester where young male hackers slept and were fed; emotionally, professionally, and physically cared for; and ultimately trained in for-profit cybersecurity work. In interviews, she spoke maternally about her wards and worried about their mental and physical health as much as their diet and future employability. Its handful of employees would live or crash there, and it was the only place Love was allowed to sleep other than his parents' house per his bail conditions. The house also served as a consulting space for corporate clients, a meeting point for hack-a-thons, and a site for tinkering with technologies of every stripe. In Arcuri's telling, Hacker House could help reorient the sometimes disruptive online behavior of her employees into a prosocial package of very much in demand cybersecurity professionals with extensive penetration-testing skills.

Since then, Hacker House has shed the "house" and nimbly reoriented itself into a flexible cybersecurity consultancy firm and an ethical hacking training academy. Its unique approach promises to be hands on: instead of spending hours learning the theory of hacking, we will learn by doing. Over the next three days we will be scanning systems, profiling vulnerabilities, and deploying exploits using cutting-edge attack platforms in sandboxed but realistic systems and scenarios. Indeed, things were so realistic that on day two we found ourselves playing with the EternalBlue exploit that just the week before had paralyzed the British NHS.

Matthew Hickey, our instructor and a cofounder of Hacker House, is standing in front of the room talking to Dragos, one of Hacker House's resident hackers, who will help run the course. Apart from sporting a sus-piciously clean black Hacker House hoodie, Hickey, who goes by the Twit-ter handle @HackerFantastic, looks nothing like the popular stereotype. He is clean shaven, with close-cropped blond hair and large expressive eyes. Indeed, one wonders whether he actually likes wearing a hoodie at all or whether it is just part of the professional dress code. The other participants are seemingly as diverse as their motivations. Two local police officers talk quietly on one side of the room; they work in the computer forensics unit and are exploring penetration-testing and systems-probing skills as a respite from the doldrums of securing digital evidence. There is also a quiet young teenage whizz who is already familiar with many of the platforms and open source tools that we will be learning to use. She hopes to become a pro-fessional security researcher. There's also an ex-air force officer who spent time working with the US Army in Nevada and who seeks to develop his "interest" in hacking. Finally, some web designers and coders contemplat-ing lateral moves into web security round out our class group.

After downloading VirtualBox (an application that allows you to run vir-tual machines on your laptop from which to practice launching attacks in a sandboxed environment) and Kali Linux (a free penetration-testing platform that bundles more than six hundred tools in a point-and-click-style interface), HackerFantastic takes us through a presentation on the complex of legal issues, ethics, and professional norms that apply to the field of offensive security. His discussion of the relevant UK legislation (e.g., the Computer Misuse Act, the Data Protection Act, the Human Rights Act, the Wireless and Telegraphy Act) is perfunctory, but his depiction of the potential criminal consequences attached to what we are about to learn is serious.

From the computer system's point of view, a security researcher testing a system and a hacker or criminal trying to access that system for illegitimate or illegal reasons look exactly the same. The only thing separating them is intent, which can be gleaned from whether the researcher has secured authorization prior to testing the system. Hickey recommends that this authorization should include an explicit written declaration from the client that they will not seek charges under the Computer Misuse Act. This is because the legal status of the attack techniques we are about to learn is ambiguous: even an active scan of a system can be considered offensive and potentially illegal (Herr and Rosenzweig 2016). The software tools themselves are outlawed in some countries, and the tactics we will deploy can be used to commit criminal acts and generate significant damage.

Hickey's introduction underscores the high-wire act ethical hackers must perform and the fact that in offensive security, the line between criminal and legitimate researcher can be easily blurred. But it also illustrates the necessary practical and normative orientations that ethical hackers must assume to signal the competence and professionalism that comes with contracting for government and corporate boundary work. What we learn over the course of the next three days provides a window into the field of ethical hacking, a space of material practice anchored by unique markers of prestige, clearly defined hierarchies of informational capital, and a well-defined security habitus. Unlike the radical transparency practices described in chapter 3, ethical hacking practice is apolitical, ascetic in orientation, and firmly oriented toward an offensive modality of defense.

As David Wall (2007, 43–44) argues, hacking is undergoing a dual process of deskilling and reskilling that characterized other technical practices (most notably factory work) as technological innovations were introduced: established skills and technologies undergo automation through rationalization processes, which make carrying out routine tasks more efficient and economical (deskilling), while a reduced cohort of workers take control of new, more complete and automated production processes to tackle more complex problems (reskilling). For Wall this shift is evident in the transition from early forms of hacking, which required a high level of proficiency in programming and coding, to the advent of "scripts"—small programs that automate tasks that were once individually executed by a human operator—and finally, to the automatization of the process and development of as-a-service business models for the distribution of malware and exploits.

The contrast between ongoing processes of digital deskilling and reskilling produce tension in the hacking community. On the one hand, they are responsible for the advent of the so-called script kiddie (Honeynet Project 2000), a disparaging term for inexperienced individuals with low technical skill who use hacking programs in blunt or unsophisticated ways to attack vulnerable computer systems for bragging rights, curiosity, or fun (Barber 2001). Script kiddies typically have a poor understanding of the underlying mechanics involved as well as the potential consequences of their incursions. In this sense, the above process has not only increased the prevalence of cyberattacks but also broadened the kinds of actors (i.e., script kiddies, cyber criminals, etc.) perpetrating them, as well as generating the sort of protracted criminalization and stigmatization effort described in chapter 2, which has affected hackers of all stripes. As Hickey told us:

> Hacking is seeing a fundamental shift in that the technical barrier to entry is much lower than before. Once you have one clever person solve a problem [and] write an exploit, everyone else can just download and use her tool. This lower barrier to entry means that more attacks are being performed online, and often the perpetrators are not Russian-backed state spies—it's a teenager who downloaded some tools while playing Xbox, knocking millions [of pounds] off the valuation of a prominent UK business in the process. [But] we need to accept that it's the computer which is broken not the teenager; we have to move away from seeing hacking as a negative force and instead embrace it for its problem-solving abilities.[7]

Evidence of this transformation, as well as the status and knowledge hierarchies it sustains in hacker communities, is visible in the security researcher's toolkit. Our main toolbox was Kali Linux, a freely available yet very advanced penetration-testing and security-auditing platform. Kali Linux bundles several freeware, open source, and subscription attack tools into an intuitive and easy to use graphical user interface (GUI). It contains tools for reconnaissance, or *scanning* (e.g., Nmap, SPARTA); vulnerability analysis (e.g., Powerfuzzer, Sqlninja); exploitation (e.g., Armitage, Backdoor Factory, Metasploit); wireless attacks (e.g., Aircrack-ng, Pyrit); password attacks (e.g., john the ripper, Burp Suite); as well as forensics, stress testing, sniffing, and spoofing.

Many of the above tools have multiple uses and straddle more than one functional category. The one such framework we trained on extensively was Metasploit—a platform that allows for the configuration of exploits (it comes loaded with exploits that target bugs in Windows, Unix/Linux, and Mac OS), information gathering on a target's vulnerabilities, choosing and executing payloads (for example, loading a shell or backdoor on a remote server), and masking the encoded payload so it is not detected.[8] Like Kali Linux, the framework is a prominent example of the wider proliferation of open source and "free" vulnerability exploitation tools, which automate, significantly simplify, and powerfully augment the penetration-tester (and hence hacking and cyber-criminal) toolkit.

When Metasploit was first released in 2003 by the prominent security researcher HD Moore, it came with only eleven exploits.[9] The following year, when Moore and colleague spoonm detailed version 2.0 at security conference DEF CON 12, in a talk entitled "Metasploit: Hacking Like in the Movies," the platform had grown to nineteen exploits and twenty-seven payloads; the current free version boasts more than fifteen hundred exploits. Metasploit streamlined the assembly of exploits and their customization while simultaneously lowering the degree of skill necessary to launch attacks (Engebretson 2011; Ramirez-Silva and Dacier 2007). Once a new vulnerability is discovered, a researcher can quickly develop a new attack script using the platform's built-in components (Wang et al. 2013). Newly discovered exploits and vulnerabilities in the wild are incorporated within the framework's modules at a breakneck pace. And often exploits are released soon after vulnerabilities are disclosed and sometimes before a patch for the software bug is released (e.g., in 2005 a zero-day exploit for the Windows operating system was available on Metasploit before Microsoft released a patch; Krebs 2012; Kerner 2005). One early multiyear study of Metasploit-related attacks found that as soon as a new plugin or release is distributed in hacking forums and communities, there is a pronounced two-day spike in the use of these exploits against as many targets as possible worldwide (Ramirez-Silva and Dacier 2007, 210). And even when a patch is released, as in the case of the WannaCry outbreak, the temporal gap between its publication and the patching of vulnerable systems can be significant. Just days after the release of the WannaCry bug, the exploit EternalBlue, which the bug is based on, was available on Metasploit (Kerner 2017).

The platform is a "dual-use security tool" (Hulme 2012) that is widely adopted across legitimate and illegitimate research communities. In 2006, Moore estimated that ninety thousand unique IP addresses had downloaded the latest version (Greenemeir 2006); in 2012, that number had swelled to one million (Hulme 2012). Even law enforcement has been known to use it: the FBI famously used the Metasploit Decloaking Engine to identify Tor users of child pornography sites on the dark web in Operation Torpedo (Poulsen 2014). It should be underscored, however, that although platforms like Metasploit and Kali Linux are powerful frameworks that lower the degree of skill required to launch attacks, using them with sophistication, consistent success, and while avoiding criminal prosecution requires discipline, mastery of craft, and a particular epistemological approach. As our instructor explained when we asked why he insisted on teaching us to use the text-based command-line interface (the DOS-looking screen) rather than the more intuitive GUI (e.g., point-and-click mouse functions, graphic icons, etc.),

> Whilst graphical components are an excellent time saver they often remove any technical barrier to use them entirely. Hacking is the art of subtly crafting or engineering a new means to solve a problem, usually gaining access to a computer or resource without authority. Hacking will often require some automation and dynamic solutions that when working from the command line are more accessible. You can access detailed schematics, instructions, compilers and linkers for practically any computer on earth and to use it you will most certainly need to get as close to the machine as possible.

The scope and functionality of security auditing toolkits trace the arc that begins with researching a system from the outside and progressively shifts to actually attacking and taking control of it. This process begins with a reconnaissance and research stage, when the abundance of publicly available information about a target is searched, compiled, and analyzed. In this context, the tremendous impact of networked technology on the way we work, interact, and relax helps to outline vectors of exposure: social media and professional forums are rich sources of data, as are front-facing company and personal websites, and hacked or leaked data available on the dark web or via torrent dumps also contain valuable pieces of the puzzle. This mastery of open source intelligence (OSINT) is a powerful skill in its own right and is often central to the work of law enforcement and investigators seeking to attribute responsibility for cybercrimes or to uncover the real-world identity of cyber actors (cf. Fish and Follis 2016 on hacker "selfie-incrimination"). Indeed, as former FBI special agent Chris Tarbell (who worked on the Silk Road and LulzSec cases) told us,

> Perfect anonymity is kind of like perfect communism. It sounds ideal but it's really tough. You would have to have a computer that you never touch [with] any of your social media, any of your bank accounts. You'd have to pay for it through an anonymous payment system like Bitcoins or something like that. . . . I have observed people hacking into things, once they get going . . . they get excited about what they have broken into. They make that one mistake. Like a robber taking a glove off in the house to pick up the jewels, he accidentally touches the door and there's his fingerprint. You know, one simple mistake.
>
> I go back historically, and the key to my investigations were always details, details, details. You dig through as much as you can and you will find that glaring mistake somewhere in there. Finding the little small thing. Like finding Ross [Ulbricht, a.k.a. Dread Pirate Roberts, the creator and operator of the dark net drug market Silk Road]: the frosty thing didn't click in anyone's brain, but as soon as I was told . . . I knew that all the stuff online was frosty @frosty, so I knew that was our guy.[10]

Tarbell's depiction of the difficulties criminals and hackers face trying to remain anonymous only underscores the overwhelming amount of data that we (who are not necessarily trying to remain anonymous) daily and willingly disclose about ourselves. But it is also a recognition of the fact that in the digital world, everything seemingly leaks: PowerPoint presentations and Word documents proliferate with metadata, rejected emails (i.e., delivery status notification reports) can betray information about antivirus software or the IP addresses for email services, email addresses are often "tells" for usernames, and images and photos promise GPS coordinates. A host of open source tools are widely available to automate the work of mining these rich datasets. For example, a tool like MetaGooFil can scour the internet for an impressive range of document formats associated with the owner of a file or a username, download them, and extract relevant metadata from them. But even more mundane artifacts of daily use like the Google search engine can return shockingly detailed information on a target using queries and well-known "hacks."

Ultimately the goal of reconnaissance is to draw up a list of IP addresses to target for more active probes; DNS (domain name system) servers are favored research points, because they will provide access to the architecture of the site (the treelike structure of internal IP addresses), and there are numerous well-known vulnerabilities and bugs in the software that runs them. Scanning the system to gauge possible vulnerabilities (e.g., what software type and version a server is running), actively probing (e.g., what documented and existent bugs the system could be vulnerable to), as well as preparing to launch an attack—which involves determining which vulnerability to exploit and how to maintain a foothold in the system once in—are subsequent steps. Finally, once inside the system, the main concern is *getting root* or *privilege escalation*. That is, leveraging one's usually tenuous (a user with limited privilege) foothold into a full-fledged administrator account. On the way out of the system, there is also the technically difficult work of cleaning up any evidence of the breach itself.

The abbreviated set of processes and steps described above fall under the broader umbrella term *methodology*. Throughout our course, we were taught the value of developing a robust methodological framework and adhering to it. The term has a double meaning: it refers to a set of discrete, sequential, and technical operations that a researcher must engage in to successfully perform a necessary task in penetrating a system (e.g., performing a scan, setting a target, setting a host, loading a payload, using a payload, etc.). But it also describes an overarching heuristic process, whose steps progressively narrow the possibilities and options available, filtering the layers of choice and decision making in the direction of the most efficient and effective modality of attack. Methodologies focus the mind and structure the trajectory of security research.

In chapter 2, we drew on Michel de Certeau's (1984) reinterpretation of military strategy to argue that cyberspace is predominantly a "tactical" space, where states, hackers, and security professionals are forced to embrace contingency and seek openings in the shadows of power. In this context, hacker methodologies bring order to the tactical moment; they provide the iterative structure and conceptual mobility essential to capitalize on chance openings, unexpected opportunities, and predictable exposures.

The very fact that most enterprise and smaller computer systems are networked makes them vulnerable, as does the exponential growth in the capacity to access work or other systems from home or on the go. This is not necessarily the fault of the IT team; the large, complex software, web-based applications, and custom platforms that are the building blocks of a system may contain bugs, mistakes, configuration errors, or security loopholes. Moreover, legacy systems (i.e., outdated and nonupgraded computer systems, application software, or even programming languages) retain a large digital footprint even though they are vulnerable to well-known exploits and cannot be easily patched. As we were told more than once, bugs and worms like the 2014 Heartbleed bug continue to "swim and live in the wild." Long after patches have been released and the news cycle has stopped reporting them, the exploits still work.

Besides the extensive list of already known vulnerabilities, new vulnerabilities continue to be disclosed at an exponential rate. When the Mitre Corporation began cataloging, describing, and assigning unique identifiers (i.e., CVE—Common Vulnerabilities and Exposures) to publicly disclosed vulnerabilities in 1999, there were 894 that year. In 2014, a five-digit CVE was introduced so that the CVE ID format would no longer cap the number of vulnerabilities at 10,000 per year (Mitre 2019). In 2017, the number of vulnerabilities disclosed broke 10,000 for the first time, reaching 14,714 (an average of 40 disclosures per day) compared with 6,447 the previous year (CVE Details 2018).

The CVE database forms one of the core epistemological pillars hackers and professionals can draw on in their security practice, but seasoned professionals seem to have an almost taxonomic knowledge of many vulnerabilities based on their use of the penetration-testing tools themselves, which are regularly updated and which target for known vulnerabilities. The disclosure of vulnerabilities, much like the writing and publishing of exploits that take advantage of those vulnerabilities, also form important markers of prestige and sources of informational capital in researcher communities. There are various professional accreditation and certification services, but the core mode of accruing and growing prestige remains proving one's technical skills through "proof of concept"-style research (where one shows theoretically how to exploit a vulnerability to illustrate one's claim of it being genuine) and the reverse engineering of exploits available in the wild (that is, already in use in cyberspace) so that they are stable and can be used as research tools.

Developing Talent and Shedding Outlaw Identities

The burgeoning market in ethical hacking thrives in the context of a global industry-wide skills shortage in the public and private cybersecurity sectors. According to a 2015 survey, 35 percent of sampled organizations could not fill security jobs even though most (82 percent) expected imminent attack (Vogel 2016, 35). Similarly, even though the FBI recognized the importance of breaches to national security as early as 2012 and established cyber task forces in each of its fifty-six field offices to focus on this, it remains under-resourced (OIG 2015). A 2015 audit of the FBI's Next Generation Cyber Initiative by the Office of Inspector General found that even the relatively modest goal of having one computer scientist assigned to each cyber task force remained elusive (five of fifty-six field offices did not have any computer scientists) and that the agency had only managed to fill 62 percent of its open computer science posts (OIG 2015, 11–12). Perhaps more importantly, the FBI also suffers from attrition and retention issues: the private sector offers much higher salaries, less intrusive background investigations, and less stringent drug-testing policies, a point acknowledged by former FBI director James Comey in a 2014 interview with the *Wall Street Journal* about the difficulties in filling two thousand open cybersecurity posts: "A lot of the nation's top computer programmers and hacking gurus are also fond of marijuana. . . . I have to hire a great work force to compete with those cyber criminals and some of those kids want to smoke weed on the way to the interview" (quoted in Levinson 2014).

Retention and recruitment have also been a long-term problem for the UK's GCHQ. As early as 2010, the agency's director told Parliament's Intelligence and Security Committee,

> I need some real internet whizzes in order to do cyber and I am not even sure they are even on the contractor market, so I need to work on that. They will be working for Microsoft or Google or Amazon or whoever. And I can't compete with their salaries; I can offer them a fantastic mission but I can't compete with their salaries. . . . [W]e do have a steady drip, I am afraid. Month-on-month, we are losing whizzes who'll basically say: "I'm sorry, I am going to take three times the salary and the car and whatever else." (ISC 2011, 20)

By 2012, the agency reported that it was expending considerable effort recruiting, training, and employing specialists only to lose them a short time later to private industry at a rate that was three times the corporate average; many of these staff members possessed high-end technology skills and were in critical positions (ISC 2012, 67). In 2013, GCHQ began piloting a "flexible reward packages" program for cybersecurity specialists (ISC 2013, 21), and while the agency had managed to stem some of the skills drain by 2017, it still faces considerable resourcing challenges in the security field: "[This] has worked to a point. It stemmed the flow of people going out in particular areas at particular stages of their career [but] we do lose people for salaries. We couldn't possibly compete with four, five times what they are getting from us" (ISC 2017, 40). It should be noted in assessing this shortage, however, that the cybersecurity field remains focused on a very small segment of the population: perhaps even more so than the rest of the IT sector, cyber security remains overwhelmingly white and male in demographic composition.

The above problematic has led states to embark on a series of adaptive solutions to populate and grow the next generation of state hackers. The most ambitious of these projects is the approach currently piloted by the United Kingdom. It seeks to tackle the dearth in cyber skills by targeting students interested in computers (and hence potentially at risk for engaging in hacktivism or cyber crime), as well as teenagers that have come to the attention of the NCA for their problematic online activity. For the former, the approach entails getting students involved in computer science early and steering their activities in progovernment or promarket directions. These initiatives are diverse and include a joint collaboration between the NCSC and GCHQ in three Gloucestershire high schools, where Cyber Schools Hubs have been set up to develop "the pipeline that is necessary to meet the UK's future cyber security needs" (NSCS 2018b). If the pilot is successful, the government's plan is to roll out the program in schools across the country. Similarly, through its CyberFirst initiative, the NCSC is piloting a series of in-school and extracurricular activities and programs targeting students between eleven and nineteen years old. Across the country, it also hosts free five-day residential courses in the summer for fourteen- to fifteen-year-olds (Cyber Defenders), fifteen- to sixteen-year-olds (CyberFirst Futures), and sixteen- to seventeen-year-olds (CyberFirst Advanced)—as well as providing funding for university scholarships and apprenticeships.

What is striking about this state-driven project is that it is directly managed, developed, and significantly funded by the NCSC, which is an arm of GCHQ, the country's premiere spy agency. In this sense, it is the equivalent of the NSA seeding a series of recruitment pathways, trajectories, and training sites within the public-school system to identify and shape a politically malleable (or even depoliticized) talent pool and prime it for work defending government computers. This ideological cooption is evident in the content of the courses and activities available; the wide and very rich field of computer science is reduced to a singular, myopic focus: preventing and fighting cyberattacks. Students learn how to "protect small networks and devices" and explore "advanced cyber security threats to devices, apps and software and investigate ways of protecting them" (NSCS 2018a).

A corollary of the above program involves interventions with teenagers who have come to the attention of the NCA for their online behavior and activity. Since November 2013, the National Cyber Crime Unit Prevent Team, in collaboration with the NCA, has been engaged in gathering intelligence debriefs (short, semistructured interviews) with individuals who have received a caution, community sentence, or prison term for cyber crime. It has also performed "cease and desist" home calls to teenagers identified as on the "fringes of cyber criminality" to collect information about them and warn them of the possible criminal consequences of their online behavior (e.g., downloading an automated DDoS tool) before they commit an offense that could land them in prison (NCA 2017, 2). In 2015, the agency performed 50 such home visits (Chellel 2015). In its 2017 report *Pathways to Cyber Crime*, the NCA noted that several UK teenagers who would rate low on a risk score for conventional (i.e., non-computer-assisted) crime were increasingly becoming involved in cyber crime. The agency linked this phenomenon to the wide availability of hacking tools, the perceived likelihood of low law enforcement intervention, and the social experience of participating in online hacking forums and gaining reputation among peers. Moreover, the study argued that "targeted interventions" and mentoring at an early stage could steer individual pathways from crime to more positive outcomes (NCA 2017, 1).

In a series of public safety advertisements and webisodes the agency produced to target the parents of twelve- to fifteen-year-olds, it has sought to dramatize this process (NCA 2015a, 2015b). One advert titled "Teenage cybercrime: Help your child make the right #CyberChoices" opens with the camera facing two parents sitting on a couch with their serious, pale-faced son between them. They are sitting in a middle-class living room, and the parents are gushing about how bright and clever he is. The father pats him on the head and brags: "You know those shooter games? The other day he was losing, so he crashed the server. Proper whiz kid." The mother continues, "It's amazing what kids can do these days . . . DDOSing, that's it? I saw it on the telly." And the father interjects, "He's no dosser though, our Robbie, a hundred percent in maths, every single exam for the last two years." The camera cuts and we see Robbie in front of his computer hacking into the school's servers and downloading his coursework at night. Eventually, as the parents continue to rave about how "smart" he is with money (cut to Robbie hacking into someone's bank account), it begins to dawn on them that maybe all this is not exactly legal. The camera shifts to reveal their interlocutors: two dead serious NCA agents who tell them to start again from the beginning. The camera shifts again, and now Robbie and his parents are in a police interview room. The slogan "cybercrime wrecks lives" appears before cutting to a shot of Robbie's empty desk and the line "Help your child make the right choices." Another webisode, entitled "#CyberChoices—Drifting into Cybercrime," features Ryan Ackroyd, a former member of LulzSec who was convicted in 2013 and served ten months of a thirty-month prison sentence, reflecting on his choices and the legitimate opportunities his computer skills could have provided for him had he not engaged in hacktivist activities.

More recently, the agency has piloted a weekend "cyber rehab camp" for youths caught committing a cyber crime (Cyber Security Challenge UK, 2017). The rehab camp flowed directly from the NCA research project that sought to measure the difference in skills between people gainfully employed in the industry and the cohorts of hackers that came to the agency's attention: "What we found was that the only sole difference within the stories was that the industry members, at some point, had an intervention. The skills are so transferable with this criminal type, if you have good cyberskills there are many, many qualifications you can take" (quoted in Ward 2017).

The process of security professionalization is but one facet of a larger political economic reorientation in which talented proto-hackers with technological and economic utility are depoliticized and primed for work in the market or the state. We have already seen how this process unfolds in the context of ethical hacking and the UK state. We now turn to the equally diverse efforts of US authorities, which range from scouring hacker conventions like DEF CON and cybersecurity conferences for talent to opening up the US Army, US Air Force, DOD, Department of Homeland Security, and others to bug bounty programs. As in the UK example, the long-term aim is to recruit and grow an internal cyber army that is disciplined and ideologically reliable while adopting neoliberal logics and strategies (i.e., responsibilization initiatives, bug bounty programs, private contractors, and state proxies) to bridge cyber-skill shortages in the short term. This is a problematic that was succinctly put by former NSA chief Michael V. Hayden in an interview with the *Australian Financial Review* in 2013:

> [W]e Americans and Australians need to recruit from Edward Snowden's generation. The problem is that this is a generation of people whose views on secrecy, privacy, transparency, and government accountability are a bit different from the folks supervising them, and certainly different from my generation. We nonetheless need to recruit from this group because they have the skills that ASIO, ASIS, DSD, NSA and CIA require to fulfil their lawful mandates. So the challenge is how to recruit this talent while also protecting ourselves from the very small fraction of that population that has this romantic attachment to absolute transparency at all costs. (Joye 2013)

Thus one part of this solution has been to keep ideology at a distance through short-term forms of boundary work, by allowing hackers to work for the state through intermediaries, crowdsourced hacking collectives, and volunteers. But the overall larger project involves the mainstreaming, commodification, co-optation, and professionalization of hacking—not as a radical, revolutionary, or antihegemonic activity but one that is increasingly situated within the center of the state's defensive posture, its neoliberal collaborative relationship with global capitalism, and the pedagogical entities that feed personnel to this complex. At certain physical sites and events, such as DEF CON, the tangle of states and hackers can be viscerally felt.

Come Meet the Feds

While this was our first DEF CON, it seemed that after twenty-five years—and judging by the high-profile sponsorships, steep registration fees, and an increasingly open stance toward the state—the conference's more radical days were over. It is true that fugitives and criminals have attended DEF

CON in the past, yet it is difficult to stage a conference in Caesars Palace, Las Vegas, and maintain any semblance of counterculture or resistance. This is not to say that the sort of oceanic togetherness, joyful tinkering, lock picking, and creative system administration—in short, the "social enchantment and moral solidarity" that characterizes DEF CON and other hacker events where people can meet and have co-presence—was absent (Coleman 2010, 47). In fact, it was plentiful. Yet community aside, the event was also deeply dominated by capitalism and its increasingly close proximity to the state. While other well-known hacker conventions (e.g., Hackers on Planet Earth [HOPE] or the Chaos Computer Club in Berlin) might retain a subversive and regressive vibe, DEF CON's twenty-five-thousand conference goers faced expensive registration fees ($450), lodging ($150 per night), and extracurricular activities. This is not an underground scene but a space where IT professionals can recreate while still being on the job. It makes sense, then, that this would be a location where transitioning gray hat hackers would congregate. It is also logical that the cybersecurity state would come here to gather cultural capital in a relatively safe space dominated by professionals but still capable of proclaiming its proximity to the edge. Why not give a few talks and try to recruit these wanna-be white hat hackers? Who among us escaping the blazing heat and blinding facades of Las Vegas for the air-conditioned corridors of the Caesars Palace was a fed?

The faux radicality at DEF CON paralleled the illusion of Las Vegas itself. The City of Sin works hard to retain its outlaw image. Working- and middle-class families know that what happens in Las Vegas stays here, or so the cliché goes. This usually means little more than losing money at the slots, paying overpriced tickets for shows, and indulging in surf and turf buffets. The more tangible sins—prostitution, poverty, bankruptcy, drug addiction, homelessness (and we might add the waste of precious Colorado River water)—are usually not included in the tally of illicit good times had. The only sin remaining is against your bank account, your future savings, and the legacy you leave for your future generations. The IT professionals who can afford it are proud of these officially sanctioned transgressions. Morning beers and afternoon shopping sprees for official DEF CON garb are capped by quirky late night raves (with unsubtle IT samples) that can be accessed only with the clunky DEF CON pass. This carnival-like atmosphere is pregnant with liminality and transgression. It is meaningful for the hackers who attend DEF CON every year. The above rituals of togetherness blend with the felt experience of a punishing marathon pace set by the conference.

The air-conditioned environment is one relief to an otherwise confusing, exhausting, and infuriating several days of geekdom. Nearly every panel is packed; lines begin well before the entry and involve as much as a half-hour long queue before reaching the door. Inside, the talks are direct and fiercely delivered. The speakers wear the markers of subcultural identity—jeans, black shirts, and a neck weighed down by previous DEF CON badges—like a uniform. In one panel, after taking a shot of whiskey or some other spirit (a DEF CON first-time speaker tradition), cybersecurity researcher Josh Corman used alliteration to introduce US congressmen James Langevin (D-RI) and Will Hurd (R-TX) to the different reasons people attend DEF CON. Participants are one and sometimes many of the following: *protectors*, who want to make the internet safer; or *puzzlers*, who enjoy tinkering and solving problems. Many are in it for *prestige, power, pride, profit*, and *professional* development as well. Some hackers are motivated by *protest*—for or against a cause. Corman revealed himself as a protector, but he also identifies as a puzzler and one that has pride in the increasing professionalization and legitimation of hackers through their recognition by the state.

Corman celebrated the transfer of hacker ideals into government policy and law: he cited a new government vulnerability disclosure program that will allow hackers to reveal vulnerabilities without fear of legal prosecution as one way in which hacker practices are increasingly decriminalized and positively influencing policy. Corman was also effusive in his appreciation of Hurd and Langevin, who both serve on the US Homeland Security Committee, and he repeatedly solicited applause for them from the audience. After the congressmen took their ceremonial shots of spirits, the appreciation became mutual. Rep. Hurd emphasized "the excellent work of hackers like y'all" no less than ten times in a twenty-minute talk. Langevin was instrumental in starting the Hack the Pentagon bug bounty program, where over the course of a month, as many as 1,400 hackers found and revealed more than 125 security vulnerabilities. According to Langevin, this crowdsourced effort was undertaken "at a fraction of the cost per bug of existing programs."[11] He told the audience that the Pentagon had plans to expand the program, and that the Internal Revenue Service was also on board. The panel ended with a standing ovation. It was clear, from this panel at least, that DEF CON had been bridged by the feds.

"Meet the Fed" panels such as this have been commonplace at DEF CON for decades now, but this was not always the case. For example, DEF CON organizer Jeff Moss, otherwise known as Dark Tangent, disinvited government officials and law enforcement from attending the 2013 DEF CON. According to one journalist, this was symbolically powerful, "coming after years during which the lines separating 'hackers' and 'the FEDS' got ever more blurry" (Roberts 2013). A collective antagonism toward "the feds" is summed up by the colloquialism "the feds" and the game of "Spot the Feds," which is encouraged by DEF CON speakers (the prize for both hunter and hunted was a hacker T-shirt).

The presence of the feds also threatened the inclusivity of DEF CON. Wanted criminals have attended the conference in the past and have been arrested here. Stephan Watt, the Unix terrorist, gave a talk at DEF CON 10 before being arrested for hacking a credit card company and subsequently serving two years in prison (Zetter 2009, 2014). Soon, however, the antagonistic "Spot the Fed"—game and panel title from DEF CON 17—became the more collaborative and nonironic "Meet the Feds" panel the following year. In this friendlier environment, the feds are not tracking hackers for arrest, but rather they "keep tabs on hacking craft and the latest attacks and exploits . . . [and come] with job offers in hand for the most talented and in-demand security folks" (Roberts 2013).

Yet in 2013 and in the wake of the Snowden revelations, Dark Tangent disinvited the feds with the following message:

> "When it comes to sharing and socializing with feds, recent revelations have made many in the community uncomfortable about this relationship . . . Therefore, I think it would be best for everyone involved if the feds call a 'time-out' and not attend DEF CON this year." The time off, he said, will "give everybody time to think about how we got here, and what comes next." (quoted in Whitney 2013)

Responses were mixed. Jeffrey Carr, CEO of Taia Global (a company that sponsors a Suits and Spooks event), said, "It doesn't make any sense to me, especially since so many hackers have built up a close relationship with the government over the years" (Mello 2013). The year before the temporary fed prohibition in 2013 may have been "peak" fed: General Keith Alexander, then head of the NSA and US Cyber Command, gave the keynote address. Alongside his talk, the NSA organized a vendor booth and created a special recruitment website. The irony of the spy chief wearing a black T-shirt with the logo of privacy advocate EFF (Electronic Frontier Foundation) was not lost on many journalists (Jue and Brownell 2012). "Sometimes you guys get a bad rep," Alexander said to the crowd. "From my perspective, what you guys are doing to figure out vulnerabilities in systems is absolutely needed." "Then stop arresting us!" one heckler in the audience replied. Another carried a small cardboard sign that said "Bullshit," to be used for just such an occasion (Kopfstein 2012).

After the PRISM revelations and Dark Tangent barring the Feds from attending that year's DEF CON, journalist Jordan Keenan conducted an informal but informative survey of attendees to see if they would work for the NSA. Rejections included "Hell no!"; "They don't want me"; "Yes, but only if I was in charge. Otherwise, fuck no." More sanguine responses followed: "Someone has to protect us, and sometimes you have to get your fingers dirty to do that"; "I have already applied for a job there"; "I like crypto analysis; I love big data. Working there appeals to me because it is more intelligence driven. The datasets would be bigger, and more meaningful"; "Yeah, I would have no problem with that. I'm a retired army officer." Others had more nuanced motives. One attendee said they see people with "mohawks, dyed hair, piercings, you name it. And they whisper, 'I need to get my doctorate because I can't get a government grant without it.' I guess the prevailing attitude is one of, 'I can work for the feds, but I don't have to like it.'" Another responded: "At the end of the day, there is no freedom, anyway. I need to pay my mortgage; I need to feed my family. Guys living in the bushes might be better off, but is that even freedom? Who knows. Here, have a beer. I'm off" (Keenan 2013).

By our attendance at DEF CON 25 in 2017, the feds were back in full force. A recurring phrase at DEF CON is that this event serves as a "bridge" between cybersecurity researchers and the federal government. In between panels titled "Meet the Feds" and "Hacking Democracy"—two panels that featured former or present federal employees at odds to explain to the audience of hundreds of hackers how their work does or should overlap—we had a discussion with a geeky lawyer who had been attending DEF CON for years and had also worked with the federal government. Our conversation meandered and touched on the subversive nature of *Playboy*; the recent arrest of NSA whistleblower Reality Winner, a hacker who bought and hacked decommissioned NASA laptops; and the government's harboring of software vulnerabilities. He ended the chat with a DEF CON joke: "Don't worry, little hacker. [The government] is not going to blow a zero day on your IOS phone," meaning any fed who was there was after big fish, not script kiddies. He was impressed with what the feds said in this year's "Meet the Feds" panel: they are "genuinely good folks who are trying to build bridges and communicate." After hearing his enthusiasm for the candor and honesty of the fed panelists, we departed for the greener pastures of beer, slot machines, and Caesar busts.

The staging of this event at Caesars Palace among an army of largely white and male attendees, its corporate-inspired recreational activities and the general mood (captured most eloquently by the *Playboy* aficionado described above) offers an opportunity to reflect on gender more generally in hacker culture. Hacker communities reflect (if not amplify) the gender disparities prevalent in the larger world. Men remain prevalent in computer science as a hobby and profession. And although research and data on gender and racial disparities in cybersecurity are scant, one relatively recent survey of 19,641 cybersecurity workers in 170 countries found that women make up only 11 percent of the information security workforce, despite having on average higher educational levels than men (Center for Cyber Safety and Education 2017).

Online hacking ecologies where men dominate—4chan, certain IRCs, and other trolling dominions—can be misogynist, racist, crude, and mean. We spoke with one long-standing hacktivist about why this toxic speech exists in hacker culture, and he admitted that hacking is often framed as "a particular form of masculinity."[12] He noted that unlike classical forms of "machoism," in hacker culture "you don't have to be strong; you have to be clever." Thus rather than celebrating masculine brawn, hackers prize brainy activity, such as "mastery, logic, and intellect, which are more 'geek' than the usual patriarchal stereotypes." He agreed that heterosexual women and traditional forms of feminine performativity are often made to feel unwelcome in the geek machoism of hacker culture and speculated that this antagonistic stance might reflect the traditional masculine shortcomings of geeks themselves: they lack "big dicks, muscles, being cool, and dressing well." From this perspective, the hacker brand of clever and brainy masculinity is undervalued in the world of *manly* men, a world in which they see manly attributes as the only currency and a view that provides license to react cruelly online, in trolling operations, and in meat space against women.

As our respondent pointed out, this is a reductionist male view of the hacker ethic, and it has come to sometimes unreflexively dominate its culture, providing justifications not just for toxic behavior but also for gender disparities in the security field itself. Nonbinary genders, however, can find a surprising welcome within hacker culture. While our respondent argued that hackers have a difficult time with and can be antagonistic toward traditional femininity, he noted that transgendered individuals "do much better in the hacker scene than other hacker milieus." This is an insight confirmed by other observers. For example, Coleman writes, "The social boundaries erected by hackers also exhibit contradictions: while the gender gap is vast, some identities—such as transgender, queer, or disabled— are more common and accepted" (2014, 331). And this is confirmed by our attendance a year later at the HOPE security conference in New York, which, perhaps because of its deliberately open and inclusive framing, exhibited much greater levels of gender and racial diversity (in terms of attendees, talks, and presenters). Yet the fact remains that the cybersecurity and state-hacker professionals shaping our contemporary digital environment are more likely to subscribe to the "geek machoism" identified by our informant, and this poses important and unaddressed questions about the overall conceptual and strategic framing of our cybersecurity choices.

The bug bounty program Hack the Pentagon that we encountered at DEF CON 25 is but one of many such programs to channel the "puzzlers" toward pro-state ends. Since the middle of this century's first decade, there has been a veritable boom in (in)security markets of every stripe. For example, although two dozen states have cyber defense and offense divisions, many more outsource this work to intermediaries or proxies, creating a lucrative market for off-the-shelf attack software (Maurer 2018, 27). The US government spent $1 billion on cyber-threat intelligence in 2017—up from $250 million in 2013 (Maurer 2018, 73). ManTech's $250 million contract to "prepare the next generation of cyberwar fighters for the Department of Defense" in 2015, or Raytheon's purchase of a US Cyber Command subsidiary for $420 million, illustrate the immense investments and profitability in this field.

A brief overview of this sector is necessary before moving on to discuss how these sites inform the logics of responsibilization and insecurity that allow state hacking to thrive. Very briefly, researchers often distinguish between legitimate and illegitimate, legal and illegal, as well as among white, gray, and black vulnerabilities markets (cf. Fidler 2015; Allodi 2017). A typical example of white markets is the numerous bug bounty, or bug-hunting, programs sponsored by software vendors like Google, Facebook, and Microsoft. Although the rules and parameters vary significantly, "hunters" generally look for bugs in software code that can be exploited and disclose those vulnerabilities to the software vendor or client in return for a variable monetary reward; they also agree on a timeframe for the public disclosure of the vulnerability (usually after the vendor has produced a patch). These are legal and legitimate markets that conform with the ethics of responsible disclosure and have proliferated in recent years. In contrast, black markets describe transactions involving vulnerabilities where the aim of the seller or the buyer is criminal. They are illegal and illegitimate. Finally, gray markets occupy a liminal position between the two. Whereas white markets are in direct competition with black markets, the term gray market describes transactions between state actors or elite cybersecurity firms and professional vulnerabilities merchants. Although these transactions are "legal" (in the sense that they by definition do not involve criminal activity), their ethical status is uncertain and questionable.

Netscape launched the first bug bounty program in 1995, but the surge in popularity began when Google launched its own (still ongoing) program in 2010. Microsoft has had a bounty program since 2013. Other big tech companies soon followed, and as time wore on, intermediaries like the Zero Day Initiative, HackerOne, Synack, Cobalt, and Bugcrowd began offering their brokering services to organize and manage bug bounty events for participating companies. The size of the bug-hunting marketplace is large. For example, HackerOne boasts access to a community of 166,000 security researchers that have cumulatively submitted 72,000 valid vulnerabilities and received more than $23.5 million in awarded bounties.

The US government has recently accelerated the pace with which it crowdsources vulnerability testing. The DOD launched its Hack the Pentagon initiative with HackerOne from April 18 to May 12, 2016, through which 1,400 participants reported 138 "unique and actionable" vulnerabilities and were paid a total of $100,000. The following year the US Army and the US Air Force both ran their own versions of the bug bounty programs, with similar results, and in 2017, the General Services Administration announced the first ongoing nonmilitary bug bounty program, with bounties ranging from $200 to $2,000.

Earlier in this chapter, we describe how responsibilization strategies inform and frame cybersecurity practices, spurring novel configurations of

crime-control and neoliberal agendas. Bug bounty, or bug-hunting, programs increasingly represent the most refined expression of this project.
The programs are appealing to private and public companies because they
address the security under-resourcing associated with the global skills gap
described above. They are also marketed as cost effective in the sense that
they are payment-by-results driven. Bounties are awarded only if a researcher
is the first to disclose the vulnerability and follows the fairly detailed rules
of engagement and the vulnerability is eligible for reward (e.g., it is not
uncommon for a vulnerability to already be known by vendors for some
time without being scheduled for patching for different reasons).

What is striking about this process is how the logic of ethical hacking is
operationalized and put in service of neoliberal business practices. Indeed,
the recent DOD vulnerability disclosure policy, introduced in 2017, has
been described by former defense secretary Ash Carter as "a 'see something,
say something' policy for the digital domain" (US Senate 2018, 4). And the
CEO of HackerOne, in his testimony before the US Senate Commerce Subcommittee on Consumer Protection, Product Safety, Insurance, and Data
Security, likened vulnerability disclosure—and by extension what his company does—as "a neighborhood watch for software" (Mickos 2018). One
might further argue that a similar logic inflects both responsible disclosure
and full disclosure. And there are clear parallels here with the "volunteer
firefighters" Lauri Love describes at the beginning of this chapter.

What is elided by the above civic-minded and voluntaristic slogans is the
calculating neoliberal capture of hacker labor that remains unquantified in
the operation of legitimate, legal white bug bounty markets. Indeed, the
entire discursive and symbolic effort of these programs is to shift the model
away from any parallels one might draw with traditional capitalist relationships, even though in important respects, the programs represent its
highest expression. They create a symbolic economy in lieu of the obliga-
tions and complexities that come bundled with actual economies. Hunters
are not "paid"; they receive "rewards." If they report a bug or vulnerability
that is not eligible for a reward (or a bounty), they might get a "mention"
or some other form of status commendation from the company they have
reported the bug to. They are not employees or even freelancers and have
little status from the point of view of employment law. Indeed, these practices flow from wider shifts in the digitalization of work and the uncertain
legal status and protections of workers in the gig economy and in other

crowdsourced, microwork, and on-demand platforms (cf. de Stefano 2016; Cherry 2016).

Penetration testing and vulnerability analysis is skilled, time consuming, and extremely repetitive work. It may take hours or days of applying one's methodology or repeating a particular set of analytical steps to find a vulnerability, if one is found at all. In this sense, crowd-sourced penetration-testing practices significantly radicalize the practices of the Taskrabbits and Ubers of the world, because they uncouple the payment for services from the actual material work hackers perform, regardless of whether they discover a genuine bug or nothing at all. Payment itself is contingent and an unexpected boon.

Bug bounties leverage tropes of responsibilization to co-opt hacker labor. But they also fold the social experience of garnering reputation, status, and prestige in hacker communities—as well as the more general fascination with tinkering and solving puzzles—into a tightly formulated business model, a cynical business practice that is completely out of step with the motivations that animate security researchers like HackerFantastic:

> It's always fun to share something cool you learned with other people, something you enjoyed can then spread enjoyment to others. I have always published exploits to highlight risk, show a problem existed and to demonstrate something I found interesting. Once you find an exploit or a new 0day, it's exciting because you have this information that you almost want to be secret forever but your proud of the discovery so of course you tell your friends, who tell their friends and so on and so on.[13]

Finally, paralleling other state and corporate short-term solutions to the pervasive shortage in cybersecurity talent, such efforts depoliticize hacking and keep its ideological instability at a distance by turning it into a capture the flag game or a hacking marathon. In so doing, they also empty *ethical hacking* of its normative content. Phineas Fisher, who hacked Hacking Team, FinFisher, and Gamma Group because of their complicity with authoritarian states, ended its "hack back" manifesto with the following missive:

> Hacking guides often end with a disclaimer: this information is for educational purposes only, be an ethical hacker, don't attack systems you don't have permissions to, etc. I'll say the same, but with a more rebellious conception of "ethical" hacking. Leaking documents, expropriating money from banks, and working to secure the computers of ordinary people is ethical hacking. However, most people

that call themselves "ethical hackers" just work to secure those who pay their high consulting fees, who are often those most deserving to be hacked. (Phineas Fisher 2016, 17)

More broadly, the trajectories of ethical hacker formation described in this chapter should be understood as solutions to the neoliberal paradox that emerges at the point of intersection between hacktivist radical democratic action, state criminal prosecution, and the commercial logic of cyber (in)security. As we argue in chapters 2 and 4, one aspect of the state's increasingly monopolistic stance toward cyberspace has been to crowd out, prosecute, or co-opt the large field of third-party actors (i.e., hacktivists, cybercriminals, cyberterrorists, etc.) that can now act with effect in the field of geopolitics since the advent of networked technology. This chapter has explored how state strategies of co-option have facilitated the emergence of twin paths for would-be or reformed hackers. On the one hand, governments like that of the United Kingdom are formally and informally drawing technological talent from at-risk or potential hackers that come under their purview through the criminal justice system to motivate them to work for the state or the market. On the other, there is an increasing effort to penetrate the professional and voluntary meetups and organizations where security researchers and techies congregate to directly recruit new talent.

6   High Breach Societies

In *Hacker States* we track the contradictory relationships that emerge when states develop armies of hackers while working to quell dissident hacking at home, and document what happens to the state, journalism, and political action in this radical new world. This book tells a story of how hackers and the state are reshaping each other in an entangled network of law, activism, conflict, and computer code. We chart a shift from late twentieth-century concerns about rogue hackers as transnational vigilante groups to a world where state hacking is not only incredibly visible but an increasingly legitimate way for states to project force.

Initially, technology leveled the playing field between hackers and the state: it gave individuals and activists the capacity to act with impact on a global scale for criminal or disruptive purposes but also (and more importantly) for traditionally liberal purposes (e.g., dissent, transparency, protest, and to spur political change or democratic debate). At the same time, though, this technological leveling effect also shifted the strategic and tactical playing field between larger and smaller, democratic and non-democratic states. Countries like the United States or the UK may adopt hacking tactics because they help secure state interests and avoid the political, public, and international pitfalls of sustained troop deployments. But they do so in a field where one's tactical footprint is no longer necessarily determined by the scale of armies or the number of bases.

One contribution of this book is the development of the concept of state boundary work and its application to this new reality. Hacking, the prosecution of hackers, the enrollment of private hackers as proxies— these are among the governance tactics adopted by networked states to harness intrusion and exfiltration technologies. We chart a new arena of state activity where hacking becomes an important resource in the expression of state power. Each chapter of this book explores one aspect of the networked state's boundary work. Chapter 2 surveys the varied strategic and organizational forms boundary practices take among different states and illustrates their deployment in the international field of state hacking. Chapter 3 situates state hacking within the recent history of leaks, whistleblowing, and digital dissent. It shows how the very tactics adopted by transparency activists became new attack vectors for the Russian state and exposed the difficulties inherent in doing boundary work through congressional regulation. Chapter 4 focuses on how criminal justice frameworks (already important elements in the governance of hacking) have now been coupled with extradition treaties and international partnerships to project the state's boundary practices internationally. Finally, chapter 5 considers state efforts to privatize boundary work through corporate security firms and proxies, alongside its adoption of crowdsourced cybersecurity in an effort to harness hacking capacities while keeping hackers at a distance. Boundary work is a core feature of the networked state, and it enrolls the full dynamism of its constituent parts—individuals and institutions, as much as software and hard infrastructures—in its defense.

Drawing boundaries and marking categories of difference are integral components of the state's historical function. States have long sought to govern their subjects through the erection, manipulation, and transformation of borders, whether this helped police the margins of inclusion, formed the threshold for going to war, or served as the basis for taxation and other modes of resource extraction. The rise of a globally networked society—and the attendant challenges it poses to state-centric notions of sovereignty when applied to tech economies or an emergent cyberspace—mean that these boundary practices are applied in updated form to this new reality.

In chapter 2 we develop a historical account of how hacking became an object, problem, and resource of governance across various US state domains. In each of these areas (law enforcement, the military, and national security), and according to the different logistical and strategic imperatives that animate them, the United States came to fold hackers and hacking into a complex assemblage for the projection and deployment of state power. We then examine how different states (China and Russia) differentially mobilized similar boundary work strategies to project their own distinctive variants of state hacking and cyber power. Finally, we consider the private hackers and cyber mercenaries—both boundary workers in their own right—who provide technological resources, attack platforms, and surveillance capabilities for hire in this zone of state activity.

Chapter 3 looks closely at the Russian hacking of the 2016 US presidential election, the manipulation of networked public spheres, and the complicity (however inadvertent) of social media companies in opening a new front in the arena of state hacking. We revisit the prodemocracy leaks of Edward Snowden, Chelsea Manning, and Daniel Ellsberg alongside the weaponized data dumps and doxing campaigns of Anonymous, LulzSec, and Phineas Fisher in an effort to theorize how different methodologies of scale and time affect networked public spheres and media ecologies to provide differential opportunities for debate, dissent, resistance, and, increasingly, state disruption. Manning, Snowden and Ellsberg crossed state boundaries to further transparency and spur public debate about the role, breadth, and limit of government activities pursued in the name of national security. Anonymous, LulzSec, and Phineas Fisher engaged in hacktivist operations that targeted state authorities, and their associated boundary workers and proxies, in the name of resistance and dissent. In the law enforcement response that followed, both sets of actors (and the networked publishing platforms that supported them) came to function as *boundary objects* against which new representations of danger, criminality, and subversion were projected. One combined consequence of these years, and the dump- and disclosure-driven headlines that chronicled them, was that they normalized an age of disinformation (and the richly speculative and doubt-laden terrain that nurtures it) and formed a prime vector of attack for Russian state hacking. In the 2016 presidential election, we see the full spectrum of Russian boundary practices on display, and we also note that one of the enduring difficulties associated with narrowing the attack topology of democratic states is the way in which democracies function.

One obvious resource for state boundary work is the law. The expansion of state criminal justice apparatuses through international assistance and extradition agreements are important vehicles for the projection of state power beyond its geographic domain. In chapter 4 we discuss the extradition case of Lauri Love, an Anonymous-associated hacktivist accused of hacking into and exfiltrating data from numerous US federal agencies. Here we see how law enforcement practices the United States historically developed to deal with domestic hacking have been internationalized and broadened.

Working through proxies in the NCA and the CPS, federal authorities built a multiyear criminal case that culminated in Love's extradition hearings. Ironically, although Love's extradition seemed inevitable, and was appealed all the way to the high court, the US request was ultimately rejected because the court considered the conditions of confinement Love would face in the United States (throughout his multiple criminal trials and eventual incarceration) inhumane. To fight his extradition, Love's defense team drew on his fragile state—his depression, Asperger syndrome, and painful eczema—as well as the copious evidence concerning the systemic dysfunction and enforced brutality of the sites where he would likely be confined.

Chapter 4 also illustrates the indeterminate nature of state boundary work. As we note early in this book, although we have used the term *state* throughout in the singular sense, we have actually been describing an assemblage of multiple state domains. At times these entities are logistically coordinated, but at others, they are in open conflict, competition, or contradiction. These logistical disjunctures can force interruptions in the circuitry of power. US authorities sought to extradite Love and pursued a multiyear campaign to have him tried in American courts, yet they were thwarted by the casual brutality of the US penal system and their inability to guarantee that Love would be treated any differently despite the state of his physical and mental health. Similarly, although the NCA and the CPS served as proxies for the United States and worked to develop the evidentiary case for Love's extradition and US trial, their efforts were resisted in another state domain, the high court, where the status of their claims and of those made by the defense had a different currency.

In chapter 5 we look closely at the privatization of state hacking as one way that hacking has been operationalized into a state resource. We present ethnographic data from an ethical hacking workshop in the UK and a large cybersecurity conference in the United States. Here the discussion moves from the abstract boundary work of the state to the actual practices of boundary workers. In experimenting with the hacker toolkit—including vulnerability, exploitation, attack, forensic, stress testing, sniffing, and spoofing tools—we develop a firsthand account of the blurred terrain between the inside and the outside of the networked state's boundary. The tools we grew accustomed to deploying in our safe and sandboxed environment in the Hacker House workshop were the same tools used by supposed cyber criminals, as well as politically motivated hacktivists. Hacker tools like the Kali Linux suite of penetration and attack applications are "boundary objects" (Star and Griesemer 1989, 393), adaptive materials with common yet distinct meanings to allow translation and mutual understanding across potentially conflicting cultures. They bridge multiple competing spaces of practice (state hacking, ethical hacking, cybersecurity, hacktivism, cyber crime), opening multiple vectors of recognition and grooming for would-be state boundary workers. Chapter 5 also considers how state boundary practices have continued to evolve and multiply in response to an ongoing global shortage of cybersecurity personnel. We see bug bounties and crowdsourced penetration testing as new boundary practices, which allow state agencies to selectively draw on hacker skillsets and capacities while keeping them at a distance from the actual state. A similar process is at work in hacker rehabilitation and reeducation programs, where we see a reversal of the criminalization process we describe in earlier chapters. Here criminal behavior and political ideology are filtered through criminal justice interventions to transform would-be hackers into state resources.

Finally, in our discussion of DEF CON, we witnessed and engaged in conversations at the boundary between networked state functionaries and hacking practitioners. While the interactions between these actors have not always been seamless—particularly after the Snowden revelations in 2013—we witnessed a renewed commitment between state officials and the hacker community toward mutual cooperation on information and job security. State assemblages require hackers within their boundaries (not simply at a distance), and hackers need jobs, access to sophisticated tools, and big data. In this sense events like DEF CON are themselves boundary objects, spaces where differently motivated actors come together around a singularly framed opportunity—to cocreate the hacking world. While their professional affiliations might be distinct, the hackers and the state representatives at DEF CON are there for camaraderie, knowledge, and networking. Through events like DEF CON and the Hacking House workshop, the former distinctions separating hackers and the state evaporate through shared interests, practices, and the need for social, economic, and informational capital.

The Mobilities of Code

The final story we tell, although it has been told before, remains difficult to follow. In August 2016 the world was introduced to the seemingly hacktivist and likely Russian Shadow Brokers, who claimed to have breached the Equation Group. The latter is a division within TAO, the US NSA's hacking department, which boasts highly sophisticated and in-house-designed tools, recruitment pools of the most talented hackers, and partnerships with telecommunications giants like Verizon, AT&T, and Sprint (Aid 2013). The NSA's Equation Group may have infected more than five hundred targets from as many as forty-two countries, including Russia, Pakistan, Afghanistan, India, Mali, Syria, and Iran (Goodin 2015). Its code weapons are state of the art, and its attack platforms are universal, modular, and customizable.

After hacking into the NSA, the Shadow Brokers attempted to auction their spoils for bitcoin. It remains unclear whether this auction failed because it lacked willing buyers or whether it was actually a hoax. Nonetheless, after the failure of the auction, the group began releasing as much as a gigabyte of its hacked NSA tools for free between November and January 2017. On April 14, 2017, they released a 300 MB (Goodin 2017b) dump of premier hacking tools, including the famous five zero-day vulnerabilities that affected most versions of Microsoft Windows and Fuzzbunch— the Equation Group's multipurpose cyber-weapon attack platform (Goodin 2017a). One of the exploits loaded into Fuzzbunch was EternalBlue, a remote code execution vulnerability that allowed attackers to gain access to millions of Windows machines.

Eventually, EternalBlue evolved into a more serious threat to global cybersecurity as it morphed into WannaCry and was released on May 12, 2017 (Brenner 2017). The first WannaCry infections appeared in India, Hong Kong, and the Philippines, yet by the end of the day, the tally of infected computers had spread to more than two hundred thousand in one hundred countries. This included sixty UK NHS boards and trusts, which caused the cancellation of nonemergency procedures across the country (Reynolds 2017). Other estimates have put the figure of affected machines significantly higher, somewhere between three hundred thousand and four hundred thousand computers globally (National Audit Office 2018). The largest number of infections reported were in Russia—followed by Ukraine, India, and Taiwan. WannaCry took over computers using certain versions of the Microsoft Windows operating system and encrypted all the data they contained until a bitcoin ransom was paid.

The crisis was contained on the same day the ransomware appeared through the efforts of malware researcher Marcus Hutchins. Hutchins, a twenty-three-year-old security researcher at Kryptos Logic, stopped the attack by creating a domain name that redirected the attacks to a sinkhole (MalwareTech 2017). Three months later, he was attending DEF CON 25 in Las Vegas and relishing the accolades he received for defusing the worm. A few days later, Hutchins was arrested at McCarran International Airport while trying to board a flight home to the UK. He was served an indictment by federal authorities and charged with six computer crimes.[1] As of this writing, he is awaiting sentencing in the United States, after pleading guilty to criminal charges associated with writing and selling the notorious "Kronos" banking trojan.

In the aftermath of the attack, the NSA claimed that the North Korean cyber-espionage department, the Reconnaissance General Bureau, built the WannaCry worm around its tool (Nakashima 2017). To date, the ransomware generated $140,000 in bitcoins that have yet to be redeemed for regular bankable currency. The North Korean state has been linked to cyber attacks for profit before (e.g., they exfiltrated $81 million from a bank in Bangladesh; Lennon 2014), and such excursions may represent an important tactic for the state in the context of punishing international sanctions.

Yet the story does not end there. A few months after WannaCry was disabled, Ukrainian banks, airports, and energy firms were hit with a ransomware attack. Petya (or NotPetya, Nyetya, or Goldeneye), as this new malware was called, would either encrypt data and request a ransom or wipe the infected computer's hard drive and reboot the system. Ukrainian cyber researchers believe the attack originated from Russia as part of a long-running cyber war between the two states. It has been attributed to Sandworm, a Russian state-linked hacking group that targeted the Ukrainian media, government offices, and transportation services, as well as generating blackouts by infecting electrical facilities in late 2015 (Greenberg 2017). The target of the Petya malware provides further evidence of its state-sponsored nature: it appeared directed at users of the Ukrainian accounting software MeDoc, which is widely used for tax filings and financial transactions within the Ukrainian government. It exploited the same Microsoft vulnerability as WannaCry.

We began with the exfiltration of highly sophisticated hacking tools and zero days from NSA servers by a hacking group linked to Russia. This group then made a sizable arsenal of these tools and weapons universally available in a series of data dumps. A short time later, one of the dumped exploits was reengineered by hackers linked to North Korea into a powerful ransomware attack, which disproportionately affected Russian computer networks. A short time later, yet another recoded version of the same exploit appeared (this time associated with Russian hackers) and targeted Ukrainian economic and transportation infrastructures, as well as government computers.

The above scenario underscores the diffuse, open-ended, and scalable character of exposure and criminal victimization in high breach societies. More so than the bulk exfiltration of user data (which the NSA, for example, has had to build new data centers to store), the entire NSA arsenal hacked by the Shadow Brokers fits on a memory stick. It can be downloaded, copied, reengineered, and recoded multiple times for as long as the vulnerability exists. In chapter 2 we argue that boundary work has emerged as a core state strategy for governing hacking technologies. Yet the Shadow Brokers episode (and its attendant fallout) also illustrates the point that, as much as states may selectively and logistically manipulate borders and boundaries to harness hacking, code obeys no boundaries. Information is mobile, and once it crosses state thresholds, it gains a momentum of its own.

When the first auction began in late 2016, several commentators argued that the Shadow Brokers were Russian operatives. A former NSA subcontractor wrote, "Circumstantial evidence and conventional wisdom indicates Russian responsibility," driven more by "diplomacy than intelligence," and timed as an escalation to the leaks of emails from the DNC (Sanger 2016). Others see the timing as suspiciously Russian as well. A post falsely claiming to be the final message by the group was released eight days before Donald Trump's inauguration, so that if the exploits were released during his tenure, they would not have negatively affected the Trump presidency (Goodin 2017c).

As agents of creative destruction and known disruptors of US politics, Russians are a convenient source and scapegoat for such hacks. And it is clear that the circumstances surrounding the original data release display a sophisticated understanding of how to maximize the impact of a dump by manipulating its scale and timing. In terms of the media and news cycle, Friday releases are a well-known political tactic to deemphasize or bury the ramifications of a disclosure: interest in the story generally dies down by the end of the weekend, and Monday begins with a new news cycle (Weaver 2017). And this is, to a certain extent, what did occur, given that the most important "newsworthy" items contained in the dump (e.g., extensive evidence of the NSA's hacking into the SWIFT banking system) did not really get the sort of response the material warranted. Indeed, the Shadow Brokers did not even emphasize that the material was contained in the dump. Yet, April 14, 2017, wasn't just any Friday, it was Good Friday, and this meant that in addition to the general short staffing on most weekends, the holiday ensured that many, if not most, security professionals were enjoying the time off and that if anyone was active, it was probably only script kiddies. In this sense, the goal of the release seems to be neither a new version of radical transparency nor some weaponization of visibility, as discussed in chapter 3 but rather an adoption of these same methodologies to maximize disruption.

Finally, there is an alternative theory about the Shadow Brokers' origins that also illustrates the pervasive mobility of exfiltrated code and sensitive information in high breach societies. On August 27, 2016, Harold Thomas Martin III was arrested at his Maryland home by a small army of federal agents (nine SWAT officers and eight FBI agents; US DOJ 2016b). In his home and vehicle, investigators found a staggering cache of classified documents that dwarfs the Panama Papers and Paradise Papers leaks combined. Martin allegedly exfiltrated 50 TB of top-secret data going back a decade, while working for the NSA's TAO and later Booz Allen Hamilton (the same contractor Edward Snowden worked for; Shane 2018). The *New York Times* as well as cybersecurity expert Bruce Schneier suggest a connection between Martin and the Shadow Brokers, given that the material leaked by this group was among the data Martin exfiltrated (Becker et al. 2016; Schneier 2017). If Martin is the source of the leaked NSA exploits, he is certainly no longer in control of the code—no one is. And prosecutors have been unable to materially link Martin to the Shadow Brokers despite his guilty plea (Shane 2018). Yet linguists who have analyzed the texts announcing the Shadow Brokers auction believe it was likely written by a native English speaker pretending to write in broken, vaguely Russian English (Franceschi-Bicchierai 2016).

In a further twist, it was not the NSA that uncovered evidence of Martin's compulsive hoarding but the Russian cybersecurity company Kaspersky Labs, known for its popular antivirus program. In 2016, Kaspersky Labs received five odd Twitter messages from user @HAL999999999 requesting a conversation with Yevgeny (Yevgeny is the first name of the firm's founder, anglicized as Eugene Kaspersky). The profile picture for this user was a man in a chair with his back turned, next to a CD-ROM with the phrase TAO2 on it. Thirty minutes later, the Shadow Brokers dumped the NSA tools online and began their auction. The term HAL999999999 was connected to an individual seeking female sexual partners and featured Martin's real picture. The firm tipped off the NSA and sent the agency Martin's tweets along with his real identity (Zetter 2019).

This is all remarkable given that at the time, the US government was in the midst of officially banning Kaspersky's services as a government contractor (Zetter 2019). And on December 12, 2017, President Trump signed the National Defense Authorization Act, which includes a prohibition on the use of Kaspersky software on government computers. US authorities accuse the cybersecurity firm of working as a double agent, engaging in proxy work for both the United States and Russia (Volz 2017; Webb 2018). This claim is connected to yet another exfiltration case involving the NSA's TAO. On September 25, 2018, Nghia Pho, a network exploitation specialist employed by TAO, was sentenced to five years and six months for hoarding a "massive trove" of source code and software for the agency's hacking operations at his home (Gerstein 2018). Pho's lawyers argued that he was ambitious and wanted to move up the promotion ladder, so he took the tools home to work on them in his free time. Yet the government is fairly certain that, perhaps unknowingly, Pho was one of the sources of the Shadow Brokers data dump, and that the software and tools were exfiltrated by the Kaspersky virus protection software he had installed on his home system (Zetter 2019).

In some respects, this is the story of a single exploit and its multiple afterlives (although many similar stories could be told). The Microsoft bug that the exploit uses was mined by the NSA. They used the bug to create an exploit that targets the vulnerability exposed by the bug. The Shadow Brokers hacked the agency and dumped the exploit on the world stage. North Korean hackers built a ransomware worm out of it and set off a seeming global computer apocalypse. Yet the same day, a malware researcher stopped the attack and was subsequently arrested for past transgressions. Later, Russian hackers repurposed the exploit and used it to target Ukrainian government computers and infrastructure during the invasion of Crimea. But it turned out that the code had been mobile for some time. Searching for evidence of how the Shadow Brokers acquired the exploit led authorities back to the NSA and down a rabbit hole of exfiltrated data. Two NSA workers—and who knows how many others—brought the exploit home and were knowingly or unknowingly the probable Shadow Brokers' source.

We want to emphasize the circular and destructive path this single exploit cuts across the world and its institutions, as well as the number of antagonistic characters using this meandering and weaponized code to fulfill ambiguous ambitions. Once the code is mobile, it traverses a circuit that links together several hacking states, the federal courts, foreign banks, government infrastructures, cybersecurity conferences, national health services, and countless other institutions. Here hacktivism, whistleblowing, covert cyber operations, and hostile state cyber incursions are inevitably scrambled, interwoven, and recombined on a global stage with fearsome scale.

The US state shares responsibility for the above crisis. It mined the bug and built a weapon out of it rather than disclose the vulnerability to Microsoft so that computers all over the world using Windows could be patched. The Russian state also bears responsibility: it may be behind the Shadow Brokers and may have weaponized the exploit to support its aggressions in Ukraine. North Korea is responsible as well: it created WannaCry. In this sense, EternalBlue and its afterlives represents one singular example of the sort of boundary work that states increasingly turn to in an attempt to harness hacking technologies and deploy them as a resource for the expression of state power. Yet as we discuss in chapter 2, such boundary exercises are by definition indeterminate and capable of being subverted from within and without the hacker state. At the same time, the effects and targets of such efforts remain fluid and open to contingency. The United States mined the exploit, but its reappearance as WannaCry severely paralyzed the National Health Service of a strategic ally (the UK) and led to the discovery of one of the largest national security breaches in American history. More recently the EternalBlue exploit has reappeared in the United States, where it has served as a vector for crippling ransomware attacks on city government infrastructures from Philadelphia to San Antonio (Perlroth and Shane 2019). And Russia may have exfiltrated the code, but its networks were among the hardest hit by the exploit's weaponization by North Korea. States actively generate exploits on popular operating systems, but they are also the recipients of unintended blowbacks whose potential impact is hard to gauge and even more difficult to defend against. How did we get here? Who is ultimately in control in this situation? The virus-producing state? The code itself? The Shadow Brokers who freed the code? The states that reproduced it into a weapon? Or is this expansive high breach ecology merely a global petri dish, within which action and counter-action occur?

The Shadow Brokers story and the other cases in this book illustrate the entanglements generated by the hacker state. There is an inherent fuzziness that results from indiscreet but entangled forces that have one foot in the physical and another in the virtual. For French sociologist Pierre Bourdieu, the description of social practices is inherently difficult because of their "irregularities and even incoherencies" (1990, 87). He warns scholars against a reductive approach that cleanly snaps the "messiness" of social practices into simplistic systems, theories, and frames. A more empirical approach, he claims, is to articulate the "fuzzy coherence" (1990, 87) in the way institutions and social practices are enmeshed. The relationship between online identity, motivation, and institutions is inherently fuzzy because of the fluidity between online and offline worlds.

Like most of the social science literature that examines digital culture, we reject the "digital dualism" that affirms a separateness between the virtual and the actual. As anthropologist Tom Boellstorff (2008) clearly explains, the physical world is increasingly augmented through digital tools; the virtual world is dependent on physical strata of natural resources, hardware, and infrastructure. In this formulation, the actual and the virtual coexist in a state of asymmetrical cocreation. Further, the scale of actual/virtual conflation continues on a seemingly runaway exponential path through the expansion of digitally powered gig economies and the networking of everyday objects.

The entangled field of hacker state relations represents one horizon in this convergence. It exists as an attempt to make the physical world transformable through code. Hacker activists struggle to make political change through coded protests and computer-aided transparency projects. States hack technological infrastructures and computer networks looking for repositories of data and code that will serve as the basis for new political technologies and pressure points. In the courts, a different set of state authorities draw on digitally derived (and often hacked) evidence to indict, extradite, and sometimes prosecute the hacktivists, state hackers, and cyber criminals who have penetrated its firewalls. Hacker-state entanglement represents one edge in the wider convergence of the virtual and the actual.

Hacktivists as well as the state exist in the liminal space between flexible practices, boundary-making institutions, and fluidity between the actual and the virtual.

While hacker-state relations are signified by an entangled relationship, the state is also in the best position to dominate this chaotic knot. This state dominance may have consequences for the legitimacy of a range of institutions, from democracy and international relations to the courts and cybersecurity. In this conclusion, we consider potential repercussions of state hacking.

State Hacking and the Dark State

Some argue that state hacking threatens the legitimacy of the state because it empowers an opaque dark state whose activities often take place outside congressional or executive oversight. The NSA has a classified budget estimated at $10.8 billion in 2013 (Shane 2013) and conducts top-secret attack and defense missions throughout the world. Warrantless wiretaps, internet monitoring, data mining, exfiltrated evidence, metadata collection, package tampering, and interception, as well as ransomware attacks, are just some of the controversial practices associated with the NSA and their tools. The NSA uses the submarine USS *Jimmy Carter* to tap undersea fiber-optic cables (Khazan 2013), and TAO, the NSA branch within which the Equation Group is situated, has been in operation since 1998 (Aid 2013).

A fifty-page classified document, "NSA ANT," lists the available tools designed and used by TAO to target Apple, Cisco, Dell, Seagate, and other hardware. The targets of these cyber weapons include the governments of China and Mexico, Tor, and Firefox users, as well as intergovernmental heavyweights such as OPEC (Organization of the Petroleum Exporting Countries; Thomson 2013). Moreover, the United States' involvement in cyber operations is expanding. Between 2012 and 2016, the US Army Cyber Command grew to include 133 new cyber-command teams (GAO 2019). The US Army, Navy, Air Force, and Marines now each have their own cyber divisions. And this is just what is known. The budgets, attacks, and successes of these state cyber squads become visible only through whistleblowing or hackers like the Shadow Brokers. As a new tool for boundary expansion into the underterritorialized areas of cyberspace, hacking has seduced both public and clandestine institutions of the state. The expansion of hacking materializes not only the development of boundary-defining technologies but also the growth of the dark state.

Hackers in Court

It could be argued that state hacking affects the courts and the judicial system because it intensifies their use as mechanisms of political and social control rather than as arbiters for the rule of law. To a certain extent, as we argue throughout this book, criminal justice processes and criminalization campaigns have always lent themselves to the expression of political aims. Yet one is struck by the overt manner in which the criminal justice process has been marshaled to support the governance of hacking. In the Shadow Brokers case, Harold Thomas Martin III and Marcus Hutchins are both awaiting sentencing. While the verdict is still out on their fate, it is clear that their arrest and prosecution—despite any other legitimate aims it may serve—performs important governance work. Martin has pleaded guilty to exfiltrating 50 TB of information from the CIA, US Cyber Command, US DOD, and other agencies (Goldman 2017). His defense team argues that he suffers from a mental illness associated with document hoarding (Gerstein 2018). Whether or not this is a legitimate defense, he joins an expanding list of notorious individuals—Chelsea Manning, Edward Snowden, Jeremy Hammond, and Julian Assange—whose outlaw status signals an ongoing crackdown on digital dissent and transparency activism. Marcus Hutchins's ordeal in particular could have a chilling effect on others working in the gray area of cybersecurity, where teenage black hat resumes are routinely converted into ethical hacking success stories. Ethical volunteers in one moment can be cast aside and reframed as criminals with astonishing rapidity.

One way in which hacker states have expanded into the digital domain has been to channel official power through the court system: aggressive prosecution in multiple jurisdictions, high-stakes plea-bargain negotiations, and the threat of lengthy consecutive criminal sentences and protracted extradition processes loom large over the cyber landscape. As in the examples of Love and Hutchins, these hacking prosecutions extend the legal, juridical, and extraterritorial boundaries of the state. Some would argue that this criminalization approach comes at the expense of legitimate forms of political dissent, protest, assembly, and speech, eroding civil liberties and the rule of law (Sauter 2014).

Software Vulnerabilities

Ethical hacking as a business is flourishing, and with it the trade in software vulnerabilities. While the cliché is that what is good for American business is good for America, and while critical academics have grown conditioned to think that a neoliberal cabal conjoins American business and regulators, one topic where this is challenged concerns the software vulnerabilities state security services discover and hoard. The story of the Shadow Brokers begins with an undisclosed vulnerability in the Microsoft operating system. These little-known vulnerabilities give the NSA an advantage in offensive espionage operations. But the bugs are weaknesses that affect not only NSA targets and potential criminals but everyone else using the software.

Consider, for example, that Microsoft Windows is the operating system currently running on 88 percent of computers and laptops. Although it is difficult to map how many PCs and laptops are in use globally, we know that the number of computers in use worldwide surpassed 1 billion in 2008 and that this figure was predicted to double in 2014 or 2016. So conservatively, and using 2 billion as a working estimate, 88 percent works out to 1.76 billion computers running a Windows operating system. At risk of contagion by the WannaCry bug were all Windows operating systems that were not running Windows 10. That represents about 60 percent of Windows' market share and, using the above estimates, translates to roughly 1.2 billion computers worldwide. The lion's share of these computers were patched if they had automatic updates enabled, and if not, they could have downloaded the update in the two months prior to the release. Yet what is also important to underscore here is that although XP was one of the most vulnerable operating systems to the bug, more than 90 percent of the computers affected were running the still-supported Windows 7. Clearly many users did not have automatic updates enabled or did not understand the difference between this threat and the cascade of near-weekly security updates that our networked devices increasingly need to function securely.

It is impossible to have software weaknesses that enable surveillance while having secure software. Some have argued that government agencies should always report vulnerabilities to vendors (Doctorow 2014; Clarke and Swire 2014). And the question of why technical solutions (such as legally mandating that dual-factor authorization protocols be the default setting for passwords) continue to be so elusive has been a long-running source of bafflement in the computer security community. The question is not whether states should protect their citizens through the use of hacking technologies. To the extent that some states adopt an aggressive posture in using these technologies, others must protect themselves and have the means for self-defense. Yet as the Shadow Brokers story illustrates, the use of vulnerabilities in one state domain (e.g., in the dark state) by definition generates insecurities in other state domains that are poorly understood and for which contingency and escalation models are woefully underdeveloped. This fact generates global insecurity on an apocalyptic scale.

Ethical Hacking

The Shadow Brokers exist in that space between state hackers, cyber criminals, transparency hacktivists, and cyber-war entrepreneurs. The market for their services empowers the market for vulnerabilities, zero-day exploits, and other tools of state cyber power. This market creates a need for cyber mercenaries, wherein the distinctions between explicit and implicit forms of state-sponsored hacking are often intentionally blurred. As the American military has long understood (Scahill 2008), there are several advantages of having a private military force unaccountable to government and opaque from the public. The privatization of cybersecurity unleashes market forces and the profit motive into the development of new methods and software for cyber espionage.

Consider Hacking Team, the Italian surveillance technology company that builds and retails tools for governments, some of them authoritarian. Hacking Team is an equal opportunity privateer, providing surveillance tools to the governments of Egypt, Italy, Russia, Ethiopia, Bahrain, and Sudan. Documents hacked from the company show that their business dealings extend to a host of countries with a questionable record on human rights and online privacy, including Azerbaijan, Morocco, United Arab Emirates, and Kazakhstan (Weissman 2015). Although they have been dubbed the "enemies of the internet" (Moini, Ismail, and Vialle 2015), Hacking Team's business thrives in a market where building, customizing, and selling penetration suites, surveillance platforms, and exploit frameworks to dictators is a legitimate business practice. Hacking Team's chief crime from this perspective is selling its wares to the wrong state—not necessarily what it was actually selling. Some might argue that this market-driven module of contractual exfiltration, which brings the private and public sectors together in a tight embrace, furthers a secret conclave that systematically subverts the entire notion of the state as a public authority, an entity whose legitimacy is bound up with questions of accountability. In this way, instead of encouraging the development of ethical hacking, state hacking may be seen to incentivize unethical hacking.

State Hacking, Democracy, and Digital Citizenship

Some have argued that hacking threatens democracy. It is not just about tampering, information warfare, or influence campaigns, but it is also about the very physical infrastructures and complex systems responsible for everything from healthcare to tallying votes. In the 2016 US presidential elections, Russian hackers targeted the electronic voting systems of more than one hundred local elections (Fessler 2017; Cole et al. 2017). Even when the tampering is not successful or when damning information is not exfiltrated, the suspicion generated by the discovery of malicious code (or reports of systems penetration) speaks to a new conspiratorial and anxious politics, in which the question of democratic legitimacy is left open and unanswered.

Democracies are certainly not perfect institutions, and we do not here want to advance the notion that as a political system, it is without faults. Indeed, one central point we make in chapter 3 speaks precisely to the structural incapacity of bicameral, deliberative legislatures to keep pace with the acceleration of social, political, and technological change. In fact, this disjuncture represents one important precondition that enables state hacking to thrive. Yet what is rapidly vanishing in high breach societies (perhaps even before it has fully materialized) is the notion that we can be digital citizens—with a range of rights and responsibilities translated for the networked age. Citizenship is an ambivalent concept, both valued in debates about nationalism and migration and debased in a postmodern world skeptical about the validity of formerly powerful institutions such as the state, labor unions, and the family. As individuals align more with political tribes, subcultures, work cultures, causes, and other niche politics, our digital practices have contributed to the fragmentation of institutions and the traditional concepts that undergird them like citizenship.

The attraction of fast and free social media has created billion-dollar technology companies soliciting and retailing the personal information of users to advertisers. This form of "surveillance capitalism" (Zuboff 2015) also has a powerful state component: state security agencies quickly learned to augment their data collection activities through collaborating with technology industries. Yet the fragmentation of the individual from public communities into difficult to recognize microtribes has also posed a problem for surveillance practices. In this sense, the development of digital surveillance and hacking practices gives the state new abilities to refilter the population into categories for monitoring and—ultimately—control (Hintz, Dencik, Wahl-Jorgensen 2017, 733). Here, security is an excuse for the "quiet expansion and adoption of offensive information warfare capabilities by states" (Deibert 2003, 518). Digital citizenship involves the ability "for political subjects to make rights claims about how their digital lives are configured, regulated and organized by dispersed arrangements of numerous people and things such as corporations and states but also software and devices as well as people such as programmers and regulators" (Isin and Ruppert 2015, 5).

State hacking erodes digital citizenship, which requires the "security of (and trust in) infrastructure, an enabling policy framework, freedom to enact citizenship through expression and protest, knowledge of characteristics of the infrastructure and its affordances, and informed consent" (Wahl-Jorgensen, Bennett, and Taylor 2017, 3). Instead, state hacking requires vulnerabilities in consumer software, which it encourages, fails to disclose, and exploits. For example, the NSA engineered backdoors into cryptographic standards, allowing them to guess passwords and decrypt messages (Rogers and Eden 2017, 807). These efforts, in league with the hacking of citizens and feeble consumer protection regulations of technology industries, makes for a state of insecurity, antithetical to the stable conditions necessary for digital citizenship to arise—let alone thrive. Where digital citizenship requires fearless debate, passive surveillance, and active recognizance by governments, it makes internet users more frightened, compliant, and wary of digital expression. Despite this lack of security, governments do not miss an opportunity to discursively capitalize on the fear of hackers and cyber war to expand their surveillance powers. Truncated transparency over select government programs is the feeble trade-off as the state assumes more power over digital citizens (Birchall 2016, 152). Digital citizenship declines as a result.

After Hacker States

Those who are concerned about a future internet dominated by hacker states are not alone. Protest, refusal, obfuscation, and regulation are all legitimate and important activities for those worried about the repercussions of state hacking on the self, society, and democracy. Some protests did follow the Snowden revelations, and some governments did seek (however ineffectually) to regulate state surveillance and hacking practices. Some have called for the breakup of the NSA (Schneier 2014), and the sanctions on Russia for hacking the 2016 US election have begun to target the companies and individuals involved but have thus far been inconsequential (Chiacu 2018). Yet no groundswell of protest or grassroots activity has emerged to challenge state hacking, signaling perhaps "ambivalence, confusion, and lack of knowledge about not just the operations of digital surveillance but also what can actually be done about them" (Dencik and Cable 2017, 777).

Others have traded the prospect of digital citizenship—the rights to liberal values online—(Isin and Ruppert 2015) for different forms of "surveillance realism" (Dencik 2015), the belief that state hacking and surveillance is permanent and perhaps necessary. From this "realist" point of view, the internet is a medium that supports a wide spectrum of serious and toxic threats—internet bullies, misogynist trolls, and hate speech, but also cybercriminals and terrorists—and the state must work in the shadows to keep citizens safe. For many, curbing digital civil liberties and allowing some measure of state monitoring and tracking is a legitimate trade-off for the state's protective mantle. Media systems may reinforce this view since mainstream newspapers tend to normalize surveillance while deemphasizing the loss of digital civil liberties (Wahl-Jorgensen, Bennett, and Taylor 2017, 19).

Against this "realism," some have sought more structured and socially grounded solutions. For example, Hintz, Dencik, and Wahl-Jorgensen have called for "self-determination in a data field environment, provided by secure infrastructure, an enabling regulatory environment, adequate public knowledge, and an informed use of relevant platforms and applications" (2017, 735). Yet the centralized and monopolized social media platforms that are best poised to support this also seem resistant to this form of self-determination. State-harbored software vulnerabilities make security difficult, and Silicon Valley remains largely unregulated. Botnet fabrication continues on an industrial scale, and shallow polemics dominate networked public spheres. All the while, technology companies and their proprietary algorithms continue to shape more and more of our collective environment, even as much of what they are doing remains shrouded in trade secret. Poor, politicized, marginalized, differently gendered, and ethnic communities remain the first and worst hit in high breach societies.

Laws of Digitalization

Computational power grows daily, as does the geographic scope and infrastructural penetration of the internet—not just PCs and mobile devices but increasingly everyday objects and things—a set of developments that pose new questions of scale: as networks multiply, thicken, and become denser, so too do the data that are exchanged within them. Indeed, the internet is now so deeply embedded in all facets of life, culture, and even nature that it is difficult to conceive how a social movement or national regulation directed at a single technology company or government agency, or the forced transparency of the dark state, could solve the potential harms associated with the hacker state. State hacking will continue as an alternative to and augmentation of traditional conflict; hacktivism, small state hacking, and for-profit "ethical hacking" will as well. Extreme technological accidents—perhaps on a scale more pronounced than the WannaCry worm and its deviations—will continue to sporadically affect global communities, and cyber attacks will increasingly carry kinetic potential (e.g., the weaponized Stuxnet virus designed by the United States and Israel to shut down the Natanz nuclear facility in Iran).

Some have argued that this emergent order could be addressed or at least regulated through international legislation, perhaps even through a nonproliferation agreement akin to what was pursued for nuclear weapons. In November 2018, French president Emmanuel Macron announced that Google, Facebook, Microsoft, and IBM, along with fifty nations, one-hundred and thirty corporations and groups, as well as ninety nonprofits and universities, had signed the "Paris Call for Trust and Security in Cyberspace" (Matsakis 2018). The initiative's signatories pledge to work together toward the realization of nine principles that include the coordination and responsible disclosure of vulnerabilities as well as the disavowal of election tampering and "hack back" retaliatory strikes for state hacking incursions. Even though the initiative is a largely symbolic and diplomatic effort (and hence has no legal standing), it is notable that the most active hacker states (the United States, Russia, China, Iran, Israel, North Korea) all refused to sign it. This state of affairs undercuts whatever motivation small and large states, democratic and authoritarian alike, might have to sign an act with legal teeth that would limit these new capacities. Moreover, such an act would have no effect on limiting hacktivism, criminal hacking, and hacking for profit.

In another sense, the current state of "unpeace" (Kello 2017) among hacker states is likely so visible and prominent precisely because we are living through a protracted anomic phase, a transitional moment in the geopolitical order when humans are still the main operators behind these machines. Yet this situation is rapidly vanishing. The developmental curve of machine learning will eventually lead to some form of artificially intelligent machines, and one of the important areas this shift to automation will transform is the terrain of state hacking. To guide the development of AI in a collaborative and generative direction, some, including the likes of engineer Elon Musk (Dowd 2017) and statesman Henry Kissinger (2018), have proposed that now is the time for an international treaty to regulate AI, not some date in the future.

Fifty years ago, world governments agreed to a Treaty on the Non-Proliferation of Nuclear Weapons, and some have argued that it provides a working template for limiting the weaponization of computational power. For example, at the time, nations without nuclear weapons agreed not to acquire them, and nuclear states mutually agreed to significantly reduce their existing arsenals. The irony of the above situation is that what is needed to avoid the larger problems associated with state hacking is more activity on the part of states themselves, greater partnerships with the corporate and technological sectors, and significantly more state regulation. In lieu of such a state of affairs, and by way of summation, we want to focus on the technological innovations that brought us to the hacker state and prospect what the future might hold for a world following this path.

One goal of this book has been to integrate literature on the political science of the state, theories from STS, and specific accounts of hacker practice and hacker lives. Such an account would be incomplete without a consideration of the material, technological trajectories that form both the background conditions for this book and the directions of future travel. Throughout this volume, we have argued that the rise of the hacker state is dependent on not only the proliferation of networks in society but also state projects to control how others use those networks. We now want to discuss this state-hacker complex in terms of networked technological innovation and digitalization.

Digitalization refers to how the specific affordances of bit-based media change culture. Before the bitification of communication, information was coded in language and text, in bodily movement and sounds. It was extended beyond the body through these same texts but also through books, fliers, totems, flags, smoke, and flashes of light. With electricity, wires, and control of the electromagnetic spectrum came new communication technologies, such as Morse code, telegraphs, telephones, radio, and television. Finally, binary code brought us a new form of information compression within which all other forms of media could be encoded, decoded, and resituated. This process of digital remediation—remaking the old in the form of the new—paired with the proliferation of networks and affordable and easy-to-use media production technologies contributed to the present moment of information overload. This has produced what Andrew Chadwick (2013) calls a hybrid media system, wherein old and new platforms, as well as the discursive forms associated with them, collapse. Since the first decade of this century, in terms of our collective cultures, digitalization has made media more accessible, more excessive, and infinitely more malleable. But this process has also resulted in a manifold increase across various indices of vulnerability and precarity.

Although some have argued that digitalization is largely a beneficial process, others have been warier of the unintended effects this process has generated in its collision with established forms of social and economic organization. These critics might cite the ongoing shift of human labor to more automated forms, the rise of decision-making software and resulting eclipse of human judgment, and the increasing ubiquity of predictive policing, but also the rise to prominence of the self and its cult. This list is certainly not exhaustive. Indeed, the scope of change is as difficult to quantify as the scale of the data that support and further it. Consider just video and visual culture. Five-hundred hours of content are uploaded to YouTube every minute. Three-hundred and fifty million photos are uploaded to Facebook every day. More than three trillion photos have been taken in human history. Media scholar Mark Andrejevic (2013) argues that this era of big data inevitably leads to an infoglut: a world in which truth and comprehension are increasingly evanescent. In this book we focus on states and their struggle to capitalize and remain relevant in the context of these changes, but other institutions—consider the publishing, music, education, and retail sectors—have also faced a protracted period of adaptation.

In this context it is crucial to revisit three mathematical laws of digitalization that together help us better understand how we got here and where we are going. First, by digitalization, we refer to how information and meaning are created with computers. The 1949 work of mathematician Claude Shannon (Shannon and Weaver 1949) is an important touchstone because it helps us understand the problem of big data and why we struggle to make meaning in the contemporary period. According to Shannon's Law, the emergence of information, or of signals and symbols we can understand, out of noise relies on how much information any system can take. And from this point of view, digitalization involves a quantum step up in the amount of noise in circulation, straining the capacity of existent systems to keep pace and identify signals. Indeed, developers today are focused less on producing artificial intelligence than they are on developing computer learning—that is, providing contexts where software can teach itself to solve problems and identify signals within noise.

States practiced signals intelligence for most of the twentieth century, and the contemporary period has only increased the need to differentiate signals from noise. Yet it has also (in part because of state hacking) made that process significantly more difficult. Encryption and other modes of interference and jamming continue to proliferate, and national intranets remain significant challenges for foreign surveillance. More broadly, the available modes of digital rejection—voluntarily opting out, going on technological retreats, engaging in digital detoxes, selective refusal, evasion, deliberate ambiguity, confusion, and providing misleading personal information—transform the generation of noise into a widely available strategy of resistance (Brunton and Nissenbaum 2015; Fish 2017).

States have embraced the potential of computer learning (whether or not it will lead to AI) because the automation of data collection and surveillance functions holds the potential to transcend the limited capacity of the human mind for pattern analysis. Although computer learning can leverage the scale of data routinely collected into a strategic advantage, its most important application may be in the promise of swifter and less fallible intrusion-detection systems. Monitoring frameworks that can identify a hacking breach when it occurs (rather than years later) and automatically respond to the incursion in machine time are clearly not far away. Neither are questions about the possibility of automatic escalation and the capacity of human timely intervention in the context of a runaway chain of events.

An important component in the above scenario is the growth in raw programming power. Thus by digitalization, we also want to reference ongoing advances in programming. Moore's Law is named after Gordon Moore, a semiconductor researcher who predicted in 1965 that programming power would double every year (Moore 1965). The drive for superior processing power is already a core resource of big-data analytics and pattern-recognition platforms. Yet as networks become denser with data, people, and things—and grow more sophisticated with computer learning and artificial intelligence—the impact of superior processing power will gain a different order of amplification. In the future this will involve not just the power to know, persuade, and nudge human users but will include their multiple mechanized and automated appendages (e.g., robotics, autonomous vehicles, and drones).

Already, this power is not equally distributed. In fact, there are only three categories of institutions that currently have access to quantum-level computing power: states, technology corporations, and the ultrarich, who can rent advanced computing services. States are using and will continue to use their superior processing power to augment hacking, surveillance, and disruption activities. Large technology conglomerates are developing this computational power for not altogether different ends: some future form of surveillance capitalism whereby human-generated information is amassed, collated, and retailed to other companies to generate targeted advertising or political advertisements. Here, monitoring criminal and terrorist activity, thwarting cyber incursions and disruption campaigns, but also the nearly endless monetization potential of more and more information, generates a world of decreasing privacy and increasing vulnerability. States and technology companies both benefit from advancing processing power as well as the expansion of the internet itself.

A final way we want to understand digitalization is with reference to the growth and uneven distribution of information infrastructures and the global asymmetries this situation generates. Metcalfe's Law is named after Robert Metcalfe, an electrical engineer and the inventor of ethernet. According to Metcalfe (2013), the usefulness of a network increases in proportion to the links that are generated among its users. The more users a network has, the better that network is for its users—it helps them find like-minded individuals, more diverse information sources, and other things that make networks beneficial. It is instructive to consider Metcalf's Law in relation to the global internet. Digitalization has resulted in the expansion of information infrastructure in some regions and for some people— consider the geography of undersea fiber-optic cables—much more so than others. And while mobile data is becoming more widespread, control over these networks is an undeniable source of power for infrastructure owners.

In the contemporary period, the global information infrastructure has continued to expand under the sea and with new data centers around the world. This infrastructural growth has renewed questions of technological equity, digital literacy, and the problem of how to apply technology in meaningful ways because networked technology is unequally distributed. Yet nonnetworked locations are quickly vanishing, even as the problems posed by years of uneven technological development remain pressing and largely unaddressed. The slowing adoption rate of social media platforms such as Facebook in the United States and Europe (where individuals are increasingly wary of trading their data for access to services and platforms) has been matched by a renewed drive to sign up more users in other parts of the globe, and with it to expand information infrastructures. Predictably, for more technologically advanced states, the question of who will build these new networks and hence wield power and influence through them has become a pressing geopolitical and strategic concern (e.g., the current diplomatic standoff between the United States and China over the latter's proposals to build 5G mobile networks in countries the United States considers allies).

The three laws of digitalization signal a future of geographically expansive networks fused into the fabric of contemporary reality and dominated by automated tools and machine-learning algorithms, augmented by the advancement of raw computational power, to serve as gatekeepers, intrusion systems, and digital sentries. To dismiss this as science fiction is to turn a blind eye to the technological acceleration all around us. This is not technological determinism or a claim that technology becomes autonomous from human agency and intervention (Winner 1977). Following STS scholar Thomas Hughes, this study of the hacker state supports an argument that societies and technologies coevolve, and "after prolonged growth and consolidation, technological systems do not become autonomous but acquire momentum" (1987, 76). Media studies scholar Leah A. Lievrouw (2014, 12) calls Hughes's theory *technological momentum*, a theory of path dependency in which once set in motion, large-scale technological systems—Hughes's example was a massive riverwide dam—tend to draw to itself people, projects, energy, and capital, in the process reinforcing themselves. Technological momentum describes the powers of the global assemblage that is internet and how major players like states are drawn to attempt to control its aura, promise, and potency. The way the internet goes, at this point, so too does humanity.

Consider how the momentum of networks affects workers. Already, workers at some Amazon distribution hubs must dodge high-speed robots racing around the factory floor to collect items for delivery. And when these workers venture on the factory floor, they need handheld devices to navigate the "chaotic storage" system of its computationally more-efficient-than-human storage algorithm (Bridle 2018). And governments in the UK and the United States have nodded approvingly at Facebook's and Instagram's proposals to solve the intractable problems of time and scale—which take the form of misinformation, fake news, misogynist and racist posts, as well as socially harmful content—through the greater use of machine learning and automatization. The world of the near future involves bigger data, quantum programming power, and hegemonic control over the backbone of communication flows. Fritz Machlup in the 1960s and Daniel Bell in the 1970s called this world the information society, and Manuel Castells in the 1980s labeled it the networked society. Welcome home.

We have traveled fairly far down this path but we have yet to arrive. There will likely be less privacy and security, as well as more surveillance, intrusions, exfiltrations, and hacked institutions and elections ahead of us. Yet the chaotic field of state hacking we have documented in this transitional moment will likely be less visible as automation brings less transparency and shortens the window between attack and response. Indeed, rather than surrender to a bleak vision of a technologically determined and dystopic future, our best strategy is to think the future in the present. That is, we need to think seriously about how to support and develop mechanisms of algorithmic justice; about how the legal, criminal, and ethical systems we have come to rely on will govern human and nonhuman interactions; and how to narrow the gap between our rapid adoption of new technologies and our slow and imperfect understanding of how these technologies are reshaping the human condition.

Notes

Chapter 1

1. In 2017 the NSA collected 500 million phone messages despite targeting only 40 people (Dellinger 2018).

2. US v. Sterling, 818 F. Supp. 2d 945 (2011); US v. Sterling, 724 F.3d 482 (2013).

3. Lauri Love Extradition Hearing Transcript, day 2, June 29, 2016.

Chapter 2

1. For example, one area where states have sought to wield influence and extend their prerogative that we do not explore is the backbone of internet security provided by decentralized networks of internet governance.

2. As we discuss in chapter 4, this is a problem that continues to plague the contemporary period: Gary McKinnon, who hacked into ninety-seven US military and NASA computers between 2001 and 2002, gained entry because administrators had failed to change the default passwords.

3. US v. Ferizi, Sentencing Memo, p. 5 (E.D. Virginia 2016). https://www.justice.gov/opa/file/896326/download.

4. US v. Ferizi, No. 1:15mj515 (E.D. Virginia 2015). https://www.databreaches.net/wp-content/uploads/ferizi_complaint_final.pdf.

Chapter 3

1. The Afghan War logs included 77,000 secret and restricted reports authored between 2004 and 2010; the Iraq War logs comprised 391,832 reports written between 2004 and 2009; and the Cablegate leak involved 251,287 US diplomatic cables covering the period between 1966 and 2010.

2. For example, the Iraq and Afghanistan War logs, or "diaries," were made up of raw field reports (SIGACTS, describing "significant actions" that occurred in the field), written in terse shorthand and punctuated with military terminology, acronyms, and abbreviations. Indeed, the complexity, scale, and potential impact of the material dictated that collaborative publishing partnerships form to help make the data digestible by the public.

3. The reports can be released after the first forty-eight to seventy-two hours, because a unit will either no longer be in the area or the military will publicly release the information on its own (Manning 2013, 3, 30, 31).

4. In our usage, there is an important distinction between *news dumps* and *data dumps*. The former refers to the prepackaged and prewritten news stories about a leak or a data dump that appear all at once on the day the revelations are made public. The latter refers to the actual data or leaked material in its unredacted and original form. News dumps can have the same (or greater) impact as the actual release of the raw data and may hold back the data in part or in full.

5. Digital disobedience is clearly a larger category than transparency activism. Transparency is one component of the digital disobedience that LulzSec and particularly Anonymous engaged in, but they used other tactics, such as denial of service attacks, digital graffiti or website defacement, trolling, video, performance art, and others. A brief antisecurity movement flourished at the beginning of the century, targeting security professionals for disclosing exploits and zero days. It, like the new AntiSec, deployed tactics ranging from doxing to email spool dumps.

6. WikiLeaks (@WikiLeaks), Twitter, April 6, 2016, 9:39 a.m., https://twitter.com/wikileaks/status/717753531483168768.

7. Brian Acton (@brianacton), Twitter, March 20, 2018, 4:00 p.m., https://twitter.com/brianacton/status/976231995846963201?lang=en.

8. All quotations from the Zuckerberg testimony are drawn from the Washington Post (2018a, 2018b) transcripts of the hearings.

Chapter 4

1. McKinnon v. Secretary of State for the Home Department and Director of Public Prosecutions [2009] EWHC 2021 (Admin), 6–8.

2. McKinnon v. USA [2008] UKHL 59, 34.

3. McKinnon v. USA [2007] EWHC 762 (Admin), 41–48.

4. *McKinnon* [2007], 3–5.

5. *McKinnon* [2007], 3–5.

6. McKinnon v. Secretary of State [2009], 18.

7. McKinnon v. Secretary of State [2009], 25–26.

8. *McKinnon* [2007], 39.

9. Skeleton Argument of the Claimant, Lauri Love v. National Crime Agency [2016], Application No. 011503187270, 4.

10. Skeleton Argument of the Respondent, Lauri Love v. National Crime Agency [2016], Application No. 011503187270, p.5.

11. Author notes, opening statements in extradition hearing, USA v. Love [2016], June 28, 2016.

12. Author notes, opening statements in extradition hearing, *USA* [2016], June 28, 2016.

13. Author notes and Defense Counsel Transcript, Professor Simon Baron-Cohen testimony, day 1 of extradition hearing, *USA* [2016], June 28, 2016.

14. Author notes and Defense Counsel Transcript, Professor Simon Baron-Cohen testimony, day 1 of extradition hearing, *USA* [2016], June 28, 2016.

15. Author notes and Defense Counsel Transcript, Peter Caldwell on cross-examination of Professor Simon Baron-Cohen, day 1 of extradition hearing, *USA* [2016], June 28, 2016.

16. Author notes and Defense Counsel Transcript, Peter Caldwell on cross-examination of Professor Michael Kopelman, day 1 of extradition hearing, *USA* [2016], June 28, 2016.

17. Author notes and Defense Counsel Transcript, Professor Michael Kopelman on cross-examination by Peter Caldwell, day 1 of extradition hearing, *USA* [2016], June 28, 2016.

18. Author notes and Defense Counsel Transcript, Peter Caldwell on cross-examination of Lauri Love, day 2 of extradition hearing, *USA* [2016], June 29, 2016.

19. Author notes and Defense Counsel Transcript, Lauri Love testimony, day 2 of extradition hearing, *USA* [2016], June 29, 2016.

20. Criminal Complaint (Oxley Affidavit), US District Court of New Jersey, Mag. No. 13-8172, Case 2:13-cr-00712-SDW, USA v. Lauri Love, May 16, 2013 (filed).

21. Author notes and Defense Counsel Transcript, Lauri Love testimony, day 2 of extradition hearing, *USA* [2016], June 29, 2016.

22. See Turkmen v. Ashcroft, No. 1:02-cv-02307-JG-SMG (E.D. New York 2002).

23. Podius v. Federal Bureau of Prisons, No. 1:16-cv-06121 (E.D. New York 2016).

24. Love v. USA [2018] EWHC 172 (Admin), 107.

25. *Love* [2018], 32.

26. *Love* [2018], 119–120.

27. *Love* [2018], 104.

Chapter 5

1. Author notes and Defense Counsel Transcript, Lauri Love testimony, day 2 of extradition hearing, USA v. Love [2016], June 29, 2016.

2. Author notes and Defense Counsel Transcript, Lauri Love testimony, day 2 of extradition hearing, *USA* [2016], June 29, 2016.

3. US v. Paras Jha, No. 3:17-cr-00164 (D.C. N.J. 2017). https://www.justice.gov/usao -nj/press-release/file/1017616/download.

4. US v. Dalton Norman, No. 3:17-cr-00167-TMB (D.C. Alaska 2017). https://www .justice.gov/opa/press-release/file/1017591/download.

5. *Paras Jha.*

6. Criminal indictment, US v. Marcus Hutchins, No. 17-cr-00124 (E.D.C. Wisc. 2017). https://www.documentcloud.org/documents/3912520-Marcus-Hutchinson-Indict ment.html.

7. Matthew Hickey (HackerFantastic), interview by the authors, June 20, 2018.

8. Exploits are essentially code that can enter a targeted system by making use of a vulnerability, or "bug," in a code base. Payloads are code commands that are executed upon entry into a system through an exploit. In other words, if exploits are the code packages that allow one to take remote control of another system, payloads are what that penetration is designed to accomplish. Preloaded payloads include things like creating a new local administrator on the target machine, opening a shell (backdoor), and installing a VNC (virtual network computing) connection— essentially allowing the attacker to view and manipulate the mouse and keyboard of the target computer as if standing in front of it.

9. Script-based attack platforms existed before Metasploit. Two of the most prominent at the time were CORE Impact and Canvas, but licensing was expensive and hence the programs were only used by professionals or wealthier users. Researchers could also develop their own code by combining available exploits and payloads in the wild, but this was time consuming and required a high level of skill.

10. Chris Tarbell, interview by the authors, July 15, 2015.

11. Author notes, remarks of James Langevin, "DC to DEF CON" panel, DEF CON 25, August 26, 2017.

12. Maxigas, interview by the authors, November 21, 2018.

13. Hickey (HackerFantastic), interview.

Chapter 6

1. Criminal indictment, US v. Marcus Hutchins, No. 17-cr-00124 (E.D.C. Wisc. 2017). https://www.documentcloud.org/documents/3912520-Marcus-Hutchinson-Indictment.html.

References

Aas, Katja Franko. 2013. *Globalization and Crime*. London: Sage.

Abbate, Janet. 2000. *Inventing the Internet*. Cambridge, MA: MIT Press.

Abrams, Philip. (1977) 1988. "Notes on the Difficulty of Studying the State." *Journal of Historical Sociology* 1 (1): 58–89.

Ackerman, Spencer, Ewen MacAskill, and Alice Ross. 2015. "Junaid Hussain: British Hacker for Isis Believed Killed in US Air Strike." *Guardian*, August 27, 2015. https://www.theguardian.com/world/2015/aug/27/junaid-hussain-british-hacker-for-isis-believed-killed-in-us-airstrike.

AFP. 2014. "Obama Warns North Korea Over Sony Hack: 'We Will Respond.'" *Security Week*, December 19, 2014. https://www.securityweek.com/obama-warns-north-korea-over-sony-hack-we-will-respond.

Aid, Matthew M. 2013. "The NSA's New Code Breakers." *Foreign Policy*, October 15, 2013. http://foreignpolicy.com/2013/10/15/the-nsas-new-code-breakers/.

Allo, Awol, and Beza Tesfaye. 2015. "Spectacles of Illegality: Mapping Ethiopia's Show Trials." *African Identities* 13 (4): 1–18.

Allodi, Luca. 2017. "Economic Factors of Vulnerability Trade and Exploitation." In *Proceedings of the 2017 ACM SIGSAC Conference on Computer and Communications Security*, 1483–1499. New York: ACM. https://arxiv.org/pdf/1708.04866.pdf.

Almousa, Hamoud. 2015. "Cyber Caliphate Leader Junaid Hussain Is Killed." *Raqqa Is Being Silently Slaughtered*. August 26, 2015. https://www.raqqa-sl.com/en/?p=1349.

Andrejevic, Mark. 2013. *Infoglut: How Too Much Information Is Changing the Way We Think and Know*. London: Routledge.

Anonymous. 2011. "Shooting Sheriffs Saturday." Pastebin, August 5, 2011. https://pastebin.com/iKsuRkUj.

Antonakakis, Manos, Tim April, Michael Bailey, Matthew Bernhard, Elie Bursztein, Jaime Cochran, Michalis Kallitsis, Damian Menscher, Zakir Durumeric, Deepak Kumar, Chad Seaman, J. Alex Halderman, Luca Invernizzi, Chaz Lever, Zane Ma, Joshua Mason, Nick Sullivan, Kurt Thomas, and Yi Zhou. 2017. "Understanding Mirai Botnet." In *Proceedings of the 26th USENIX Security Symposium*, 1093–1110. Berkeley, CA: USENIX Association. https://www.doc.ic.ac.uk/~maffeis/331/mirai.pdf.

Arendt, Hannah. 1966. *Crisis of the Republic*. New York: Harcourt, Brace.

Arnell, Paula. 2013. "The Forum Bar to Extradition." *Scots Law Times* 24:169–171.

Assange, Julian. 2014. *When Google Met WikiLeaks*. New York: OR Books.

Atlantic Council. 2012. "Lessons from Our Cyber Past: The First Military Cyber Units." Transcript of Cyber Statecraft Initiative event held on March 5, 2012, at the Atlantic Council in Washington, DC. https://www.atlanticcouncil.org/?view=article &id=9088:transcript-lessons-from-our-cyber-past-the-first-military-cyber-units.

Aupers, Stef. 2012. "'Trust No One': Modernization, Paranoia and Conspiracy Culture." *European Journal of Communication* 27 (1): 22–34.

Baack, Stefan. 2011. "A New Style of News Reporting: WikiLeaks and Data-Driven Journalism." *Cyborg Subjects*. https://www.ssoar.info/ssoar/handle/document/40025.

Baack, Stefan. 2016. "What Big Data Leaks Tell Us about the Future of Journalism." *Internet Policy Review*, July 26, 2016. https://policyreview.info/articles/news/what-big -data-leaks-tell-us-about-future-journalism-and-its-past/413.

Baker, Scott. 2011. *A Review of the United Kingdom's Extradition Arrangements*. London: Home Office.

Ball, James. 2012. "LulzSec Court Papers Reveal Extensive FBI Co-Operation with Hackers." *Guardian*, March 6, 2012. https://www.theguardian.com/technology/2012/ mar/06/lulzsec-court-papers-sabu-anonymous.

Ball, James. 2014. "Angry Birds and 'Leaky' Phone Apps Targeted by NSA and GCHQ for User Data." *Guardian*, January 28, 2014. https://www.theguardian.com/ world/2014/jan/27/nsa-gchq-smartphone-app-angry-birds-personal-data.

Barber, Richard. 2001. "Hackers Profiled: Who Are They and What Are Their Motivations?" *Computer Fraud and Security* 2001 (2): 14–17.

Baumard, Philippe. 2017. *Cybersecurity in France*. Charm, Switzerland: Springer.

Becker, Jo, Adam Goldman, Michael S. Schmidt, and Matt Apuzzo. 2016. "N.S.A. Contractor Arrested in Possible New Theft of Secrets." *New York Times*, October 5, 2016. https://www.nytimes.com/2016/10/06/us/nsa-leak-booz-allen-hamilton.html.

Benkler, Yochai. 2011. "A Free Irresponsible Press: WikiLeaks and the Battle Over the Soul of the Networked Fourth Estate." *Harvard Civil Rights-Civil Liberties Law Review* 46 (2): 311–397.

Benkler, Yochai. 2013. "WikiLeaks and the Networked Fourth Estate." In *Beyond WikiLeaks: Implications for the Future of Communications, Journalism, and Society*, edited by Benedetta Brevini, Arne Hintz, and Patrick McCurdy, 11–34. New York: Palgrave Macmillan.

Bennett, Brian. 2019. "President Trump's Threats to Former Staffers Reveal a Problem at the White House." *Time*, February 1, 2019. http://time.com/5518135/donald-trump-non-disclosure-agreements/.

Beyer, Jessica. 2014. *Expect Us: Online Communities and Political Mobilization*. Oxford: Oxford University Press.

Bigo, Didier. 2000. "When Two Become One: Internal and External Securitisations in Europe." In *International Relations Theory and the Politics of European Integration: Power, Security, and Community*, edited by M. Kelstrup and M. Williams, 171–204. London: Routledge.

Birchall, Claire. 2016. "Managing Secrecy." *International Journal of Communication* 10:152–163.

Blake, Andrew. 2016. "Islamic State Hacker Sentenced for Assisting Terrorist Group with 'Kill List.'" *Washington Times*, September 24, 2016. https://www.washingtontimes.com/news/2016/sep/24/ardit-ferizi-hacker-who-aided-islamic-state-senten/.

Boellstorff, Tom. 2008. *Coming of Age in Second Life: An Anthropologist Explores the Virtually Human*. Princeton, NJ: Princeton University Press.

Borger, Julian. 2013. "NSA Files: Why the Guardian in London Destroyed Hard Drives of Leaked Files." *Guardian*, August 20, 2013. https://www.theguardian.com/world/2013/aug/20/nsa-snowden-files-drives-destroyed-london.

Bourdieu, Pierre. 1975. "The Specificity of the Scientific Field and the Social Conditions of the Progress of Reason." *Sociology of Science* 14 (5): 19–47.

Bourdieu, Pierre. 1990. *The Logic of Practice*. Cambridge: Polity.

Bourdieu, Pierre. 1994. "Rethinking the State: Genesis and Structure of the Bureaucratic Field." *Sociological Theory* 12 (1): 1–18.

Brenner, Bill. 2017. "WannaCry: The Ransomware Worm that Didn't Arrive on a Phishing Hook." *Naked Security*, Sophos Labs, May 17, 2017. https://nakedsecurity.sophos.com/2017/05/17/wannacry-the-ransomware-worm-that-didnt-arrive-on-a-phishing-hook/.

Bridle, James. 2018. *New Dark Age: Technology and the End of the Future*. New York: Verso.

Broadbridge, Sally. 2009. *The US/UK Extradition Treaty: Requests by US*. Research briefing, SN/HA/4980, July 31, 2009. London: House of Commons Library. http://researchbriefings.parliament.uk/ResearchBriefing/Summary/SN04980#fullreport.

Brownlee, Kimberley. 2016. "The Civil Disobedience of Edward Snowden: A Reply to William Scheuerman." *Philosophy and Social Criticism* 42 (10): 965–970.

Brunton, Finn, and Helen Nissenbaum. 2015. *Obfuscation: A User's Guide to Privacy and Protest*. Cambridge, MA: MIT Press.

Buchanan, Ben. 2017. *The Cybersecurity Dilemma: Hacking, Trust, and Fear between Nations*. New York: Oxford University Press.

Bumiller, Elisabeth. 2010. "Records Shows Doubts on '64 Vietnam Crisis." *New York Times*, July 14, 2010. http://www.nytimes.com/2010/07/15/world/asia/15vietnam.html.

Bump, Philip. 2018. "Roger Stone's Connection to WikiLeaks Just Got Murkier, Not Clearer." *Washington Post*, February 28, 2018. https://www.washingtonpost.com/politics/2019/02/28/roger-stones-connection-wikileaks-just-got-murkier-not-clearer.

Burning Glass. 2015. *Job Market Intelligence: Cybersecurity Jobs, 2015*. Boston: Burning Glass. https://www.burning-glass.com/wp-content/uploads/Cybersecurity_Jobs_Report_2015.pdf.

Cadwalladr, Carole. 2018. "'I Made Steve Bannon's Psychological Warfare Tool': Meet the Data War Whistleblower." *Guardian*, March 18, 2018. https://www.theguardian.com/news/2018/mar/17/data-war-whistleblower-christopher-wylie-faceook-nix-bannon-trump.

Cadwalladr, Carole, and Emma Graham-Harrison. 2018a. "How Cambridge Analytica Turned Facebook 'Likes' into a Lucrative Political Tool." *Guardian*, March 17, 2018.

Cadwalladr, Carole, and Emma Graham-Harrison. 2018b. "Revealed: 50 Million Facebook Profiles Harvested for Cambridge Analytica in Major Data Breach." *Guardian*, March 17, 2018.

Callon, Michel. 1984. "Some Elements of a Sociology of Translation: Domestication of the Scallops and the Fishermen of St. Brieuc Bay." *Sociological Review* 32 (1): 196–233.

Carlin, John P., and Garrett M. Graff. 2018. *Dawn of the Code War: America's Battle Against Russia, China, and the Rising Global Cyber Threat*. New York: Public Affairs.

Carroll, Patrick. 2006. *Science, Culture, and Modern State Formation*. Berkeley: University of California Press.

Carroll, Patrick. 2009. "Articulating Theories of States and State Formation." *Journal of Historical Sociology* 22:553–603.

Carroll, Patrick. 2012. "Water and Technoscientific State Formation in California." *Social Studies of Science* 42 (4): 489–516.

Castells, Manuel. 2000. "Grassrooting the Space of Flows." In *Cities in the Telecommunications Age: The Fracturing of Geographies*, edited by James O. Wheeler, Yuko Aoyama, and Barney L. Warf, 18–30. London: Routledge.

Castells, Manuel, and Matthew Carnoy. 2001. "Globalization, the Knowledge Society and the Network State: Poulantzas at the Millennium." *Global Networks* 1 (1): 1–18.

Center for Cyber Safety and Education. 2017. *2017 Global Information Security Workforce Study.* Center for Cyber Safety and Education. https://www.isc2.org/-/media/B7E003F79E1D4043A0E74A57D5B6F33E.ashx.

Celikates, Robin. 2016. "Rethinking Civil Disobedience as a Practice of Contestation—Beyond the Liberal Paradigm." *Constellations Journal* 23 (1): 37–45.

Chadwick, Andrew. 2013. *The Hybrid Media System: Politics and Power.* New York: Oxford University Press.

Chatterjee, Pratap. 2012. "WikiLeaks' Stratfor Dump Lifts Lid on Intelligence-Industrial Complex." *Guardian*, February 28, 2012. https://www.theguardian.com/commentisfree/cifamerica/2012/feb/28/wikileaks-intelligence-industrial-complex.

Chellel, Kit. 2015. "U.K. Cops Are Trying to Scare Teen Hackers with House Calls." *Bloomberg Businessweek*, December 10, 2015. https://www.bloomberg.com/news/articles/2015-12-10/u-k-cops-are-trying-to-scare-teen-hackers-with-house-calls.

Cherry, Miriam A. 2016. "Beyond Misclassification: The Digital Transformation of Work." *Comparative Labour Law and Policy Journal* 37 (3): 577–603.

Chiacu, Doina. 2018. "U.S. Sanctions Russians over Military, Intelligence Hacking." *Reuters*, June 11, 2018. https://www.reuters.com/article/us-usa-russia-sanctions/u-s-sanctions-russians-over-military-intelligence-hacking-idUSKBN1J71T5.

Clarke, Richard, and Peter Swire. 2014. "The NSA Shouldn't Stockpile Web Glitches." *Daily Beast*, April 18, 2014. https://www.thedailybeast.com/the-nsa-shouldnt-stockpile-web-glitches.

Cohen, Jean L., and Andrew Arato. 1999. *Civil Society and Political Theory.* Cambridge, MA: MIT Press.

Cohen, Julie. 2007. "Cyberspace as/and Space." *Columbia Law Review* 107 (1): 210–256.

Cohen, Stanley. (1972) 2002. *Folk Devils and Moral Panics: The Creation of the Mods and Rockers.* London: Routledge.

Coker, Margaret, Eric Schmitt, and Rukmini Callimachi. 2017. "With Loss of Its Caliphate, ISIS May Return to Guerrilla Roots." *New York Times*, October 18, 2017. https://www.nytimes.com/2017/10/18/world/middleeast/islamic-state-territory -attacks.html.

Cole, Matthew, Richard Esposito, Sam Biddle, and Ryan Grim. 2017. "Top-Secret NSA Report Details Russian Hacking Effort Days before 2016 Election." *Intercept,* June 5, 2017. https://theintercept.com/2017/06/05/top-secret-nsa-report-details -russian-hacking-effort-days-before-2016-election/.

Coleman, E. Gabriella. 2010. "The Hacker Conference: A Ritual Condensation and Celebration of a Lifeworld." *Anthropological Quarterly* 83 (1): 47–72.

Coleman, E. Gabriella. 2013a. "Anonymous and the Politics of Leaking." In *Beyond WikiLeaks: Implications for the Future of Communications, Journalism, and Society*, edited by Benedetta Brevini, Arne Hintz, and Patrick McCurdy, 209–228. New York: Palgrave Macmillan.

Coleman, E. Gabriella. 2013b. *Coding Freedom: The Ethics and Aesthetics of Hacking*. Princeton, Oxford: Princeton University Press.

Coleman, E. Gabriella. 2014. *Hacker, Hoaxer, Whistleblower, Spy: The Many Faces of Anonymous*. London: Verso.

Coleman, E. Gabriella. 2015. *Hacker, Hoaxer, Whistleblower, Spy: The Many Faces of Anonymous*. London: Verso.

Connell, Michael, and Sarah Vogler. 2017. *Russia's Approach to Cyber Warfare*. CNA Analysis and Solutions, March 2017. https://www.cna.org/CNA_files/PDF/DOP-2016 -U-014231-1Rev.pdf.

Connolly, William E. 2009. "Speed, Concentric Cultures and Cosmopolitanism." In *High-Speed Society: Social Acceleration, Power, and Modernity*, edited by Hartmut Rosa and William Scheuerman, 261–286. University Park: Pennsylvania State University.

Connor, J. D. 2015. "The Sony Hack: Data and Decision in the Contemporary Studio." *Media Industries* 2 (2): 42–58.

Cox, Joseph. 2015. "The FBI Spent $775K on Hacking Team's Spy Tools Since 2011." *Wired*, July 6, 2015. https://www.wired.com/2015/07/fbi-spent-775k-hacking -teams-spy-tools-since-2011/.

Cox, Joseph. 2016. "A Notorious Hacker Just Released a How-To Video Targeting Police." *Motherboard*, May 19, 2016. https://motherboard.vice.com/en_us/article/ vv77y9/phineas-fisher-sme.

Cox, Joseph. 2018. "New Tool Automatically Finds and Hacks Vulnerable Internet-Connected Devices." *Motherboard*, January 31, 2017. https://motherboard.vice.com/ en_us/article/xw4emj/autosploit-automated-hacking-tool.

Crosthwaite, Paul. 2013. "Accident." In *The Virilio Dictionary*, edited by John Armitage, 17–19. Edinburgh: Edinburgh University Press.

CVE Details. 2018. "Browse Vulnerabilities by Date." CVE Details. https://www.cve details.com/browse-by-date.php.

Cyber Security Challenge UK. 2017. "CyberSecurity Challenge UK Hosts UK's First Cyber Crime Intervention Workshop." Cyber Security Challenge UK, July 26, 2017. https://www.cybersecuritychallenge.org.uk/news-events/cyber-security -challenge-uk-hosts-uks-first-cyber-crime-intervention-workshop.

Davies, Hugh. 2013. "Catastrophe." In *The Virilio Dictionary*, edited by John Armitage, 42–45. Edinburgh: Edinburgh University Press.

Davis, Angela J. 2007. *Arbitrary Justice: The Power of the American Prosecutor*. New York: Oxford University Press.

Dean, Jodi. 2001. "Publicity's Secret." *Political Theory* 29 (5): 624–650.

Dean, Jodi. 2009. *Democracy and Other Neoliberal Fantasies: Communicative Capitalism and Left Politics*. Durham, NC: Duke University Press.

Dean, Jodi. 2010. *Blog Theory: Feedback and Capture in the Circuits of Drive*. Cambridge: Polity.

Dean, Mitchell. 1999. *Governmentality: Foucault, Power, and Social Structure*. Thousand Oaks, CA: Sage.

de Certeau, Michel. 1984. *The Practice of Everyday Life*. Berkeley: University of California Press.

Deibert, Ronald J. 2003. "Black Code: Censorship, Surveillance, and the Militarisation of Cyberspace." *Millennium: Journal of International Studies* 32:501–530.

Deibert, Ronald J., Rafal Rohozinski and Masashi Crete-Nishihata. 2012. "Cyclones in Cyberspace: Information Shaping and Denial in the 2008 Russia-Georgia War." *Security Dialogue* 43 (1): 3–24.

Dellinger, A. J. 2018. "The NSA Managed to Collect 500 Million US Call Records in 2017 Despite Targeting Just 40 People." *Gizmodo*, May 4, 2018. https://gizmodo .com/the-nsa-managed-to-collect-500-million-us-call-records-1825789394.

Dencik, Lina. 2015. "The Advent of Surveillance Realism." *Journalism, Media and Culture* (blog), January 23, 2015. http://www.jomec.co.uk/blog/the-advent-of -surveillance-realism-2/.

Dencik, Lina, and Jonathan Cable. 2017. "The Advent of Surveillance Realism: Public Opinion and Activist Responses to the Snowden Leaks." *International Journal of Communication* 11:763–781.

Department of Defense (DOD). 1992. *Conduct of the Persian Gulf War: Final Report to Congress*. Washington, DC: Pentagon.

de Stefano, Valerio. 2016. "The Rise of the 'Just-In-Time Workforce': On-Demand Work, Crowdwork, and Labor Protection in the 'Gig Economy.'" *Comparative Labor Law and Policy Journal* 37 (3): 471–505.

Doctorow, Cory. 2014. "If GCHQ Wants to Improve National Security It Must Fix Our Technology." *Guardian*, March 11, 2014. https://www.theguardian.com/technology/2014/mar/11/gchq-national-security-technology.

Doe, John. 2019. "John Doe's Manifesto." *Sueddeutsche Zeitung*. Accessed May 14, 2019. https://panamapapers.sueddeutsche.de/articles/572c897a5632a39742ed34ef/.

Domscheit-Berg, Daniel. 2011. *Inside WikiLeaks: My Time with Julian Assange at the World's Most Dangerous Website*. New York: Crown.

Donner, Frank J. 1980. *The Age of Surveillance: The Aims and Methods of America's Political Intelligence System*. New York: Knopf.

Dopp, Terence. 2018. "Islamic State Threat Endures after Defeats, US General Warns." *Bloomberg*, January 1, 2018. https://www.bloomberg.com/news/articles/2018-01-01/u-s-general-citing-gains-warns-islamic-state-still-a-danger.

Dowd, Maureen. 2017. "Elon Musk's Billion-Dollar Crusade to Stop the AI Apocalypse." *Vanity Fair*, April 2017. https://www.vanityfair.com/news/2017/03/elon-musk-billion-dollar-crusade-to-stop-ai-space-x.

Duffy, Helen. 2005. *The "War on Terror" and the Framework of International Law*. New York: Cambridge University Press.

Easton, Nina. 2013. "The CEO Who Caught the Chinese Spies Red-Handed." *Fortune*, July 8, 2013. http://fortune.com/2013/07/08/the-ceo-who-caught-the-chinese-spies-red-handed/.

Edgett, Sean. 2017. "Testimony of Sean J. Edgett, Acting General Counsel, Twitter, Inc." *Hearings on "Extremist Content and Russian Disinformation Online: Working with Tech to Find Solutions," before the Subcommittee on Crime and Terrorism*. United States Senate Committee on the Judiciary, October 21, 2017.

Electricity Information Sharing and Analysis Center (E-ISAC). 2016. *Analysis of the Cyber Attack on the Ukrainian Power Grid*. Defense Use Case. March 18, 2016. https://ics.sans.org/media/E-ISAC_SANS_Ukraine_DUC_5.pdf.

Ellsberg, Daniel. 2002. *Secrets: A Memoir of Vietnam and the Pentagon Papers*. New York: Penguin.

Engebretson, Patrick. 2011. *The Basics of Hacking and Penetration Testing: Ethical Hacking and Penetration Testing Made Easy*. New York: Elsevier.

Erikson, Kai T. 1966. *Wayward Puritans: A Study in the Sociology of Deviance.* New York: Wiley.

Fakhoury, Hanni. 2013. "How the Sentencing Guidelines Work against Defendants in CFAA Cases." Electronic Frontier Foundation, April 9, 2013. https://www.eff .org/deeplinks/2013/03/41-months-weev-understanding-how-sentencing-guidelines -work-cfaa-cases-0.

Feeley, Malcolm. 1992. *The Process Is the Punishment: Handling Cases in a Lower Criminal Court.* New York: Russell Sage.

Fessler, Pam. 2017. "Russian Cyberattack Targeted Elections Vendor Tied to Voting Day Disruptions." *National Public Radio,* August 10, 2017. https://www.npr .org/2017/08/10/542634370/russian-cyberattack-targeted-elections-vendor-tied-to -voting-day-disruptions?t=1561613608345.

Fidler, Mailyn. 2015. "Regulating the Zero-Day Vulnerability Trade: A Preliminary Analysis." *I/S: A Journal of Law and Policy for the Information Society* 11 (2). https:// papers.ssrn.com/sol3/papers.cfm?abstract_id=2706199.

FireEye. 2013. *Report: APT37 (Reaper): The Overlooked North Korean Actor* https:// www2.fireeye.com/rs/848-DID-242/images/rpt_APT37.pdf.

FireEye. 2016. *Redline Drawn: China Recalculates Its Use of Cyber Espionage.* Special report, June 2016. https://www.fireeye.com/content/dam/fireeye-www/current -threats/pdfs/rpt-china-espionage.pdf.

Fish, Adam R. 2017. "Technology Retreats and the Politics of Social Media." *Triple C: Communication, Capitalism and Critique* 15 (1): 355–369.

Fish, Adam R., and Luca Follis. 2016. "Gagged and Doxed: Hacktivism's Self-Incrimination Complex." *International Journal of Communication* 10:3281–3300.

Fisher, Max. 2012. "Stratfor Is a Joke and So Is WikiLeaks for Taking It Seriously." *Atlantic,* February 27, 2012. https://www.theatlantic.com/international/archive/2012/ 02/stratfor-is-a-joke-and-so-is-wikileaks-for-taking-it-seriously/253681/.

Follis, Luca. 2013a. "Of Friendless and Stained Men: Grafting Medieval Sanction onto Democratic Law." In *Comparative Law: Engaging Translation,* edited by Simone Glanert, 173–190. London: Routledge.

Follis, Luca. 2013b. "Resisting the Camp: Civil Death and the Practice of Sovereignty in New York State." *Law, Culture, and the Humanities* 9 (1): 91–113.

Follis, Luca, and Adam R. Fish. 2017. "Half-Lives of Hackers and the Shelf Life of Hacks." *Limn* 8: 46–49.

Fong, Glenn R. 2001. "ARPA Does Windows: The Defense Underpinning of the PC Revolution." *Business and Politics* 3 (3): 213–237.

Foucault, Michel. 1977. *Discipline and Punish: The Birth of the Prison*. New York: Pantheon Books.

Foucault, Michel. 1991. "Governmentality." In *The Foucault Effect: Studies in Governmentality*, edited by Graham Burchell, Colin Gordon, and Peter Miller, 87–104. Chicago: The University of Chicago Press.

Franceschi-Bicchierai, Lorenzo. 2016. "The NSA Data Leakers Might Be Faking Their Awful English to Deceive Us." *Motherboard*. https://motherboard.vice.com/en_us/article/gv5d93/the-shadow-brokers-nsa-leakers-linguistic-analysis.

Franceschi-Bicchierai, Lorenzo. 2017. "Newly Leaked Hacking Tools Were Worth $2 Million on the Gray Market." *Motherboard*, April 14, 2017. https://motherboard.vice.com/en_us/article/mgye4v/leaked-nsa-hacking-tools-were-worth-2-million.

Franceschi-Bicchierai, Lorenzo. 2018. "Hacking Team Is Still Alive Thanks to a Mysterious Investor From Saudi Arabia." *Motherboard*, January 31, 2018. https://motherboard.vice.com/en_us/article/8xvzyp/hacking-team-investor-saudi-arabia.

Frenkel, Sheera. 2017. "Hackers Find 'Ideal Testing Ground' for Attacks: Developing Countries." *New York Times*, July 2, 2017. https://www.nytimes.com/2017/07/02/technology/hackers-find-ideal-testing-ground-for-attacks-developing-countries.html.

Gadher, Dipesh. 2015. "British Hacker is No 3 on Pentagon 'Kill List.'" *Times* (London), August 2, 2015. https://www.thetimes.co.uk/article/british-hacker-is-no-3-on-pentagon-kill-list-6g95bfqwfnz.

Garfinkel, H. 1956. "Conditions of Successful Degradation Ceremonies." In *Sociological Theory: A Book of Readings*, edited by Lewis A. Coser and Bernard Rosenberg, 455–462. Long Grove, IL: Waveland Press.

Garland, David. 2001. *The Culture of Control: Crime and Social Order in Contemporary Society*. Chicago: University of Chicago Press.

Geller, Amanda. 2016. "The Process Is Still the Punishment: Low-Level Arrests in the Broken Windows Era." *Cardozo Law Review* 37:1025–1058.

Gerstein, Josh. 2018. "Ex-NSA Contractor Accused of Hoarding Classified Info to Plead Guilty." *Politico*, January 3, 2018. https://www.politico.com/story/2018/01/03/nsa-harold-martin-guilty-plea-322113.

Gieryn, Thomas F. 1983. "Boundary-Work and the Demarcation of Science from Non-Science: Strains and Interests in Professional Ideologies of Scientists." *American Sociological Review* 48 (6): 781–795.

Ginsburg, Faye. 1997. "'From Little Things, Big Things Grow': Indigenous Media and Cultural Activism." In *Between Resistance and Revolution: Counter Politics and Social*

Protest, edited by Richard D. Fox and Orin Starn, 118–144. Rutgers, NJ: Rutgers University Press.

Goffman, Alice. 2014. *On the Run: Fugitive Life in an American City.* New York: Picador Press.

Goffman, Erving. 1959. *The Presentation of Self in Everyday Life.* Garden City, NY: Doubleday.

Goffman, Erving. 1967. *Interaction Ritual: Essays on Face-to-Face Behavior.* Garden City, NY: Doubleday.

Goldman, Adam. 2017. "Government Contractor Indicted in Theft of Top-Secret Documents." *New York Times,* February 8, 2017. https://www.nytimes.com/2017/02/08/us/politics/harold-martin-nsa.html.

Goode, Erica. 2012. "Stronger Hand for Judges in the 'Bazaar' of Plea Deals." *New York Times,* March 22, 2012. http://www.nytimes.com/2012/03/23/us/stronger-hand-for-judges-after-rulings-on-plea-deals.html.

Goodin, Dan. 2015. "How 'Omnipotent' Hackers Tied to NSA Hid for 14 Years—and Were Found at Last." *Ars Technica,* February 16, 2015. https://arstechnica.com/information-technology/2015/02/how-omnipotent-hackers-tied-to-the-nsa-hid-for-14-years-and-were-found-at-last/.

Goodin, Dan. 2017a. "Mysterious Microsoft Patch Killed 0-Days Released by NSA-Leaking Shadow Brokers." *Ars Technica,* April 15, 2017. https://arstechnica.com/information-technology/2017/04/purported-shadow-brokers-0days-were-in-fact-killed-by-mysterious-patch/.

Goodin, Dan. 2017b. "NSA-Leaking Shadow Brokers Just Dumped Its Most Damaging Release Yet." *Ars Technica,* April 14, 2017. https://arstechnica.com/information-technology/2017/04/nsa-leaking-shadow-brokers-just-dumped-its-most-damaging-release-yet/.

Goodin, Dan. 2017c. "NSA-Leaking Shadow Brokers Lob Molotov Cocktail before Exiting World Stage." *Ars Technica,* January 12, 2017. https://arstechnica.com/information-technology/2017/01/nsa-leaking-shadow-brokers-lob-molotov-cocktail-before-exiting-world-stage/.

Goodwin, Bill. 2017. "Lauri Love: how Reformed Hackers Halted the WannaCry Virus." *Computer Weekly,* November 29, 2017. https://www.computerweekly.com/video/Laurie-Love-how-reformed-hackers-prevented-the-spread-of-NHS-malware.

Graff, Garrett M. 2017. "How a Dorm Room Minecraft Scam Brought Down the Internet." *Wired,* December 13, 2017. https://www.wired.com/story/mirai-botnet-minecraft-scam-brought-down-the-internet/.

Graham, Chris. 2017. "Cyber Attack Hits German Train Stations as Hackers Target Deutsche Bahn." *Telegraph*, May 13, 2017. https://www.telegraph.co.uk/news/2017/05/13/cyber-attack-hits-german-train-stations-hackers-target-deutsche/.

Graham, David A. 2018. "The Coincidence at the Heart of the Russia Hacking Scandal." *Atlantic Monthly*, July 13, 2018. https://www.theatlantic.com/politics/archive/2018/07/russia-hacking-trump-mueller/565157/.

Green, Kieran Richard. 2016. "People's War in Cyberspace: Using China's Civilian Economy in the Information Domain." *Military Cyber Affairs* 2 (1). https://scholarcommons.usf.edu/mca/vol2/iss1/5/.

Greenberg, Andy. 2016. "How Reporters Pulled Off the Panama Papers, the Biggest Leak in Whistleblower History." *Wired*, April 4, 2016. https://www.wired.com/2016/04/reporters-pulled-off-panama-papers-biggest-leak-whistleblower-history/.

Greenberg, Andy. 2017. "Petya Ransomware Epidemic May Be Spillover from Cyberwar." *Wired*, June 28, 2017. https://www.wired.com/story/petya-ransomware-ukraine/.

Greenemeier, Larry. 2006. "Is the Metasploit Hacking Tool Too Good?" *Information Week*, October 20, 2006. https://www.informationweek.com/is-the-metasploit-hacking-tool-too-good/d/d-id/1048120.

Greenwald, Glenn. 2014. "The U.S. Government's Secret Plans to Spy for American Corporations." *Intercept*, September 5, 2014. https://theintercept.com/2014/09/05/us-governments-plans-use-economic-espionage-benefit-american-corporations/.

Greenwald, Glenn. 2015. *No Place to Hide: Edward Snowden, the NSA, and the Surveillance State.* London: Penguin.

Greenwald, Glenn. 2016. "The Intercept Is Broadening Access to Snowden's Archive: Here's Why." *Intercept*, May 16, 2016. https://theintercept.com/2016/05/16/the-intercept-is-broadening-access-to-the-snowden-archive-heres-why/.

Gregory, Julia, and Niels Ladefoged. 2018. "Lauri Love Plans to Use 'Internet as a Force for Good.'" *Computer Weekly*, February 5, 2018. https://www.computerweekly.com/news/252434465/Lauri-Love-plans-to-use-internet-as-a-force-for-good.

Hackett, Robert. 2016. "China's Cyber Spying on the U.S. Has Drastically Changed." *Fortune*, June 25, 2016. http://fortune.com/2016/06/25/fireeye-mandia-china-hackers/.

Hafner, Katie, and Matthew Lyon. 1998. *Where Wizards Stay Up Late: The Origins of the Internet.* New York: Simon and Schuster.

Halbert, Debora. 1997. "Discourses of Danger and the Computer Hacker." *Information Society* 13 (4): 361–374.

Hall, Stuart, Charles Critcher, Tony Jefferson, John Clarke, and Brian Roberts. (1978) 2013. *Policing the Crisis: Mugging, the State, and Law and Order*. Basingstoke: Palgrave Macmillan.

Halpern, Micah. 2015. "Iran Flexes Its Power by Transporting Turkey to the Stone Age." *Observer*, April 22, 2015. https://observer.com/2015/04/iran-flexes-its-power-by-transporting-turkey-to-the-stone-ages/.

Hamburger, Tom, and Ellen Nakashima. 2016. "Clinton Campaign—And Some Cyber Experts—Say Russia Is Behind Email Release." *Washington Post*, July 24, 2016. https://www.washingtonpost.com/politics/clinton-campaign--and-some-cyber-experts--say-russia-is-behind-email-release/2016/07/24/5b5428e6-51a8-11e6-bbf5-957ad17b4385_story.html.

Hamilton, Martha M. 2015. "Whistleblower? Thief? Hero? Introducing the Source of the Data That Shook HSBC." *ICIJ*, February 8, 2015. https://www.icij.org/investigations/swiss-leaks/whistleblower-thief-hero-introducing-source-data-shook-hsbc/.

Hassan, Robert. 2008. "Network Speed and Democratic Politics." *World Futures* 64 (1): 3–21.

Hayden, Michael V. 2017. *Playing to the Edge: American Intelligence in the Age of Terror*. New York: Penguin.

Healey, Jason, ed. 2013. *A Fierce Domain: Conflicts in Cyberspace, 1986–2012*. Washington, DC: Atlantic Council.

Heard, Catherine. 2009. "A Brief Review of US-UK Extradition under the Extradition Act of 2003 from a Human Rights Perspective." *International Enforcement Law Reporter* 25:2–7.

Hedges, Chris. 2002. *War Is a Force that Gives Us Meaning*. New York: Anchor Books.

Henderson, Scott J. 2007. *The Dark Visitor: Inside the World of Chinese Hackers*. Self-published, Lulu. http://www.lulu.com/items/volume_62/2048000/2048958/4/print/2048958.pdf.

Henderson, Scott J. 2008. "Beijing's Rising Hacker Stars . . . How Does Mother China React?" *IO Sphere*, Fall, 25–30.

Herr, Trey, and Paul Rosenzweig. 2016. "Cyber Weapons and Export Control: Incorporating Dual Use with the PrEP Model." *Journal of National Security Law and Policy* 8:301–319.

Hersh, Seymour M. 1974. "Huge CIA Operation Reported in U.S. against Antiwar Forces, Other Dissidents in Nixon Years." *New York Times*, December 22, 1974. http://www.nytimes.com/1974/12/22/archives/huge-cia-operation-reported-in-u-s-against-antiwar-forces-other.html.

Hess, Amanda. 2017. "How Privacy Became a Commodity for the Rich and Power-ful." *New York Times Magazine*, May 9, 2017. https://www.nytimes.com/2017/05/09/magazine/how-privacy-became-a-commodity-for-the-rich-and-powerful.html.

Hintz, Arne, Lina Dencik, and Karin Wahl-Jorgensen. 2017. "Digital Citizenship and Surveillance Society." *International Journal of Communication* 11:731–739. http://ijoc.org/index.php/ijoc/article/view/5521/1929.

Holley, Peter. 2018. "Marriott: Hackers Accessed More Than 5 Million Passport Numbers during November's Massive Data Breach." *Washington Post*, January 4, 2018. https://www.washingtonpost.com/technology/2019/01/04/marriott-hackers-accessed-more-than-million-passport-numbers-during-novembers-massive-data-breach.

Honeynet Project. 2000. "Know Your Enemy: The Tools and Methodologies of the Script Kiddie." Honeynet Project, July 21, 2000. http://old.honeynet.org/papers/enemy/.

Hope, Christopher, and Con Coughlin. 2012. "Gary McKinnon: Eric Holder For-mally Complains to UK and Refuses to Take Theresa May's Calls." *Telegraph*, October 19, 2012.

Hopkins, Nick, and Helena Bengtsson. 2017. "What Are the Paradise Papers and What Do They Tell Us?" *Guardian*, November 5, 2017. https://www.theguardian.com/news/2017/nov/05/what-are-the-paradise-papers-and-what-do-they-tell-us.

House of Commons. 2012. *The US-UK Extradition Treaty*, vol. 1, *Report, Together with Formal Minutes, Oral, and Written Evidence*. London: Stationary Office.

Hughes, Thomas P. 1987. "The Evolution of Large Technical Systems." In *The Social Construction of Technological Systems: New Directions in the Sociology and History of Technology*, edited by Wiebe E. Bijker, Thomas P. Hughes, and Trevor Pitch, 51–82. Cambridge, MA: MIT Press.

Hulme, George V. 2012. "Metasploit Review: Ten Years Later, Are We Any More Secure?" *Search Security*, October 24, 2012. https://searchsecurity.techtarget.com/feature/Metasploit-Review-Ten-Years-Later-Are-We-Any-More-Secure.

Inkster, Nigel. 2016. *China's Cyber Power*. Abingdon: Routledge.

Intelligence and Security Committee (ISC). 2011. *Annual Report 2010–2011*. UK Parliament. London: Stationary Office. https://b1cba9b3-a-5e6631fd-s-sites.google groups.com/a/independent.gov.uk/isc/files/2010-2011_ISC_AR.pdf.

Intelligence and Security Committee (ISC). 2012. *Annual Report 2011–2012*. UK Parliament. London: Stationary Office. https://b1cba9b3-a-5e6631fd-s-sites.google groups.com/a/independent.gov.uk/isc/files/2011-2012_ISC_AR.pdf.

Intelligence and Security Committee (ISC). 2013. *Annual Report 2012–2013*. UK Parliament. London: Stationary Office. https://b1cba9b3-a-5e6631fd-s-sites.google groups.com/a/independent.gov.uk/isc/files/2012-2013_ISC_AR.pdf.

Intelligence and Security Committee (ISC). 2017. *Annual Report 2016–2017*. UK Parliament. London: Stationary Office. https://b1cba9b3-a-5e6631fd-s-sites.google groups.com/a/independent.gov.uk/isc/files/2016-2017_ISC_AR.pdf.

International Consortium of Investigative Journalists (ICIJ). 2015. "Whistleblower? Thief? Hero? Introducing the Source of the Data that Shook HSBC." *ICIJ*, February 8, 2015. https://www.icij.org/investigations/panama-papers/20160506-john-doe -statement/.

International Consortium of Investigative Journalists (ICIJ). 2016. "Panama Papers Source Offers Documents to Governments, Hints at More to Come." *ICIJ*, May 6, 2016. https://www.icij.org/investigations/panama-papers/20160506-john-doe-statement/.

International Consortium of Investigative Journalists (ICIJ). 2017. "About the Paradise Papers Investigation." *ICIJ*, November 5, 2017. https://www.icij.org/ investigations/paradise-papers/about/.

Isaac, Mike, and Daisuke Wakabayashi. 2017. "Russian Influence Reached 126 Million through Facebook Alone." *New York Times*, October 30, 2017.

ISACA. 2016. *State of Cybersecurity: Implications for 2016—An ISACA and RSA Conference Survey*. Rolling Meadows, IL: ISACA. https://www.isaca.org/cyber/Documents/ state-of-cybersecurity_res_eng_0316.pdf.

Isin, Engin, and Evelyn Ruppert. 2015. *Being Digital Citizens*. London: Rowman and Littlefield.

Jordan, Tim. 2008. "The Politics of Technology: Three Types of Hacktivism." In *Net Working/Networking Citizen Initiated Internet Politics*, edited by Häyhtiö Tapio and Jarmo Rinne, 254–280. Tampere, Finland: University of Tampere Press.

Jordan, Tim. 2009. "Hacking and Power: Social and Technological Determinism in the Digital Age." *First Monday* 14 (7). https://firstmonday.org/article/viewArticle/ 2417/2240.

Jordan, Tim. 2015. *Information Politics: Liberation and Exploitation in the Digital Society*. London: Pluto Press

Jordan, Tim. 2017. "A Genealogy of Hacking." *Convergence* 23 (5): 528–544.

Jordan, Tim, and Paul A. Taylor. 2004. *Hacktivism and Cyberwars: Rebels with a Cause?* London: Routledge.

Joyce, Patrick, and Chandra Mukerji. 2017. "The State of Things: State History and Theory Reconfigured." *Theory and Society* 46 (1): 1–19.

Joye, Christopher. 2013. "Transcript: Interview with former CIA, NSA Chief Michael V. Hayden." *Australian Financial Review*, July 19, 2013, https://genius.com/Michael-hayden-interview-regarding-edward-snowden-cyber-security-and-transparency-annotated.

Jue, Aaron, and Kellie Brownell. 2012. "Thanks for Supporting EFF in Las Vegas and Beyond!" Electronic Frontier Foundation, August 9, 2012. https://www.eff.org/deeplinks/2012/08/thanks-supporting-eff-las-vegas-and-beyond.

Kaplan, Frank. 2016. *Dark Territory: The Secret History of Cyber War*. New York: Simon and Schuster.

Kaspersky Lab. 2016. "The Equation Giveaway." *SecureList*, August 16, 2016. https://securelist.com/the-equation-giveaway/75812/.

Katz, Rita. 2016. "When ISIS Hackers Call You out by Name." *Motherboard*, June 14, 2016. https://motherboard.vice.com/en_us/article/ezpbyn/when-isis-calls-you-out-by-name.

Kean, Thomas H. 2004. *The 9/11 Commission Report: Final Report of the National Commission on Terrorist Attacks upon the United States*. New York: Norton.

Keenan, Jordan. 2013. "The Big Defcon Question: Would You Work for the NSA?" *Motherboard*, August 6, 2013. https://www.vice.com/en_us/article/3dd3dn/the-big-def-con-question-would-you-work-for-the-nsa.

Keller, Bill. 2011. "Dealing with Assange and the WikiLeaks Secrets." *New York Times*, January 26, 2011. https://www.nytimes.com/2011/01/30/magazine/30Wikileaks-t.html.

Kello, Lucas. 2017. *The Virtual Weapon and the International Order*. New Haven, CT: Yale University Press.

Kelty, Chris. 2008. *Two Bits: The Cultural Significance of Free Software and the Internet*. Durham, NC: Duke University Press.

Kerbaj, Richard, and Caroline Wheeler. 2017. "British Spy Chiefs Knew of FBI Sting on NHS Hack Attack Hero Marcus Hutchins." *Times* (London), August 20, 2017. https://www.thetimes.co.uk/article/british-spy-chiefs-knew-of-fbi-sting-on-nhs-hack-attack-hero-marcus-hutchins-hctlgbvrr.

Kerner, Sean Michael. 2005. "Windows 0-Day Helped by Open Source?" *Server Watch*, December 30, 2005. https://www.serverwatch.com/news/article.php/3574411/Windows-0Day-Exploit-Helped-by-Open-Source.htm.

Kerner, Sean Michael. 2017. "WannaCry Ransomware Worm Risk Continues as Exploit Lands in Metasploit." *eWeek*, May 18, 2017. http://www.eweek.com/security/wannacry-ransomware-worm-risk-continues-as-exploit-lands-in-metasploit.

Kerr, Orin S. 2016. "Trespass, Not Fraud: The Need for New Sentencing Guidelines in CFAA Cases." *George Washington Law Review* 84 (6): 1544–1567.

Khazan, Olga. 2013. "The Creepy, Long-Standing Practice of Undersea Cable Tapping." *Atlantic*, July 16, 2013. https://www.theatlantic.com/international/archive/2013/07/the-creepy-long-standing-practice-of-undersea-cable-tapping/277855/.

Kilday, Gregg. 2014. "Sony Hack Reportedly Includes 47,000 Social Security Numbers, Celebrity Data." *Hollywood Reporter*, December 4, 2014. https://www.hollywoodreporter.com/news/sony-hack-reportedly-includes-47000-754055.

Kissinger, Henry. 2018. "How the Enlightenment Ends." *Atlantic Monthly*, June 2018. https://www.theatlantic.com/magazine/archive/2018/06/henry-kissinger-ai-could-mean-the-end-of-human-history/559124/.

Klimburg, Alexander. 2017. *The Darkening Web: The War for Cyberspace*. New York: Penguin.

Kloc, Joe. 2014. "How Much Did Snowden Really Take? Not Even the NSA Really Knows." *Newsweek*, June 9, 2014. https://www.newsweek.com/how-much-did-snowden-take-not-even-nsa-really-knows-253940.

Kopfstein, Janus. 2012. "NSA Trolls for Talent at Def Con, the Nation's Largest Hacker Conference." *Verge*, August 1, 2012. https://www.theverge.com/2012/8/1/3199153/nsa-recruitment-controversy-defcon-hacker-conference.

Krebs, Brian. 2012. "Attackers Pounce on Zero-Day Java Exploit." *Krebs on Security*, August 27, 2012. https://krebsonsecurity.com/2012/08/attackers-pounce-on-zero-day-java-exploit/.

Krekel, Bryan. 2009. *Capability of the People's Republic of China to Conduct Cyber Warfare and Computer Network Exploitation*. McLean, VA: Northrop Grumman. https://nsarchive2.gwu.edu/NSAEBB/NSAEBB424/docs/Cyber-030.pdf.

Lacey, David. 2013. "Ditch the Triangle and Use More Technology." *David Laceys IT Security Blog*, January 20, 2013. https://www.computerweekly.com/blog/David-Laceys-IT-Security-Blog/Ditch-the-Triangle-and-use-more-technology.

Landler, Mark, and John Markoff. 2007. "Digital Fears Emerge after Data Siege in Estonia." *New York Times*, May 29, 2007. https://www.nytimes.com/2007/05/29/technology/29estonia.html.

Lapsley, Phil. 2013. *Exploding the Phone: The Untold Story of the Teenagers and Outlaws Who Hacked Ma Bell*. New York: Grove Press.

Lemert, Edwin H. 1951. *Social Pathology: A Systematic Approach to the Theory of Systematic Behavior*. New York: McGraw-Hill.

Lennon, Mike. 2014. "Hackers Used Sophisticated SMB Worm to Attack Sony." *Security Week*, December 19, 2014. https://www.securityweek.com/hackers-used-sophisticated-smb-worm-tool-attack-sony.

Levinson, Charles. 2014. "Comey: 'Grappling' with Hiring Policy Concerning Marijuana." *Wall Street Journal*, May 20, 2014. https://blogs.wsj.com/law/2014/05/20/director-comey-fbi-grappling-with-hiring-policy-concerning-marijuana/.

Levy, Steven. 2010. *Hackers: Heroes of the Computer Revolution*. Sebastpol, CA: O'Reilly Media.

Lewallen, Ann-Elise. 2003. "Strategic 'Indigeneity' and the Global Indigenous Women's Movement." *Michigan Feminist Studies* 17:105–130.

Lichtblau, Eric, and Noah Weiland. 2016. "Hacker Releases More Democratic Party Documents." *New York Times*, April 12, 2016. https://www.nytimes.com/2016/08/13/us/politics/democratic-party-documents-hack.html.

Lievrouw Leah A. 2014. "Materiality and Media in Communication and Technology Studies: An Unfinished Project." In *Media Technologies: Essays on Communication, Materiality, and Society*, edited by T. Gillespie, P. Boczkowski, and K. Foot, 21–51. Cambridge, MA: MIT Press.

LookingGlass Cyber Threat Intelligence Group. 2015. *Operation Armageddon: Cyber Espionage as a Strategic Component of Russian Modern Warfare*. Report CTIG-20150428-01. April 28, 2015. https://www.lookingglasscyber.com/wp-content/uploads/2015/08/Operation_Armageddon_Final.pdf.

Ludlow, Peter. 2013. "The Real War on Reality." *New York Times*, June 14, 2013. https://opinionator.blogs.nytimes.com/2013/06/14/the-real-war-on-reality/.

LulzSec. 2011. "Welcome to Operation Anti-Security." Pastebin, June 19, 2011. https://pastebin.com/9KyA0E5v.

Lynch, Tim. 2016. "Americans Are Bargaining Away Their Innocence." *Washington Post*, January 20, 2016.

Maass, Peter. 2018. "Reality Winner Has Been in Jail for a Year: Her Prosecution Is Unfair and Unprecedented." *Intercept*, June 3, 2018. https://theintercept.com/2018/06/03/reality-winner-nsa-paul-manafort/.

MacAskill, Ewen, Edward Snowden, and Daniel Ellsberg. 2018. "'Is Whistleblowing Worth Prison or a Life in Exile?': Edward Snowden talks to Daniel Ellsberg." *Guardian*, January 16, 2018. https://www.theguardian.com/world/2018/jan/16/is-whistleblowing-worth-prison-or-a-life-in-exile-edward-snowden-talks-to-daniel-ellsberg.

MacKinnon, Rebecca. 2012. *Consent of the Networked: The Worldwide Struggle for Internet Freedom*. New York: Basic Books.

MalwareTech. 2017. "How to Accidentally Stop a Global Cyber Attack." *Malware-Tech*, May 13, 2017. https://www.malwaretech.com/2017/05/how-to-accidentally-stop-a-global-cyber-attacks.html.

Mandiant. 2013. *APT1: Exposing One of China's Cyber Espionage Units*. https://www.fireeye.com/content/dam/fireeye-www/services/pdfs/mandiant-apt1-report.pdf.

Mann, Sylvia. 2017. "My Partner Lauri Love Could Be Saving the World from Cyber Attacks but Instead He Faces a 99-Year Prison Sentence." *Independent*, November 26, 2017. https://www.independent.co.uk/voices/lauri-love-hacker-activist-prison-sentence-extradition-america-aspergers-autism-death-sentence-a8076541.html.

Manning, Bradley [Chelsea] E. 2013. "Statement in Support of Providence Inquiry—US v. Private First Class (PFC) Bradley E. Manning (U)." *US v. PFC Bradley E. Manning: Defense Legal Filings and Statements*, January 29, 2013. https://alexaobrien.com/archives/1476.

Marcus, Ruth. 2018. "Trump Had Senior Staff Sign Nondisclosure Agreements: They're Supposed to Last Beyond His Presidency." *Washington Post*, March 18, 2018. https://www.washingtonpost.com/opinions/trumps-nondisclosure-agreements-came-with-him-to-the-white-house/2018/03/18/226f4522-29ee-11e8-b79d-f3d931db7f68_story.html.

Marczak, William R., John Scott-Railton, Morgan Marquis-Boire, and Vern Paxson. 2014. "When Governments Hack Opponents: A Look at Actors and Technology." Paper presented at the USENIX 14 Symposium, August 20–22, 2014, San Diego, California. https://www.usenix.org/conference/usenixsecurity14/technical-sessions/presentation/marczak.

Marzulli, John. 2016. "Judge Refuses to Send Women to Brooklyn Jail With 'Third World' Conditions." *National Association of Women Judges*, October 7, 2016. https://www.nawj.org/blog/newsroom/news/judge-refuses-to-send-women-to-brooklyn-jail-with-third-world-conditions.

Matsakis, Louise. 2018. "The US Sits Out an International Cybersecurity Agreement." *Wired*, November 12, 2018. https://www.wired.com/story/paris-call-cybersecurity-united-states-microsoft/.

Maurer, Tim. 2018. *Cyber Mercenaries: The State, Hackers, and Power*. Cambridge: Cambridge University Press.

Mayrl, Damon, and Sarah Quinn. 2016. "Defining the State from Within: Boundaries, Schemas, and Associational Policymaking." *Sociological Theory* 34 (1): 1–26.

McCurdy, Patrick. 2013. "From the Pentagon Papers to Cablegate: How the Network Society Has Changed Leaking." In *Beyond WikiLeaks: Implications for the Future of Communications, Journalism, and Society*, edited by Benedetta Brevini, Arne Hintz, and Patrick McCurdy, 123–145. New York: Palgrave Macmillan.

McEwen, Thomas J. 1989. *Dedicated Computer Crime Units.* Washington, DC: US Department of Justice, National Institute of Justice, Office of Justice Programs.

McMillan, Robert. 2017. "New Threats Fuel Fears of Another Global Cyberattack." *Wall Street Journal*, May 17, 2017. https://www.wsj.com/articles/new-threats-fuel-fears -of-another-global-cyberattack-1495042636.

Medvedev, Sergei A. 2017. "Offense-Defense Theory Analysis of Russian Cyber Capability." Master's thesis, Naval Postgraduate School, Monterey, California. https:// core.ac.uk/download/pdf/36737355.pdf.

Mello, John P., Jr. 2013. "The Ban on Feds at Defcon Draws a Mixed Reaction." *CIO*, July 12, 2013. https://www.cio.com/article/2384191/the-ban-on-feds-at-defcon -draws-a-mixed-reaction.html.

Meredith, Sam. 2018. "Facebook-Cambridge Analytica: A Timeline of the Data Hijacking Scandal." *CNBC*, April 10, 2018. https://www.cnbc.com/2018/04/10/face book-cambridge-analytica-a-timeline-of-the-data-hijacking-scandal.html.

Metcalfe, Robert. 2013. "Metcalfe's Law after 40 Years of Ethernet." *IEEE Computer* 46 (12): 26–31.

Mickos, Marten G. 2018. "Data Security and Bug Bounty Programs": Testimony of Marten G. Mickos before the Commerce Subcommittee on Consumer Protection, Product Safety, Insurance, and Data Security. US Congress, February 6, 2018. https://www.commerce.senate.gov/public/_cache/files/cf1e3c8c-1d90-4f85-9e11 -78271a5776a6/627FACFBD6AA202FAAA9976EF0733722.marten-mickos---hacker one---testimony.pdf.

Migdal, Joel S. 2001. *State in Society: Studying How States and Societies Transform and Constitute One Another.* Cambridge: Cambridge University Press.

Migdal, Joel S., and Klaus Schlichte. 2005. "Rethinking the State." In *The Dynamics of States: The Formation and Crises of State Domination*, edited by Joel S. Midgal, 1–40. Aldershot: Routledge.

Miller, Zeke J. 2015. "U.S. Sanctions North Korea Over Sony Hack." *Time*, January 2, 2015. http://time.com/3652479/sony-hack-north-korea-the-interview-obama-sanctions/.

Mitchell, Timothy. 1991. "The Limits of the State: Beyond Statist Approaches and Their Critics." *American Political Science Review* 85 (1): 77–96.

Mitnick, Kevin. 2012. *Ghosts in the Wires: My Adventures as the World's Most Wanted Hacker.* New York: Back Bay Books.

Mitre. 2019. Frequently Asked Questions. CVE, Mitre Corporation. Last updated March 6, 2019. https://cve.mitre.org/about/faqs.html.

Moini, Reza, Benjamin Ismail, and Elodie Vialle. 2015. *Censorship and Surveillance of Journalists: An Unscrupulous Business*. Paris: Reporters without Borders. https://rsf.org/sites/default/files/rsf_report_censorship_and_surveillance_of_journalists_0.pdf.

Moore, Gordon. 1965. "Cramming More Components onto Integrated Circuits." *Electronics Magazine* 38 (8): 114–117.

Morgan, Steve. 2016. "One Million Cybersecurity Job Openings In 2016." *Forbes*, January 2, 2016. https://www.forbes.com/sites/stevemorgan/2016/01/02/one-million-cybersecurity-job-openings-in-2016.

Morton, Timothy. 2013. *Hyperobjects: Philosophy and Ecology after the End of the World*. Minneapolis: University of Minnesota Press.

Mosco, Vincent. 2004. *The Digital Sublime*. Cambridge, MA: MIT Press.

Mosendz, Polly. 2015. "Newsweek Twitter Account Hacked by Group Claiming ISIS Affiliation." *Newsweek*, February 10, 2015. https://www.newsweek.com/newsweek-twitter-account-hacked-isis-affiliated-group-305897.

Mozur, Paul, and Jane Perlez. 2017. "China Is Reluctant to Blame North Korea, Its Ally, for Cyberattack." *New York Times*, May 17, 2017. https://www.nytimes.com/2017/05/17/world/asia/china-north-korea-ransomware.html.

Mozur, Paul, and Choe Sang-Hun. 2017. "North Korea's Rising Ambition Seen in Bid to Breach Global Banks." *New York Times*, March 25, 2017. https://www.nytimes.com/2017/03/25/technology/north-korea-hackers-global-banks.html.

Mueller, Milton L. 2010. *Networks and States: The Global Politics of Internet Governance*. Cambridge, MA: MIT Press.

Mullen, Jethro. "North Korea and the Sony hack: The War of Words Escalates." *CNN*, December 22, 2014. https://edition.cnn.com/2014/12/22/world/asia/north-korea-us-sony-hack-who-says-what/index.html.

Murillo, Luis Felipe R., and Christopher Kelty. 2018. "Hackers and Hacking." In *Digitization: Theories and Concepts for Empirical Cultural Studies*, edited by Gertraud Koch, 95–116. New York: Routledge.

Nadelmann, Ethan A. 1993. *Cops Across Borders: The Internationalization of US Criminal Law Enforcement*. University Park: Pennsylvania State University Press.

Nakashima, Ellen. 2015a. "Hacks of OPM Databases Compromised 22.1 Million People, Federal Authorities Say." *Washington Post*, July 9, 2015. https://www.washingtonpost.com/news/federal-eye/wp/2015/07/09/hack-of-security-clearance-system-affected-21-5-million-people-federal-authorities-say.

Nakashima, Ellen. 2015b. "U.S. Charges a Suspect with Terrorism and Hacking." *Washington Post*, October 16, 2015. https://www.washingtonpost.com/world/

national-security/in-a-first-us-charges-a-suspect-with-terrorism-and-hacking/2015/
10/15/463447a8-738b-11e5-8248-98e0f5a2e830_story.html.

Nakashima, Ellen. 2016a. "Guccifer 2.0 Claims Credit for DNC Hack." *Washington Post*, June 15, 2016. https://www.washingtonpost.com/world/national-security/
guccifer-20-claims-credit-for-dnc-hack/2016/06/15/abdcdf48-3366-11e6-8ff7-7b6c
1998b7a0_story.html.

Nakashima, Ellen. 2016b. "Russian Government Hackers Penetrated DNC, Stole Opposition Research on Trump." *Washington Post*, June 14, 2016. https://www
.washingtonpost.com/world/national-security/russian-government-hackers
-penetrated-dnc-stole-opposition-research-on-trump/2016/06/14/cf006cb4-316e
-11e6-8ff7-7b6c1998b7a0_story.html.

Nakashima, Ellen. 2017. "The NSA Has Linked the WannaCry Computer Worm to North Korea." *Washington Post*, June 14, 2017. https://www.washingtonpost
.com/world/national-security/the-nsa-has-linked-the-wannacry-computer-worm-to
-north-korea/2017/06/14/101395a2-508e-11e7-be25-3a519335381c_story.html.

Nakashima, Ellen, and Craig Timberg. 2017. "NSA Officials Worried about the Day Its Potent Hacking Tool Would Get Loose: Then It Did." *Washington Post*, May 16, 2017.
https://www.washingtonpost.com/business/technology/nsa-officials-worried-about
-the-day-its-potent-hacking-tool-would-get-loose-then-it-did/2017/05/16/50670b16
-3978-11e7-a058-ddbb23c75d82_story.html.

Nakoula, Basseley Nakoula, dir. 2012. *Innocence of Muslims* trailer. Video, 13:50.
https://www.youtube.com/watch?v=YJBWCLeOEaM&bpctr=1530535635.

Nash, Roderick. 1967. *Wilderness and the American Mind*. New Haven, CT: Yale University Press.

National Association of Women Judges (NAWJ). 2015. *Visit to BOP's Metropolitan Detention Center (MDC), Brooklyn, New York*. NAWJ, Washington, DC, March 20,
2015.

National Association of Women Judges (NAWJ). 2016. *Second Visit to BOP's Metropolitan Detention Center (MDC), Brooklyn, New York*. NAWJ, Washington, DC, June 3,
2016.

National Audit Office. 2018. *Investigation: WannaCry Cyber Attack and the NHS*. April 25, 2018. National Audit Office. https://www.nao.org.uk/wp-content/uploads/2017/
10/Investigation-WannaCry-cyber-attack-and-the-NHS.pdf.

National Crime Agency (NCA). 2015a. "#CyberChoices—Drifting into Cybercrime."
NCA, December 11, 2015, video, 1:21. https://www.youtube.com/watch?v=J
_GrdBMXN5k.

National Crime Agency (NCA). 2015b. "Teenage Cybercrime: Help Your Child Make the Right #CyberChoices." NCA, December 8, 2015, video, 1:27. https://www.you tube.com/watch?reload=9&v=DjYrxzSe3DU.

National Crime Agency (NCA). 2017. "Pathways into Cybercrime: Intelligence Brief." NCA, January 13, 2017.

National Cyber Security Centre (NSCS). 2018a. "CyberFirst Courses." Global Communications Headquarters, July 4, 2018. https://www.ncsc.gov.uk/information/ cyberfirst-courses.

National Cyber Security Centre (NSCS). 2018b. "Cyber Schools Hubs." Global Communications Headquarters, February 11, 2018. https://www.ncsc.gov.uk/ information/cyber-schools-hubs.

National Intelligence Council. 2017. *Background to "Assessing Russian Activities and Intentions in Recent US Elections": The Analytic Process and Cyber Incident Attribution.* Washington, DC: National Intelligence Council.

New Jersey US Attorney's Office. 2013. "Alleged Hacker Indicted in New Jersey for Data Breach Conspiracy Targeting Government Agency Networks." Press release, October 28, 2013.

New York Times. 2016. "The DCCC Responds to the Hack." *New York Times*, December 13, 2016. https://www.nytimes.com/interactive/2016/12/13/us/politics/document -DCCC-Response-to-Hack.html.

Novak, Matt. 2016. "The Untold Story of the Teen Hackers Who Transformed the Early Internet." *Paleofuture*, April 4, 2016. https://paleofuture.gizmodo.com/ the-untold-story-of-the-teen-hackers-who-transformed-th-1770977586.

Obermaier, Frederik, Bastian Obermayer, Vanessa Wormer, and Wolfgang Jaschensky. 2019. "About the Panama Papers." *Sueddeutsche Zeitung*. Accessed May 15, 2019. https://panamapapers.sueddeutsche.de/articles/56febff0a1bb8d3c3495adf4/.

Office of Inspector General (OIG). 2003. *The September 11 Detainees: A Review of the Treatment of Aliens Held on Immigration Charges in Connection with the Investigation of the September 11 Attacks.* April 2003. US Department of Justice, Washington, DC.

Office of Inspector General (OIG). 2015. *Audit of the Federal Bureau of Investigation's Implementation of Its Next Generation Cyber Initiative.* July 2015. US Department of Justice, Washington, DC. https://www.hsdl.org/?view&did=768399.

Office of Inspector General (OIG). 2017. *Review of the Federal Bureau of Prisons' Use of Restrictive Housing for Inmates with Mental Illness.* July 2017. US Department of Justice, Washington, DC.

Osborne, Charlie. 2015. "Hacking Team: We Won't 'Shrivel Up and Go Away' after Cyberattack." *ZDnet*, July 7, 2015. http://www.zdnet.com/article/hacking -team-cyberattack-aftermath-interview/.

Owen, Taylor. 2016. *Disruptive Power: The Crisis of the State in the Digital Age*. New York: Oxford University Press.

Papacharissi, Zizi. 2010. "Privacy as a Luxury Commodity." *First Monday* 15 (8). http://journals.uic.edu/ojs/index.php/fm/article/view/3075/2581.

Perlroth, Nicole. 2016. "Governments Turn to Commercial Spyware to Intimidate Dissidents." *The New York Times*, May 29, 2016. https://www.nytimes .com/2016/05/30/technology/governments-turn-to-commercial-spyware-to -intimidate-dissidents.html.

Perlroth, Nicole, and Scott Shane. 2019. "In Baltimore and Beyond, a Stolen N.S.A. Tool Wreaks Havoc." *New York Times*, May 25, 2019. https://www.nytimes .com/2019/05/25/us/nsa-hacking-tool-baltimore.html.

Peterson, Nolan. 2016. "How Russia's Cyberattacks Have Affected Ukraine." *Daily Signal*, December 16, 2016. https://www.dailysignal.com/2016/12/16/how-russias -cyberattacks-have-affected-ukraine/.

Pew Research Center. 2018. "Mobile Fact Sheet." Washington, DC: Pew Research Center. http://www.pewinternet.org/fact-sheet/mobile/.

Phineas Fisher. 2016. "Hack Back! A DIY Guide." Pastebin. https://pastebin.com/ raw/0SNSvyjJ.

Pilkington, Ed. 2014. "Burglars in 1971 FBI Office Break-in Come Forward After 43 Years." *Guardian*, January 7, 2014. https://www.theguardian.com/world/2014/ jan/07/fbi-office-break-in-1971-come-forward-documents.

Pilkington, Ed, and Amanda Michel. 2012. "Obama, Facebook and the Power of Friendship: The 2012 Data Election." *Guardian*, February 17, 2017. https://www.the guardian.com/world/2012/feb/17/obama-digital-data-machine-facebook-election.

Pirie, Fernanda. 2013. "The Limits of the State: Coercion and Consent in Chinese Tibet." *Journal of Asian Studies* 72 (1): 69–89.

Polantz, Katelyn, and Stephen Collinson. 2018. "12 Russians Indicted in Mueller Investigation." *CNN Politics*, July 14, 2018. https://edition.cnn.com/2018/07/13/ politics/russia-investigation-indictments/index.html?no-st=1551377552.

Poulantzas, Nicos. (1978) 2013. *State, Power, Socialism*. London: Verso.

Poulsen, Kevin. 2014. "The FBI Used the Web's Favorite Hacking Tool to Unmask Tor Users." *Wired*, December 16, 2014. https://www.wired.com/2014/12/fbi -metasploit-tor/.

Powers, Shawn M., and Michael Jablonski. 2015. *The Real Cyber War: The Political Economy of Internet Freedom*. Urbana: University of Illinois Press.

Priest, Dana, and William M. Arkin. 2010. "A Hidden World, Growing Beyond Control." *Washington Post*, June 19, 2010. http://projects.washingtonpost.com/top-secret-america/articles/a-hidden-world-growing-beyond-control/.

Priest, Dana, and William M. Arkin. 2011. *Top Secret America: The Rise of the New American Security State*. New York, NY: Little, Brown.

Prusak, Christina T. 2010. "The Trial of Alberto Fujimori: Navigating the Show Trial Dilemma in Pursuit of Transitional Justice." *New York University Law Review* 85 (3): 867–904.

Purcell, Kristen, and Lee Rainie. 2014. *Technology's Impact on Workers*. Pew Research Center, December 2014. http://www.pewInternet.org/2014/12/30/technologys-impact-on-workers/.

Rainie, Lee, and Janna Anderson. 2014. "The Future of Privacy." Pew Research Center, December 18, 2014. http://www.pewinternet.org/2014/12/18/future-of-privacy/.

Ramirez-Silva, E., and M. Dacier. 2007. "Empirical Study of the Impact of Metasploit-Related Attacks in 4 Years of Attack Traces." In *Advances in Computer Science—ASIAN 2007: Computer and Network Security*, edited by I. Cervesato, 198–211. Berlin: Springer.

Rawls, John. 1991. "Definition and Justification of Civil Disobedience." In *Civil Disobedience in Focus*, edited by H. A. Bedau, 103–121. London: Routledge.

Realpe, Germán, and José Luis Peñarredonda. 2016. "'Me arrepiento de haberme involucrado en política': Hacker Sepúlveda." *Enter.co*. October 4, 2016. https://www.enter.co/chips-bits/seguridad/me-arrepiento-de-haberme-involucrado-en-politica-hacker-sepulveda/.

Reardon, Marguerite. 2018. "Facebook's FTC Consent Decree Deal: What You Need to Know." *CNet*, April 14, 2018. https://www.cnet.com/news/facebooks-ftc-consent-decree-deal-what-you-need-to-know/.

Reynolds, Matt. 2017. "Ransomware Attack Hits 200,000 Computers across the Globe." *New Scientist*, May 15, 2017. https://www.newscientist.com/article/mg23431263-500-ransomware-attack-hits-200000-computers-across-the-globe/.

Rid, Thomas, and Ben Buchanan. 2018. "Hacking Democracy." *SAIS Review of International Affairs* 38 (1): 3–16.

Roberts, Alisdair. 2012. "WikiLeaks: The Illusion of Transparency." *International Review of Administrative Sciences* 78 (1): 116–133.

Roberts, Paul. 2013. "Spot the Wishful Thinker: DEF CON and the FEDS." Veracode, July 11, 2013. https://www.veracode.com/blog/2013/07/spot-the-wishful-thinker -defcon-and-the-feds.

Robertson, Jordan, Michael Riley, and Andrew Willis. 2016. "How to Hack an Election." *Bloomberg*, March 31, 2016. https://www.bloomberg.com/features/2016 -how-to-hack-an-election/.

Rogers, Michael, and Grace Eden. 2017. "The Snowden Disclosures, Technical Standards, and the Making of Surveillance Infrastructures." *International Journal of Communication* 11:802–823.

Ronfeldt, David, and John Arquilla. 2001. "Networks, Netwars, and the Fight for the Future." *First Monday* 6 (10). https://firstmonday.org/ojs/index.php/fm/article/ view/889/798.

Roose, Kevin, Cecilia Kang, and Sheera Frenkel. 2018. "Zuckerberg Gets a Crash Course in Charm: Will Congress Care?" *New York Times*, April 8, 2018. https://www .nytimes.com/2018/04/08/technology/zuckerberg-gets-a-crash-course-in-charm-will -congress-care.html.

Rosa, Hartmut. 2013. *Social Acceleration: A New Theory of Modernity*. New York: Columbia University Press.

Rosenberg, Matthew, Nicholas Confessore, and Carole Cadwalladr. 2018. "How Trump Consultants Exploited the Faceboook Data of Millions." *New York Times*, March 17, 2018. https://www.nytimes.com/2018/03/17/us/politics/cambridge -analytica-trump-campaign.html.

Sadoff, David A. 2016. *Bringing International Fugitives to Justice: Extradition and Its Alternatives*. Cambridge: Cambridge University Press.

Salgado, Richard. 2017. "Written Testimony of Richard Salgado, Senior Counsel, Law Enforcement and Information Security, Google." *Hearings on "Extremist Content and Russian Disinformation Online: Working with Tech to Find Solutions," before the Subcommittee on Crime and Terrorism*. United States Senate, Committee on the Judiciary, October 21, 2017.

Sanger, David E. 2016. "'Shadow Brokers' Leak Raises Alarming Question: Was the NSA Hacked?" *New York Times*, August 16, 2016. https://www.nytimes.com/2016/ 08/17/us/shadow-brokers-leak-raises-alarming-question-was-the-nsa-hacked.html.

Sanger, David E., and Robertson Dean. 2018. *The Perfect Weapon: War, Sabotage, and Fear in the Cyber Age*. New York: Random House.

Sanger, David E., and Steven Lee Myers. 2018. "After a Hiatus, China Accelerates Cyberspying Efforts to Obtain U.S. Technology." *New York Times*, November 29,

2018. https://www.nytimes.com/2018/11/29/us/politics/china-trump-cyberespionage.html.

Sanger, David E., Jim Rutenberg and Eric Lipton. 2018. "Tracing Guccifer 2.0's Many Tentacles in the 2016 Election." *New York Times*, July 15, 2018. https://www.nytimes.com/2018/07/15/us/politics/guccifer-russia-mueller.html.

Sauter, Molly. 2014. *The Coming Swarm*. New York: Bloomberg Press.

Savage, Charlie. 2016. *Power Wars: Inside Obama's Post-9/11 Presidency*. New York: Little, Brown.

Saward, Michael. 2017. "Agency, Design and 'Slow' Democracy." *Time and Society* 26 (3): 362–383.

Scahill, Jeremy. 2008. *Blackwater: The Rise of the World's Most Powerful Mercenary Army*. New York: Nation Books.

Scheuerman, William E. 2004. *Liberal Democracy and the Social Acceleration of Time*. Baltimore: Johns Hopkins University Press.

Scheuerman, William E. 2014. "Whistleblowing as Civil Disobedience: The Case of Edward Snowden." *Philosophy and Social Criticism* 40 (7): 609–628.

Scheuerman, William E. 2015. "Recent Theories of Civil Disobedience: An Anti-Legal Turn?" *Journal of Political Philosophy* 23 (4): 427–449.

Scheuerman, William E. 2016. "What Edward Snowden Can Teach Theorists of Conscientious Law-Breaking." *Philosophy and Social Criticism* 42 (10): 958–964.

Schmidt, Andreas. 2013. "The Estonian Cyber Attacks." In *A Fierce Domain: Conflicts in Cyberspace, 1986–2012*, edited by Jason Healey, 174–193. Washington, DC: Atlantic Council.

Schneier, Bruce. 2013. "People, Process, and Technology." *Schneier on Security*, January 30, 2013. https://www.schneier.com/blog/archives/2013/01/people_process.html.

Schneier, Bruce. 2014. "How to Save the Net: Break up the NSA." *Wired*, August 19, 2014. https://www.wired.com/2014/08/save-the-net-bruce-schneier/.

Schneier, Bruce. 2017. "Who Are the Shadow Brokers?" *Atlantic Monthly*, May 23, 2017. https://www.theatlantic.com/technology/archive/2017/05/shadow-brokers/527778/.

Schwartz, Mattathias. 2017. "Cyberwar for Sale." *New York Times*, January 4, 2017. https://www.nytimes.com/2017/01/04/magazine/cyberwar-for-sale.html.

Schwirtz, Michael, and Joseph Goldstein. 2017. "Russian Espionage Piggybacks on a Cybercriminal's Hacking." *New York Times*, March 12, 2017. https://www.nytimes.com/2017/03/12/world/europe/russia-hacker-evgeniy-bogachev.html.

SecDev Group and Citizen Lab. 2009. *Tracing GhostNet: Investigating a Cyber Espionage Network*. Ottawa, ON: SecDev Group.

Sengupta, Somini. 2012. "Criminals Exploit Stolen Customer Data from Stratfor." *New York Times*, February 15, 2012. https://bits.blogs.nytimes.com/2012/02/15/criminals-exploit-stolen-customer-data-from-stratfor/.

Shane, Scott. 2013. "New Leaked Document Outlines US Spending on Intelligence Agencies." *New York Times*, August 29, 2013. https://www.nytimes.com/2013/08/30/us/politics/leaked-document-outlines-us-spending-on-intelligence.html.

Shane, Scott. 2018. "Ex-NSA Worker Accused of Stealing Trove of Secrets Offers to Plead Guilty." *New York Times*, January 3, 2018. https://www.nytimes.com/2018/01/03/us/politics/harold-martin-nsa-guilty-plea-offer.html.

Shannon, Claude E., and Warren Weaver. 1949. *A Mathematical Model of Communication*. Urbana: University of Illinois Press.

Sheller, Mimi. 2015. "News Now." *Journalism Studies* 16 (1): 12–26.

Shue, Vivienne. 2004. "Legitimacy Crisis in China?" In *State and Society in 21st Century China: Crisis, Contention, and Legitimation*, edited by Peter Hays Gries and Stanley Rosen, 24–49. New York: Routledge.

Sifry, Micah. 2011. *WikiLeaks and the Age of Transparency*. New Haven, CT: Yale University Press.

Smith, Brad. 2017. "The Need for Urgent Collective Action to Keep People Safe Online: Lessons from Last Week's Cyberattack." Microsoft, May 14, 2017. https://blogs.microsoft.com/on-the-issues/2017/05/14/need-urgent-collective-action-keep-people-safe-online-lessons-last-weeks-cyberattack/#sm.0001f04ed012qeeaht7p5g0ous47x.

Smith, Craig S. 2001. "May 6–12: The First World Hacker War." *New York Times*, May 13, 2001. https://www.nytimes.com/2001/05/13/weekinreview/may-6-12-the-first-world-hacker-war.html.

Smith, Joan. 2016. "Julian Assange Is Nothing but a Seedy Egomaniac Who Believes Himself to Be Above the Law." *Telegraph*, February 4, 2016. https://www.telegraph.co.uk/women/politics/julian-assange-is-nothing-but-a-seedy-egomaniac-who-believes-him/.

Snider, L. Britt. 1999–2000. "Recollections from the Church Committee's Investigation of NSA: Unlucky SHAMROCK." *Studies in Intelligence*, Winter. https://www.cia.gov/library/center-for-the-study-of-intelligence/csi-publications/csi-studies/studies/winter99-00/art4.html#rft9.

Snider, L. Britt. 2008. *The Agency and the Hill: CIA's Relationship with Congress, 1946–2004*. Washington, DC: Center for the Study of Intelligence, CIA. https://

www.cia.gov/library/center-for-the-study-of-intelligence/csi-publications/books
-and-monographs/agency-and-the-hill/.

Snowden, Edward. 2015. "By my read, #SnoopersCharter legitimizes mass surveillance. It is the most intrusive and least accountable surveillance regime in the West." *Twitter*, November 4, 2015, 10:59 a.m. https://twitter.com/Snowden/status/6619 50808381128704.

Soma, John T., Paula J. Smith, and Robert D. Sprague. 1985. "Legal Analysis of Electronic Bulletin Board Activities." *Western New England Law Review* 77 (3): 571–626.

Sprang, Ronald. 2018. "Russia in Ukraine 2013–2016: The Application of New Type Warfare Maximizing the Exploitation of Cyber, IO, and Media." *Small Wars Journal*, September 11, 2018. https://smallwarsjournal.com/jrnl/art/russia-ukraine-2013-2016 -application-new-type-warfare-maximizing-exploitation-cyber-io-and.

Star, Susan Leigh, and James R. Griesemer. 1989. "Institutional Ecology, 'Translations,' and Boundary Objects: Amateurs and Professionals on Berkeley's Museum of Vertebrate Zoology." *Social Studies of Science* 19 (3): 387–420.

Steinmetz, Kevin F. 2016. *Hacked: A Radical Approach to Hacker Culture and Crime*. New York: New York University Press.

Sterling, Bruce. (1992) 2013. *The Hacker Crackdown: Law and Disorder on the Electronic Frontier*. Hamburg: Trediton Classics.

Stretch, Colin. 2017. "Prepared Testimony of Colin Stretch, General Counsel, Facebook." *Hearings on "Extremist Content and Russian Disinformation Online: Working with Tech to Find Solutions," before the Subcommittee on Crime and Terrorism*. United States Senate, Committee on the Judiciary, October 21, 2017.

Symonds, Alexandria, and Rallian Brooks. 2017. "Forget Foreign Hacking: The Big Surprise Was a Candid FBI." *New York Times*, March 13, 2017. https://www.nytimes .com/2017/03/13/insider/bogachev-russian-hacker-schwirtz-goldstein.html.

Tabarrok, Alexander. 2012. "Fugitives, Outlaws, and the Lessons of Safe Surrender." *Criminology and Public Policy* 11 (3): 461–471.

Talbot, David. 2015. "Cyber-Espionage Nightmare." *MIT Technology Review*, June 10, 2015. https://www.technologyreview.com/s/538201/cyber-espionage-nightmare/.

Terranova, Tiziana. 2004. *Network Culture: Politics for the Information Age*. London: Pluto Press.

Thomas, Douglas. 2002. *Hacker Culture*. Minneapolis: University of Minnesota Press.

Thompson, Nicholas, and Fred Vogelstein. 2018. "Inside the Two Years that Shook Facebook—and the World." *Wired*, February 12, 2018. https://www.wired.com/story/ inside-facebook-mark-zuckerberg-2-years-of-hell/.

Thomson, Iain. 2013. "How the NSA Hacks PCs, Phones, Routers, Hard Disks 'At Speed of Light': Spy Tech Catalog Leaks." *Register*, December 31, 2013. https://www.theregister.co.uk/2013/12/31/nsa_weapons_catalogue_promises_pwnage_at_the_speed_of_light.

Thomson, Iain. 2015. "Hacking Team Flash Exploit Leak Revealed Lightning Reflexes of Malware Toolkit Crafters." *Register*, August 5, 2015. https://www.theregister.co.uk/2015/08/05/hacking_team_zero_day_speedy_exploit_kit_authors/.

Thomson, Iain. 2017a. "Crackas With Attitude Troll Gets Five Years in Prison for Harassment." *Register*, September 11, 2017. https://www.theregister.co.uk/2017/09/11/crackas_with_attitude_troll_gets_5yrs/.

Thomson, Iain. 2017b. "While Microsoft Griped about NSA Exploit Stockpiles, It Stockpiled Patches: Friday's WinXP Fix Was Built in February." *Register*, May 16, 2017. https://www.theregister.co.uk/2017/05/16/microsoft_stockpiling_flaws_too/.

Timberg, Craig, Tony Romm, and Elizabeth Dwoskin. "Facebook: 'Malicious Actors' Used Its Tools to Discover Identities and Collect Data on a Massive Scale." *Washington Post*, April 4, 2018. https://www.washingtonpost.com/news/the-switch/wp/2018/04/04/facebook-said-the-personal-data-of-most-its-2-billion-users-has-been-collected-and-shared-with-outsiders/?utm_term=.e36ca85e415c.

Tocqueville, Alexis de. (1835) 2000. *Democracy in America*. Chicago: University of Chicago Press.

Torpey, John. 2000. *The Invention of the Passport: Surveillance, Citizenship, and the State*. Cambridge: Cambridge University Press.

Trottier, Daniel. 2017. "Digital Vigilantism as Weaponisation of Visibility." *Philosophy and Technology* 30:55–72.

Tsotsis, Alexia. 2011. "LulzSec Releases Arizona Law Enforcement Data, Claims Retaliation for Immigration Law." *Tech Crunch*, June 24, 2011. https://techcrunch.com/2011/06/23/lulzsec-releases-arizona-law-enforcement-data-in-retaliation-for-immigration-law/.

Tufekci, Zeynep. 2018. "The Looming Digital Meltdown." *New York Times*, January 6, 2018. https://www.nytimes.com/2018/01/06/opinion/looming-digital-meltdown.html.

Turla, Jay. 2013. "Getting to Know Kosova Hacker's Security Crew Plus an Exclusive Interview with Th3 Dir3ctorY." *Infosec Institute*, June 11, 2013. http://resources.infosecinstitute.com/getting-to-know-kosova-hackers-security-crew-plus-an-exclusive-interview-with-th3-dir3ctory/.

UK Parliament. 2018. "Evidence from Christopher Wylie, Cambridge Analytica Whistle-Blower." Fake News Inquiry. Digital, Culture, Media and Sport Committee,

March 27, 2018. https://parliamentlive.tv/Event/Index/28e9cccd-face-47c4-92b3 -7f2626cd818e.

US Air Force. 1999. *609 IWS: A Brief History, Oct 1995-Jun 1999*. Shaw AFB, SC: US Air Force. https://securitycritics.org/wp-content/uploads/2006/03/hist-609.pdf.

US Attorney's Office. 2013. "Alleged Hacker Charged in Virginia with Breaching Multiple Government Agency Computers." Press release, Eastern District of Virginia, Department of Justice, October 28, 2013.

US Attorney's Office. 2014a. "Hacker Charged with Breaching Multiple Government Computers and Stealing Thousands of Employee and Financial Records." Press release, Eastern District of Virginia, Department of Justice, July 24, 2014.

US Attorney's Office. 2014b. "U.K. Computer Hacker Charged in Manhattan Federal Court with Hacking into Federal Reserve Computer System." Press release. Southern District of New York, Department of Justice, February 27, 2014.

US-China Economic and Security Review Commission. 2009. *Report to Congress*. 111th Cong., 1st sess. Washington, DC: GPO. https://www.uscc.gov/sites/default/ files/annual_reports/2009-Report-to-Congress.pdf.

US Congress. 2017. *Hack the Department of Homeland Security Act*. S. rept. 115-209, 115th Congress, 2nd sess. https://www.congress.gov/congressional-report/115th-congress/ senate-report/209/1.

US Department of Justice (DOJ). 2014. "U.S. Leads Multi-National Action Against 'Gameover Zeus' Botnet and 'Cryptolocker' Ransomware, Charges Botnet Administrator." Press release, June 2, 2014. https://www.justice.gov/opa/pr/us-leads-multi -national-action-against-gameover-zeus-botnet-and-cryptolocker-ransomware.

US Department of Justice (DOJ). 2016a. "Computer Hacker Extradited from France." Press Release, May 20, 2016. https://www.justice.gov/usao-ndga/pr/computer -hacker-extradited-france.

US Department of Justice (DOJ). 2016b. "Government Contractor Charged with Removal of Classified Materials and Theft of Government Property." Press release, October 5, 2016. https://www.justice.gov/usao-md/pr/government-contractor-charged -removal-classified-materials-and-theft-government-property.

US Department of Justice (DOJ). 2017a. "Cybercriminal Who Created Global Botnet Infected with Malicious Software Extradited to Face Click Fraud Charges." Press Release, April 21, 2107. https://www.justice.gov/usao-edny/pr/cybercriminal-who -created-global-botnet-infected-malicious-software-extradited-face.

US Department of Justice (DOJ). 2017b. "Latvian Cybercriminal Extradited for 'Scareware' Hacking Scheme That Caused Millions of Dollars in Loss." Press Release, June 12, 2017. https://www.justice.gov/opa/pr/latvian-cybercriminal-extradited -scareware-hacking-scheme-caused-millions-dollars-loss.

US Department of Justice (DOJ). 2018a. "Alleged Operator of Kelihos Botnet Extradited From Spain." Press release, February 2, 2018. https://www.justice.gov/opa/pr/alleged-operator-kelihos-botnet-extradited-spain.

US Department of Justice (DOJ). 2018b. "Thirty-Six Defendants Indicted for Alleged Roles in Transnational Criminal Organization Responsible for More than $530 Million in Losses from Cybercrimes." Press release, February 7, 2018. https://www.justice.gov/opa/pr/thirty-six-defendants-indicted-alleged-roles-transnational-criminal-organization-responsible.

US Federal Trade Commission (FTC). 2011. "Facebook Settles FTC Charges that It Deceived Consumers by Failing to Keep Privacy Promises." Press release, November 29, 2011. https://www.ftc.gov/news-events/press-releases/2011/11/facebook-settles-ftc-charges-it-deceived-consumers-failing-keep.

US Government Accountability Office (GAO). 1991. *Computer Security: Hackers Penetrate DOD Computer Systems*. Washington, DC: GAO. https://www.gao.gov/products/GAO/T-IMTEC-92-5.

US Government Accountability Office (GAO). 2019. *U.S. Cyber Command and Services Should Take Actions to Maintain a Trained Cyber Mission Force*. Washington, DC: GAO. https://www.gao.gov/assets/700/697268.pdf.

US House of Representatives. 1983. *Computer and Communications Security and Privacy: Hearings before the Subcommittee on Transportation, Aviation, and Materials of the Committee on Science and Technology*. 98th Cong., 1st sess., September 26, October 17 and 24, 1983.

US Senate. 1976. *National Security Agency Surveillance Affecting Americans: Final Report of the Select Committee to Study Governmental Operations with Respect to Intelligence Activities*. Washington, DC: GPO. http://www.aarclibrary.org/publib/church/reports/book3/pdf/ChurchB3_10_NSA.pdf.

US Senate. 2018. *Hack the Department of Homeland Security Act. Report of the Committee on Homeland Security and Governmental Affairs*. Washington, DC: GPO. https://www.hsdl.org/?abstract&did=810833.

US Senate Committee on Homeland Security and Governmental Affairs. 2017. *State Secrets: How an Avalanche of Media Leaks Is Harming National Security: A Majority Staff Report of the Committee on Homeland Security and Governmental Affairs*. July 6, 2017. https://www.hsdl.org/?abstract&did=802117.

US Senate Intelligence Committee. 2018. *Russian Targeting of Election Infrastructure During the 2016 Election: Summary of Initial Findings and Recommendations*. May 8, 2018. https://www.burr.senate.gov/imo/media/doc/RussRptInstlmt1-%20ElecSec%20Findings,Recs2.pdf.

US Sentencing Commission. 2015. *Guidelines Manual*. §3E1.1 (Nov. 2015). https://www.ussc.gov/sites/default/files/pdf/guidelines-manual/2015/GLMFull.pdf.

Vicens, A. J. 2016. "DNC Hacker Dumps Trove of Clinton Documents." *Mother Jones*, June 21, 2016. https://www.motherjones.com/politics/2016/06/hacker-releases-another-set-dnc-documents-hillary-clinton/.

Virilio, Paul. 1986. *Speed and Politics: An Essay on Dromology*. New York: Columbia University Press.

Virilio, Paul. 1998. "Surfing the Accident" (interview by Andreas Ruby). In *The Art of the Accident*, edited by Andreas Broeckmann, 30–44. Rotterdam: NAI.

Virilio, Paul. 1999. "Virilio—Cyberesistance Fighter: An Interview with Paul Virilio." By David Dufresne. Translated by Jacques Houis. *Après Coup*. http://www.apres-coup.org/mt/title/Cyberesistance%20Fighter%20-%20An%20Interview%20with%20Paul%20Virilio.pdf.

Virilio, Paul. 2000. *The Information Bomb*. New York: Verso.

Virilio, Paul. 2007. *The Original Accident*. Cambridge, MA: Polity Press.

Virilio, Paul, and Frederich Kittler. 1999. "The Information Bomb: A Conversation." Edited and introduced by John Armitage. *Angelaki: Journal of the Theoretical Humanities* 4 (2): 81–90.

Vogel, Rebecca. 2016. "Closing the Cybersecurity Skills Gap." *Salus Journal* 4 (2): 32–46.

Volz, Dustin. 2017. "Trump Signs into Law US Government Ban on Kaspersky Lab Software." *Reuters*, December 12, 2017. https://uk.reuters.com/article/us-usa-cyber-kaspersky/trump-signs-into-law-u-s-government-ban-on-kaspersky-lab-software-idUKKBN1E62V4.

Waddell, Kaveh. 2016. "Twitter's Account Suspensions Are Surprisingly Effective Against ISIS." *Atlantic Monthly*, February 19, 2016. https://www.theatlantic.com/technology/archive/2016/02/twitters-account-suspensions-are-surprisingly-effective-against-the-islamic-state/463440/.

Wahl-Jorgensen, Karin, Lucy Bennett, and Gregory Taylor. 2017. "The Normalization of Surveillance and the Invisibility of Digital Citizenship: Media Debates After the Snowden Revelations." *International Journal of Communication* 11:740–762. http://ijoc.org/index.php/ijoc/article/view/5523/1930.

Wall, David S. 2007. *Cybercrime: The Transformation of Crime in the Digital Age*. Cambridge: Polity.

Wall, David S. 2012. "The Devil Drives a Lada: The Social Construction of Hackers as Cybercriminals," In *Constructing Crime*, edited by Christiana Gregoriou, 4–18. London: Palgrave Macmillan.

Wang, Ruowen, Peng Ning, Tao Xie, and Quan Chen. 2013. "MetaSymploit: Day-One Defense against Script-Based Attacks with Security-Enhanced Symbolic Analysis." In *Proceedings of the 22nd USENIX Security Symposium*. Berkeley, CA: USENIX Association. http://enigma.usenix.org/sites/default/files/sec13_proceedings_interior .pdf#page=73.

Ward, Mark. 2017. "Rehab Camp Aims to Put Young Cyber-Crooks on Right Track." *BBC News*, July 25, 2017. https://www.bbc.co.uk/news/technology-40629887.

Wark, McKenzie. 2004. *A Hacker Manifesto*. Cambridge, MA: Harvard University Press.

Washington Post. 2018a. "Transcript of Mark Zuckerberg's Appearance before House Committee." *Washington Post*, April 11, 2018. https://www.washingtonpost .com/news/the-switch/wp/2018/04/11/transcript-of-zuckerbergs-appearance-before -house-committee/.

Washington Post. 2018b. "Transcript of Mark Zuckerberg's Senate Hearing." *Washington Post*, April 10, 2018. https://www.washingtonpost.com/news/the-switch/wp/ 2018/04/10/transcript-of-mark-zuckerbergs-senate-hearing/.

Watts, Jonathan. 2013. "NSA Accused of Spying on Brazilian Oil Company Petrobas." *Guardian*, September 9, 2013. https://www.theguardian.com/world/2013/sep/ 09/nsa-spying-brazil-oil-petrobras.

Weaver, Nicholas. 2017. "Shadow Brokers Redux: Dump of NSA Tools Gets Even Worse." *Lawfare*, April 14, 2017. https://www.lawfareblog.com/shadow-brokers-redux -dump-nsa-tools-gets-even-worse.

Webb, Whitney. 2018. "The Media's Curious Coverage of the 'Second Snowden.'" *MPN News*, March 20, 2018. https://www.mintpressnews.com/the-forgotten-whistle blower-the-medias-curios-coverage-of-the-second-snowden/239223/.

Weissman, Cale Guthrie. 2015. "Hacked Security Company's Documents Show a Laundry List of Questionable Clients." *Business Insider*, July 6, 2015. http://www .businessinsider.com/hacked-security-companys-document-2015-7.

Westall, Claire, and Michael Gardiner. 2014. *The Public on the Public: The British Public as Trust, Reflexivity, and Political Foreclosure*. New York: Palgrave Macmillan.

White, Sarah P. 2018. "Understanding Cyberwarfare: Lessons from the Russia-Georgia War." Modern War Institute, March 20, 2018. https://mwi.usma.edu/ understanding-cyberwarfare-lessons-russia-georgia-war/.

Whitney, Lance. 2013. "Defcon to Feds: 'We Need Some Time Apart.'" CNET, July 11, 2013. https://www.cnet.com/news/defcon-to-feds-we-need-some-time-apart/.

Whittaker, Zack. 2018. "Justice Dept. Charges 36 Alleged Scammers for $530 Million Cyber-Fraud Scheme." *ZD Net*, February 7, 2018. https://www.zdnet.com/article/justice-department-indictment-february-cybercrime-ring/.

Winner, Langdon. 1977. *Autonomous Technology: Technics-out-of-Control as a Theme in Political Thought.* Cambridge, MA: MIT Press.

Wolin, Sheldon. 1997. "What Time Is It?" *Theory and Event* 1 (1): n.p. doi:10.1353/tae .1991.0003.

Woodruff, Betsy. 2017. "Leak Investigations Rise 800% under Jeff Sessions." *Daily Beast*, November 14, 2017. https://www.thedailybeast.com/leak-investigations-rise -800-under-jeff-sessions?ref=scroll.

Wylie, Christopher. 2018. "Christopher Wylie: Why I Broke the Facebook Data Story—and What Should Happen Now." *Guardian*, April 7, 2018. https://www .theguardian.com/uk-news/2018/apr/07/christopher-wylie-why-i-broke-the -facebook-data-story-and-what-should-happen-now.

Yoo, John. 2007. "The Terrorist Surveillance Program and the Constitution." *George Mason Law Review* 14 (3): 565–604.

Young, Tiffany. 2015. "Jennifer Arcuri—Hacker Extraordinaire." *New Entrepreneurs Foundation*, October 6, 2015. http://newentrepreneursfoundation.com/ jennifer-arcuri-hacker-extraordinaire/.

Zetter, Kim. 2009. "Former Morgan Stanley Coder Gets 2 Years in Prison for TJX Hack." *Wired*, December 22, 2009. https://www.wired.com/2009/12/stephen-watt/.

Zetter, Kim. 2014. "A Convicted Hacker and an Internet Icon Join Forces to Thwart NSA Spying." *Wired*, July 18, 2014. https://www.wired.com/2014/07/dark-mail -hides-metadata-from-nsa/.

Zetter, Kim. 2016. "Hacking Team's Leak Helped Researchers Hunt Down A Zero-Day." *Wired*, January 13, 2016. https://www.wired.com/2016/01/hacking-team-leak -helps-kaspersky-researchers-find-zero-day-exploit/.

Zetter, Kim. 2019. "Exclusive: How a Russian Firm Helped Catch an Alleged NSA Data Thief." *Politico*, January 9, 2019. https://www.politico.com/story/2019/01/09/ russia-kaspersky-lab-nsa-cybersecurity-1089131.

Zuboff, Shoshana. 2015. "Big Other: Surveillance Capitalism and the Prospects of an Information Civilization." *Journal of Information Technology* 30 (1): 75–89.

Zwoof. 2013. "How the FBI Was Busted for Domestic Spying in 1971: Burglary Ends Hoover's COINTELPRO." *Daily Kos*, June 14, 2013. http://www.dailykos.com/ story/2013/6/14/1216231/-How-the-FBI-was-Busted-for-Domestic-Spying-in-1971 -Burglary-Ends-Hoover-s-COINTELPRO.

Index